George Boyle

The English and American Poets and Dramatists of the Victorian Age

George Boyle

The English and American Poets and Dramatists of the Victorian Age

ISBN/EAN: 9783337029203

Printed in Europe, USA, Canada, Australia, Japan

Cover: Foto ©ninafisch / pixelio.de

More available books at **www.hansebooks.com**

THE ENGLISH AND AMERICAN
POETS AND DRAMATISTS

OF THE

VICTORIAN AGE;

WITH

BIOGRAPHICAL NOTICES.

BY

GEORGE BOYLE,

Sometime Professor of Modern Languages in the Royal Belfast Academical Institution;
Teacher of the English Language in the Royal Prussian School of Artillery.

> Poets are all who love, who feel great
> truths and tell them. —
> Bailey (Festus).

FRANKFORT o. M.
PUBLISHED BY ADOLPHUS GESTEWITZ
1886.

PREFACE.

For some years past the conviction has been gradually gaining ground in Germany, that a knowledge of the English language, as well as of the England and the Englishman of our times, is only to be acquired by a study of the popular literature of the present day. Germans who have visited England relying on their acquaintance with the writers of the seventeenth and eighteenth centuries. have found themselves in a world where everything was strange to them. They daily heard a language in many respects unlike that of the authors with whom they were familiar; they misunderstood the greater part of what was said to them, were misunderstood in their turn, and saw themselves at last necessitated to apply themselves seriously to the acquisition of a tongue, of which they had imagined themselves to be perfect masters.

From this it by no means follows, that a study of the older English writers is valueless, for the man who can trace the language back to its sources possesses an immense advantage, other circumstances being equal, over the less deeply read student. We merely mean to say, that as the purpose of school education is to fit us for some particular career in life, common sense would seem to suggest, that young people should begin by learning what is likely to be of service to them in after-years. In our bustling, work-day world, how few comparatively have leisure to devote themselves to pure philological research! We live in an age of eager competition, one in which much must be learned before a young man is thought capable of filling the most modest position; and we hear constant complaints of the overtasking of youthful minds. Is it not then the part of wisdom, in the study of languages, to proceed with as little delay as possible to the practically useful?

In this concise handbook the student will find the English of our day both in its most elegant and its most familiar form. And here it will not be out of place to observe, that the language of recent English poetry does not materially differ from that of good prose. In the older poets we meet with a superabundance of metaphors, conceits, quips, and pedantic classical allusions, which have no place in the poetry of the Victorian Age. When William Cobbett said, that if a man wrote a letter in the style of Paradise Lost, his relations would put him in a madhouse, and take his estate, he showed his ludicrous want of all poetical feeling; still the caustic pleasantry is not devoid of a grain of truth. But a man might compose an epistle in the language of Tennyson, without any risk of losing either his personal liberty or his personal property.

The production of the present volume has been truly, on the part of the author, "a labour of love", and it has been his endeavour to make it as complete as he could. He believes that he has not passed over a single name worthy of mention, and in choosing the extracts it has been his constant aim to introduce the reader to the real beauties of each writer. Many of these selections are true gems, which will be perused with delight, and always remembered with pleasure, for, to quote the words of Keats:

A thing of beauty is a joy for ever.

CONTENTS.

I. POETS.

II. DRAMATISTS.

AMERICAN POETS AND DRAMATISTS.

THE ENGLISH POETS AND DRAMATISTS OF THE VICTORIAN AGE.

If we may be permitted to draw so bold a parallel, we should be tempted to compare the Victorian Age of English literature to some one, who, by a freak of fortune, finds himself the heir to a noble inheritance and an illustrious name, and who is painfully conscious, that he must spare no efforts, and shirk no labour, to prove himself worthy of such a succession. The marvellous events of the preceding half-century — the French Revolution, the dazzling, meteoric career of Napoleon, and all the strange episodes with which these were associated — had stirred up the dullest minds, and awakened slumbering genius throughout Europe. In England, the spirit of the age embodied itself, and found a vent, not only in the enthusiastic earlier poetry of Southey, Shelley, and Wordsworth, but more or less in the leading prose-writers of the day. One great theme absorbed the universal interest — the wonderful present, with its inscrutable but inevitable influence on the future destinies of the human race. Such were the times that witnessed the amazing outburst of genius which forms the chief glory of the reigns of George III. and George IV., and was not quite exhausted till towards the close of the short reign of William IV. — a period which we shall hereafter distinguish by the simple general designation of "the Georgian Age."

The Victorian Age, on the other hand, opens with eleven years of profound peace. These, it is true, were years of great commercial activity, and till then unexampled industrial progress, but they were no less

1

distinguished by a remarkable dearth of stirring public events. Even when, in 1848, nearly the whole of the European continent was convulsed by revolutionary movements, England remained a passive and impassionate, though not an indifferent spectator; and the same remark applies to the Italian war of 1859, the political changes in Germany in the year 1866, and to the French campaign of 1870—1871. In the long interval of forty-five years, between 1837 and 1882, only two public events of immediate national importance to England can be recorded: the Crimean war and the Indian Mutiny; and strongly as both of these affected contemporary English literature, their influence, like the events themselves, was of brief duration.

In the literary aspect of the period now under consideration, we shall consequently find no traces of any influence from without, irresistibly stimulating unconscious talent to preternatural fertility and precocious ripeness. The age is not given to enthusiasm, and is rather one of sober, toilsome, and tranquil research. Hence it is, that the Victorian poets, abandoning the older models, have mostly followed in the path marked out for them by Wordsworth in his later style of poetry, seeking their subjects mainly within themselves, and uniting them with just so much action, and so much of external life, as they considered necessary to illustrate their meaning and secure the reader's attention. This leaning towards philosophical poetry will hardly surprise us when we recollect, that at the accession of Queen Victoria, in 1837, Wordsworth was the only great living poet, who still continued to write. John Keats had died in 1821, Shelley in 1822, Bloomfield and Wolfe in 1823, Byron in 1824, Bishop Heber in 1826, Crabbe in 1832, Sotheby in 1833, Coleridge and Lamb in 1834, Mrs. Hemans and Hogg in 1835. Southey, it is true, lived till 1843, but the latter years of his life were clouded by hopeless idiocy. Campbell survived till 1844, and Moore till 1852, but for a long time before their death, the chief labours of both had been biographical, critical, or historical. Rogers lived till 1855, but he produced nothing of importance after 1822; and among the few other poets, whose life was prolonged into the Victorian Age, there was not one whose intellectual caliber equalled that of Wordsworth.

The three pre-eminent dramatists of the Victorian Age are Knowles, Talfourd, and Lord Lytton. In the two former we discover a decided tendency to return to the great masters of the English and the Greek stage; while Lord Lytton seems more ambitious of emulating the flowing and musical diction of Byron's dramas. Mr. Knowles, it is true, produced a great deal previous to 1837, but as he lived for twenty-five years after the accession of Queen Victoria, and during this time his pieces, in which for several years he continued to perform himself, attained the acme of their popularity, we have not hesitated to assign him a place among the Victorian dramatists.

If it be asked: what is the great characteristic of the Victorian literature in general? we shall reply: its infinite variety, and its wideness of range. It cannot, indeed, boast of a dramatist like Shakespeare, a poet like Milton, or a philosopher like Bacon, but it has left no department of learning untouched, no sort of elegant writing unattempted. With rare exceptions, too, the literature of the period respires a genial, humanizing spirit which in the older literature we should seek in vain. Even the satire of the Victorian Age, when most pungent, will compare most favourably with the scathing sarcasm of Swift, or the acrimonious venom of Churchill.

We now proceed to our task of enumerating the English Poets and Dramatists of the Victorian Age, who can justly lay claim to literary distinction. We shall begin with the small band, who, like setting stars sparkling in the dawn, form a connecting link between the Victorian and the Georgian era, and then pass on, to reach gradually, and without abrupt transition, the writers who have shed on this age the full and continuous lustre of their genius.

I. POETS.

Miss Landon.

Letitia Elizabeth Landon [1802—1838], born at Hans Place, Chelsea, published her earliest poetical compositions in the *Literary Gazette* with the signature L. E. L. Her most important work was the Improvisatrice. In 1838 she married Mr. George Maclean, governor of Cape Coast Castle, and accompanied her husband to Africa, but about four months later was found dead in her room, in consequence, it was believed, of taking an overdose of prussic acid. Her last verses, addressed to the Pole-star, which she had watched on her voyage till it sunk below the horizon, cannot fail to awaken a tender and melancholy interest in the bosom of every reader:

THE POLE-STAR.

A star has left the kindling sky —
    A lovely northern light;
How many planets are on high,
    But that has left the night.

I miss its bright familiar face,
    It was a friend to me;
Associate with my native place,
    And friends beyond the sea.

It rose upon our English sky.
    Shone o'er our English land,
And brought back many a loving eye,
    And many a gentle hand.

It seemed to answer to my thought,
    It called the past to mind,
And with its welcome presence brought
    All I had left behind.

The voyage it lights no longer, ends
    Soon on a foreign shore;
How can I but recall the friends
    That I may see no more?

Fresh from the pain it was to part —
   How could I bear the pain?
Yet strong the omen in my heart
   That says — We meet again.

Meet with a deeper, dearer love,
   For absence shows the worth
Of all from which we then remove,
   Friends, home and native earth.

Thou lovely polar star, mine eyes
   Still turned the first on thee,
Till I have felt a sad surprise
   That none looked up with me.

But thou hast sunk upon the wave,
   Thy radiant place unknown;
I seem to stand beside a grave,
   And stand by it alone.

Farewell! ah, would to me were given
   A power upon thy light!
What words upon our English heaven
   Thy loving rays should write!

Kind messages of love and hope
   Upon thy rays should be;
Thy shining orbit should have scope
   Scarcely enough for me.

Oh, fancy vain as it is fond,
   And little needed too;
My friends! I need not look beyond
   My heart to look for you.

T. H. Bayly.

The most successful of modern song-writers, if we except Thomas Moore, was Thomas Haynes Bayly, a native of Bath, who was born in 1797, and died in 1839, at the comparatively early age of forty-two. His songs, *I'd be a Butterfly; Oh, no, we never mention her; Isle of Beauty; the Soldier's Tear; We met — 'twas in a crowd; She wore a wreath of Roses*, long maintained, and some of them still maintain, their popularity. Though educated for the church. Mr. Bayly adopted literature as a profession, and the last years of his life were years of constant care and struggle.

SHE WORE A WREATH OF ROSES.

She wore a wreath of roses,
　　The night that first we met;
Her lovely face was smiling
　　Beneath her curls of jet.
Her footstep had the lightness, ·
　　Her voice the joyous tone,
The tokens of a youthful heart
　　Where sorrow is unknown.
I saw her but a moment,
　　Yet methinks I see her now,
With a wreath of summer flowers
　　Upon her snowy brow.

A wreath of orange blossoms
　　When next we met she wore;
Th' expression of her features
　　Was more thoughtful than before;
And standing by her side was one,
　　Who strove, and not in vain,
To soothe her leaving that dear home
　　She ne'er might view again.
I saw her but a moment,
　　Yet methinks I see her now,
With the wreath of orange blossoms
　　Upon her snowy brow.

And once again I see that brow,
　　No bridal wreath was there;
The widow's sombre cap conceals
　　Her once luxuriant hair.
She weeps in silent solitude,
　　And there is no one near
To press her hand within his own,
　　And wipe away the tear.
I saw her broken-hearted,
　　Yet methinks I see her now
In the pride of youth and beauty,
　　With a garland on her brow.

ISLE OF BEAUTY.

Shades of evening! close not o'er us,
　　Leave our lonely bark a while;
Morn, alas! will not restore us
　　Yonder dim and distant isle.
Still my fancy can discover
　　Sunny spots where friends may dwell;
Darker shadows round us hover:
　　Isle of beauty, fare thee well!

'Tis the hour when happy faces
    Smile around the taper's light;
Who will fill our vacant places?
    Who shall sing our songs to-night?
Through the mist that floats above us
    Softly chimes the vesper bell,
Like the voice of those that love us,
    Breathing fondly, fare thee well!

Round our ship the waves are breaking.
    As I pace the deck along,
And my eyes in vain are seeking
    Some green leaf to rest upon.
What would I not give to wander
    Where my lov'd companions dwell!
Absence makes the heart grow fonder:
    Isle of beauty, fare thee well!

W. M. Praed.

Winthrop Mackworth Praed [1802 — 1839] was born in London, and educated at Eton and Cambridge. He was called to the bar in 1829, and obtained a seat in Parliament in the following year. About the same time his health began to fail, and he died of consumption at the early age of 37. His poems were collected, and published in 1864, preceded by a biographical notice by the Rev. Derwent Coleridge. From his numerous poems we select one which must stir the heart of every German reader. The subject is the last interview of Arminius [Hermann der Deutsche] and his unpatriotic brother Flavius, as he had chosen to call himself, on the opposite banks of the Weser, some time after the defeat of Varus, and subsequent to the capture of Thusnelda. We learn from Tacitus [Annals II. 9, 10] that at first each of the brothers endeavoured to gain over the other to his own party, but as the arguments and persuasions on both sides proved equally unavailing, they parted in resentment, but not before Arminius had overwhelmed his recreant brother with reproaches such as Praed has here attributed to him. The indignant patriot is supposed to speak at the moment when Flavius, calling aloud for his horse and his arms, made a show of crossing the river, to inflict a chastisement on his fraternal foe.

Back, back! he fears not foaming flood
    Who fears not steel-clad line:
No warrior thou of German blood,
    No brother thou of mine.
Go, earn Rome's chain to load thy neck,
    Her gems to deck thy hilt;
And blazon honour's hapless wreck
    With all the gauds of guilt.

But would'st thou have me share the prey?
    By all that I have done,
The Varian bones that day by day
    Lie whitening in the sun,
The legion's trampled panoply,
    The eagle's shattered wing,
I would not be for earth or sky
    So scorn'd and mean a thing.

Ho, call me here the wizard, boy,
    Of dark and subtle skill,
To agonise but not destroy,
    To curse, but not to kill.
When swords are out, and shriek and shout
    Leave little room for prayer,
No fetter on man's arm or heart
    Hangs half so heavy there.

I curse him by the gifts the land
    Hath won from him and Rome,
The riving axe, the wasting brand,
    Rent forest, blazing home;
I curse him by our country's gods,
    The terrible, the dark,
The breakers of the Roman rod,
    The smiters of the bark.

Oh, misery! that such a ban
    On such a brow should be;
Why comes he not, in battle's van
    His country's chief to be?
To stand a comrade by my side,
    The sharer of my fame,
And worthy of a brother's pride,
    And of a brother's name?

But it is past! — where heroes press,
    And cowards bend the knee,
Arminius is not brotherless,
    His brethren are the free.
They come around: — one hour, and light
    Will fade from turf and tide,
Then onward, onward to the fight,
    With darkness for our guide.

To-night, to-night, when we shall meet
    In combat face to face,
Then only would Arminius greet
    The renegade's embrace.
The canker of Rome's guilt shall be
    Upon his dying name;
And as he lived in slavery,
    So shall he fall in shame.

Allan Cunningham.

Allan Cunningham, born in Dumfriesshire in Scotland, in the year 1784, lived till 1842. He wrote poems and songs, chiefly but not exclusively in the Scottish dialect, and a drama with the title: *Sir Marmaduke Maxwell.* One of his finest effusions is the sea-song, *A wet sheet and a flowing sea:*

A wet sheet and a flowing sea,
    A wind that follows fast,
And fills the white and rustling sail,
    And bends the gallant mast;
And bends the gallant mast, my boys,
    While, like the eagle free,
Away the good ship flies, and leaves
    Old England on the lee. ')

Oh for a soft and gentle wind!
    I heard a fair one cry;
But give to me the snoring breeze,
    And white waves heaving high;
And white waves heaving high, my boys,
    The good ship tight and free —
The world of waters is our home,
    And merry men are we.

') The lee side of a ship is the side opposite to that against which the wind blows.

There's tempest in you horned moon,
And lightning in yon cloud;
And hark the music, mariners,
The wind is piping loud;
The wind is piping loud, my boys,
The lightning flashing free —
While the hollow oak our palace is,
Our heritage the sea.

Thomas Hood.

We now come to a poet whose merits are so manifold and strangely diverse — we mean T h o m a s H o o d [1798—1845] — that we feel puzzled to know whether we should call him a serious or a comic writer. Perhaps no man was ever at once such a consummate master of the art of provoking immoderate laughter, of eliciting sympathy with the unfortunate, and of melting his readers into tears. His friend, Charles Lamb, described him admirably in his punning application of the popular phrase, that he carried two faces [a serious and a comic one] under one *hood*. This remarkable man was born in London, though his father was a native of Dundee in Scotland. Young Hood was first sent to a private school kept by two maiden sisters with the strange name of Hogsflesh, and then transferred to a "finishing school" in the neighbourhood of London. His father died in 1811, and the boy's health becoming delicate, his mother sent him to his relations in Dundee, where he remained two years. On his return to London he was sent to his maternal uncle, Mr. Sands, to learn the art of engraving; and he made such good progress that he afterwards usually furnished the illustrations for his own poems; but it was not long till he resolved to maintain himself exclusively by his pen. His earliest productions were contributions to the *London Magazine*, in which journal the first series of his *Whims and Oddities* originally appeared. A second and a third series were given to the world between 1826 and 1828; and in 1829 he commenced the *Comic Annual*, which continued for nine years, and was very profitable. He next edited an annual called the *Gem*, and for this work be wrote the *Dream of Eugene Aram*, appending to it as an explanatory note: "The late Admiral Burney went to school at an establishment where the unhappy Eugene Aram was usher subsequent to his crime. The admiral stated that Aram was generally liked by the boys; and that he used to discourse to them about *murder* in somewhat of the spirit which is attributed to him in this poem." In 1843 Hood became editor of the *New Monthly Magazine*. His last periodical was *Hood's Magazine*, which he continued to conduct till within a few weeks of his death.

Of Hood's serious poems the most important are the *Plea of the Midsummer Fairies*, which he dedicated to Charles Lamb, and his *Hero and Leander*, dedicated to S. T. Coleridge. In the first of these it was his design, he tells us, to celebrate, by an allegory that immortality which Shakespeare has conferred on the fairy mythology by his *Midsummer Night's Dream*. "It would have been a pity," he adds, "for such a race to go extinct, even though they were but as the Butterflies that hover about the leaves and blossoms of the visible world." The subject of the second is of course borrowed from classical antiquity. The *Bridge of Sighs* tells its own story. In *Lycus the Centaur*, a waternymph, by whom the hero is beloved, desiring to render him immortal, has recourse to Circe, but the treacherous sorceress gives her an incantation to pronounce which should change him into a horse. The horrible effect of the charm causes the nymph to break off in the midst, and Lycus becomes a Centaur. Hood's last serious production was the *Song of the Shirt*, which appeared in the London *Punch*, and was intended to awaken public sympathy for the over-worked and ill-paid sempstresses of London. This now celebrated poem begins as follows:

> With fingers weary and worn,
> With eyelids heavy and red,
> A woman sat in unwomanly rags,
> Plying her needle and thread.

Stitch — stitch — stitch!
    In poverty, hunger and dirt;
And still with a voice of dolorous pitch
    She sung the Song of the Shirt!

Work — work — work!
    While the cock is crowing aloof!
And work — work — work!
    Till the stars shine through the roof!
It's oh! to be a slave,
    Along with the barbarous Turk!
Where woman has never a soul to save,
    If this is Christian work!

The forlorn needle-woman longs for the fresh air,
for a brief respite from her monotonous toil:

Oh! but to breathe the breath
    Of the cowslip and primrose sweet —
With the sky above my head,
    And the grass beneath my feet.
For only one short hour
    To feel as I used to feel,
Before I knew the woes of want,
    And the walk that costs a meal!

Oh! but for one short hour!
    A respite however brief!
No blessed leisure for love or hope,
    But only time for grief!
A little weeping would ease my heart,
    But in their briny bed
My tears must stop, for every drop
    Hinders needle and thread.

The remaining verses are almost too painful for
quotation. We prefer giving a few other specimens
of Hood's serious style.

TO A CHILD EMBRACING HIS MOTHER.

Love thy mother, little one!
Kiss and clasp her neck again, —
Hereafter she may have a son
Will kiss and clasp that neck in vain.
    Love thy mother, little one!

Gaze upon her living eyes,
And mirror back her love to thee, —
Hereafter thou may'st shudder sighs
To meet them when they cannot see.
    Gaze upon her living eyes.

Press her lips, the while they glow
With love that they have often told, —
Hereafter thou may'st press in woe,
And kiss them till thine own are cold.
      Press her lips the while they glow!

Oh! revere her raven hair!
Although it be not silver grey;
Too early Death, led on by Care,
May snatch save one dear lock away.
      Oh! revere her raven hair!

Pray for her at eve and morn
That Heaven may long the stroke defer, —
For thou may'st live the hour forlorn
When thou wilt ask to die with her.
      Pray for her at eve and morn!

THE DEATHBED.

We watch'd her breathing through the night,
    Her breathing soft and low,
As in her breast the wave of life
    Kept heaving to and fro.

So silently we seem'd to speak,
    So slowly moved about;
As we had lent her half our powers
    To eke her living out.

Our very hopes belied our fears,
    Our fears our hopes belied —
We thought her dying when she slept,
    And sleeping when she died.

For when the morn came dim and sad,
    And chill with early showers,
Her quiet eyelids closed — she had
    Another morn than ours.

THE DREAM OF EUGENE ARAM.

'Twas in the prime of summer time,
    An evening calm and cool,
And four-and-twenty happy boys
    Came bounding out of school:
There were some that ran and some that leapt,
    Like troutlets in a pool.

Away they sped with gamesome minds,
    And souls untouched by sin.
To a level mead they came, and there
    They drave the wickets in.
Pleasantly shone the setting sun
    Over the town of Lynn.

Like sportive deer they coursed about,
    And shouted as they ran. —
Turning to mirth all things of earth,
    As only boyhood can;
But the Usher sat remote from all,
    A melancholy man!

His hat was off, his vest apart,
    To catch heaven's blessed breeze;
For a burning thought was in his brow,
    And his bosom ill at ease:
So he leaned his head upon his hands, and read
    The book upon his knees.

Leaf after leaf he turned it o'er,
    Nor ever glanced aside,
For the peace of his soul he read that book
    In the golden eventide:
Much study had made him very lean,
    And pale, and leaden-eyed.

At last he shut the ponderous tome,
    With a fast and fervent grasp.
He strained the dusty covers close,
    And fixed the brazen hasp:
"O God! could I so close my mind,
    And clasp it with a clasp!"

Then leaping on his feet upright,
    Some moody turns he took, —
Now up the mead, then down the mead,
    And past a shady nook, —
And lo! he saw a little boy
    That pored upon a book.

"My gentle lad, what is't you read —
    Romance or fairy fable?
Or is it some historic page
    Of kings and crowns unstable?"
The young boy gave an upward glance.
    "It is, the Death of Abel."

The usher took six hasty strides,
    As smit with sudden pain, —
Six hasty strides beyond the place,
    Then slowly back again;
And now he sat beside the lad,
    And talked with him of Cain;

And, long since then, of bloody men,
    Whose deeds tradition saves;
Of lonely folk cut off unseen,
    And hid in sudden graves;
Of horrid stabs, in groves forlorn,
    And murders done in caves.

And how the sprites of injured men
    Shriek upward from the sod. —
Ay, how the ghostly hand will point
    To show the burial clod;
And unknown facts of guilty acts
    Are seen in dreams from God!

He told how murderers walk the earth
    Beneath the curse of Cain, —
With crimson clouds before their eyes,
    And flames about their brain.
For blood has left upon their souls
    Its everlasting stain!

"And well", quoth he, "I know for truth
    Their pangs must be extreme, —
Woe, woe, unutterable woe, —
    Who spill life's sacred stream!
For why? Methought last night I wrought
    A murder, in a dream!

One that had never done me wrong —
    A feeble man and old;
I led him to a lonely field,
    The moon shone clear and cold:
Now here, said I, this man shall die,
    And I will have his gold!

Two sudden blows with a ragged stick,
    And one with a heavy stone,
One hurried gash with a hasty knife,
    And then the deed was done:
There was nothing lying at my foot
    But lifeless flesh and bone!

Nothing but lifeless flesh and bone!
   That could not do me ill;
And yet I feared him all the more,
   For lying there so still:
There was a manhood in his look,
   That murder could not kill!

And lo! the universal air
   Seemed lit with ghastly flame;
Ten thousand, thousand dreadful eyes
   Were looking down in blame:
I took the dead man by his hand,
   And called upon his name!

O God! it made me quake to see
   Such sense within the slain!
But when I touched the lifeless clay,
   The blood gushed out amain!
For every clot, a burning spot
   Was scorching in my brain!

My head was like an ardent coal,
   My heart as solid ice;
My wretched, wretched soul, I knew,
   Was at the Devil's price:
A dozen times I groaned: the dead
   Had never groaned but twice.

And now, from forth the frowning sky
   From the Heaven's topmost height,
I heard a voice — the awful voice —
   Of the blood-avenging sprite:
Thou guilty man! take up thy dead,
   And hide it from my sight.

I took the dreary body up,
   And cast it in a stream, —
A sluggish water, black as ink,
   The depth was so extreme:
My gentle boy, remember this
   Is nothing but a dream.

Down went the corse with a hollow plunge,
   And vanished in the pool;
Anon I cleansed my bloody hands,
   And washed my forehead cool,
And sat among the urchins young
   That evening in the school.

O Heaven! to think of their white souls,
   And mine so black and grim!
I could not share in childish prayer,
   Nor join in evening hymn:
Like a devil of the pit I seemed
   With holy cherubim!

And peace went with them one and all,
   And each calm pillow spread;
But Guilt was my grim chamberlain
   That lighted me to bed;
And drew my midnight curtains round
   With fingers bloody red!

All night I lay in agony,
   In anguish dark and deep,
My fevered eyes I dared not close,
   But stared aghast at Sleep:
For Sin had rendered unto her
   The Keys of Hell to keep!

All night I lay in agony,
   From weary chime to chime,
With one besetting horrid hint
   That racked me all the time;
A mighty yearning, like the first
   Fierce impulse unto crime!

One stern tyrannic thought that made
   All other thoughts its slave;
Stronger and stronger every pulse
   Did that temptation crave, —
Still urging me to go and see
   The dead man in his grave!

Heavily I rose up as soon
   As light was in the sky,
And sought the black, accursed pool
   With a wild misgiving eye;
And I saw the Dead in the river bed,
   For the faithless stream was dry.

Merrily rose the lark, and shook
   The dew-drop from its wing;
But I never marked its morning flight,
   I never heard it sing:
For I was stooping once again
   Under the horrid thing.

With breathless speed, like a soul in chase,
  I took him up and ran;
There was no time to dig a grave
  Before the day began:
In a lonesome wood, with heaps of leaves
  I hid the murdered man!

And all that day I read in school,
  But my thoughts were otherwhere,
As soon as the mid-day task was done. —
  In secret I was there:
And a mighty wind had swept the leaves,
  And still the corse was bare!

Then down I cast me on my face,
  And first began to weep,
For I knew my secret then was one
  That earth refused to keep:
Or land or sea, though he should be
  Ten thousand fathoms deep.

So wills the fierce avenging Sprite,
  Till blood for blood atones!
Ay, though he's buried in a cave
  And trodden down with stones,
And years have rotted off his flesh,
  The world shall see his bones!

O God! that horrid, horrid dream
  Besets me now awake!
Again — again. with dizzy brain
  The human life I take.
And my right hand grows raging hot,
  Like Cranmer's at the stake.

And still no peace for the restless clay,
  Will wave or mould allow;
The horrid thing pursues my soul —
  It stands before me now!"
The fearful boy looked up, and saw
  Huge drops upon his brow.

That very night, while gentle sleep
  The urchin-eyelids kissed,
Two stern-faced men set out from Lynn,
  Through the cold and heavy mist;
And Eugene Aram walked between
  With gyves upon his wrist.

Among Hood's humorous and satirical poems, none gives us a better idea of his manysidedness and the versatility of his genius, than the story of *Miss Kilmansegg and her precious Leg;* the intention of which is to ridicule purse-pride and vulgar love of display. The heroine fractures her leg badly when out riding, and the injured limb being amputated, she insists on replacing it by a golden leg, as a means of advertising her great wealth, and at the same time of attracting suitors. She finds a husband, but soon discovers that riches are not necessarily allied with domestic happiness; and one day the gentleman, in a violent passion, seizes the costly limb, and knocks out her brains with it, while she is lying in bed. Impossible as it is to give, by a brief extract, any adequate idea of the wit, the odd fancies, and we will even add, the philosophy of this pretty long poem, we cannot refrain from quoting the description of Miss Kilmansegg's happy parents, as they appeared at her christening:

> To paint the maternal Kilmansegg
> The pen of an Eastern Poet would beg,
> And need an elaborate sonnet;
> How she sparkled with gems whenever she stirr'd
> And her head niddle-noddled at every word,
> And seem'd so happy, a Paradise Bird
> Had nidificated upon it.
>
> And Sir Jacob the father strutted and bow'd,
> And smiled to himself, and laughed aloud,
> To think of his heiress and daughter;
> And then in his pockets he made a grope,
> And then, in the fulness of joy and hope,
> Seem'd washing his hands with invisible soap
> In imperceptible water.*)

In one of Hood's minor poems, he humorously exposes some of the petty hypocrisies of social life. It is called *Domestic Asides, or Truth in Parentheses:*

> I really take it very kind,
> This visit, Mrs. Skinner!
> I have not seen you such an age —
> [The wretch has come to dinner!]

---

*) Humorous description of his rubbing his hands together to express his delight.

Your daughters, too, what loves of girls!
    What heads for painters' easels!
Come here, and kiss the infant, dears —
    [And give it perhaps the measles.]

Your charming boys, I see, are home
    From Reverend Mr. Russell's;
'Twas very kind to bring them both —
    [What boots for my new Brussels!]

What! little Clara left at home?
    Well now I call that shabby:
I should have loved to kiss her so —
    [A flabby, dabby babby!]

And Mr. S. I hope he's well;
    Ah! though he lives so handy,
He never now drops in to sup —
    [The better for our brandy!]

Come, take a seat — I long to hear
    About Matilda's marriage;
You're come of course to spend the day!
    [Thank Heaven! I hear the carriage.]

What! must you go? next time, I hope,
    You'll give me longer measure;
Nay — I shall see you down the stairs —
    [With most uncommon pleasure!]

Good-bye, good-bye, remember all,
    Next time, you'll take your dinners!
[Now, David, mind I'm not at home
    In future to the Skinners!]

Many of Hood's shorter effusions, such as, *I'm going to Bombay,* were prompted by the passing incidents of the day. A letter under a pseudonym had appeared in the *Times* newspaper, in which the writer, a lady and a mother, complained of the ever increasing difficulty of marrying young ladies at the present day. She had herself three very accomplished daughters, she added, but could find no chance of disposing of them in marriage, and was thus compelled to solicit good advice. Advice soon came, in the form of a reply from a gentleman who had just returned from India, and the counsel he gave to her and to all mothers similarly circumstanced was, to ship off their daughters to that country, where European ladies were at a premium.

I'M GOING TO BOMBAY.

My hair is brown, my eyes are blue,
    And reckoned rather bright;
I'm shapely, if they tell me true,
    And just the proper height;
My skin has been admired in verse,
    And called as fair as day —
If I am fair, so much the worse,
    I'm going to Bombay.

At school I passed with some éclat;
    I learn'd my French in France;
De Wint gave lessons how to draw
    And D'Egville how to dance;
Crevelli taught me how to sing,
    And Cramer how to play —
It really is the strangest thing,
    I'm going to Bombay!

By Pa and Ma I'm daily told
    To marry now's my time,
For though I'm very far from old,
    I'm rather in my prime.
They say while we have any sun
    We ought to make our hay —
And India has so hot a one,
    I'm going to Bombay!

My cousin writes from Hydrapot
    My only chance to snatch,
And says the climate is so hot,
    It's sure to light a match.*)
She's married to a son of Mars,
    With very handsome pay,
And swears I ought to thank my stars
    I'm going to Bombay!

She says that I shall much delight
    To taste their Indian treats,
But what she likes may turn me quite,
    Their strange outlandish meats.

---

    *) Pun on m a t c h, in German Streichhölzchen, and m a t c h, Heiratspartie.

If I can eat rupees[1]) who knows?
   Or dine, the Indian way,
On doolies and on bungalows —
   I'm going to Bombay!

She says that I shall much enjoy —
   I don't know what she means —
To take the air, and buy some toy
   In my own palankeens.
I like to drive my pony chair,
   Or ride our dapple grey, —
But elephants are horses there —
   I'm going to Bombay!

That fine new teak-built ship, the Fox,
   A 1[2]) Commander Bird,
Now lying in the London docks,
   Will sail on May the third.
Apply for passage or for freight,
   To Nichol, Scott, and Gray;
Pa has applied, and sealed my fate —
   I'm going to Bombay!

My heart is full, my trunks as well,
   My mind and caps made up;
My corsets, shap'd by Mrs. Bell,
   Are promised ere I sup;
With boots and shoes, Rivarta's best,
   And dresses by Ducé,
And a special license in my chest,
   I'm going to Bombay!

Hood's *Up the Rhine* is brimful of broad humour, and reminds us strongly of Smollett's *Humphrey Clinker*. The travellers are respectively, the hypochondriac Uncle Orchard; Mrs. Wilmot, his recently widowed sister, who wishes to be thought a very interesting personage; her talkative "woman", Martha Penny, and the sprightly nephew, Frank Somerville. Like Smollett, Hood has

---

[1]) The young lady is mistaken in supposing the r u p e e to be a sort of p e a. It is a silver coin worth about 2 s. sterling. The d o o l y and the p a l a n k e e n, or p a l a n q u i n, are two forms of a bamboo carriage, borne by four men on their shoulders. The b u n g a l o w, properly speaking, is a small one-story house; but it sometimes means a small inn or refreshment station for travellers.

[2]) A ship is classed A 1 when built of the best materials, and not more than five years old.

here adopted the epistolary form. and the letters are in
prose, but almost continually interspersed with incidental
verses. As the reader will guess, the subject is the tour
of an eccentric English family on the continent.

We shall conclude our notice of Hood's poetical
works with a specimen of his *punning* style:

FAITHLESS NELLY GRAY.

Ben Battle was a soldier bold,
    And used to war's alarms;
But a cannon-ball took off his legs,
    So he laid down his a r m s![1])

Now as they bore him off the field,
    Said he, "Let others shoot,
For here I leave my second leg,
    And the forty-second f o o t."[2])

Now Ben he loved a pretty maid,
    Her name was Nelly Gray;
So he went to pay her his d e v o u r s [devoirs]
    When he'd devoured his pay;

But when he called on Nelly Gray,
    She made him quite a scoff;
And when she saw his wooden legs,
    Began to t a k e t h e m o f f![3])

O Nelly Gray! O Nelly Gray!
    Is this your love so warm?
The love that loves a scarlet coat,
    Should be more u n i f o r m![4])

She said, "I loved a soldier once,
    For he was blithe and brave;
But I will never have a man,
    With b o t h l e g s i n t h e g r a v e!

Before you had those timber toes,
    Your love I did allow,
But then, you know, you stand upon
    Another f o o t i n g now!"

----

[1]) A r m s; in German, Arme, or Waffen.
[2]) Foot or infantry regiment.
[3]) T o t a k e o f f; in German, abnehmen, or sich über etwas
lustig machen.
[4]) U n i f o r m; in German c o n s e q u e n t, or Regimentsuniform.

"O Nelly Gray! O Nelly Gray!
    For all your jeering speeches,
At duty's call I left my legs
    In Badajos's b r e a c h e s.

O false and fickle Nelly Gray,
    I know why you refuse!
Though I've no feet, some other man
    Is standing in my shoes![1]

I wish I ne'er had seen your face!
    But now a long farewell!
For you will be my death; — alas!
    You will not be my Nell!" (knell)[2]

So round his melancholy neck
    A rope he did entwine,
And, for his second time in life,
    Enlisted in the L i n e.

One end he tied around a beam,
    And then removed his pegs,
And, as his legs were off, of course
    He soon was off his legs.

And there he hung till he was dead
    As any nail[3] in town;
For though distress had c u t h i m u p,
    It could not c u t h i m d o w n!

A dozen men sat on his corpse,
    To find out why he died —
And they buried Ben in four cross-roads,[4]
    With a s t a k e in his inside!

R. H. Barham.

T h e R e v. R i c h a r d H a r r i s B a r h a m (1788—
1845), poet and humorist, furnishes us with a striking
example of cheerfulness and the love of innocent mirth
co-existing with the exercise of one of the gravest pro-

---

[1] T o s t a n d i n o n e's s h o e s is, to take one's place
(Jemand ausstechen).
[2] Todtenglocke.
[3] Alluding to the popular simile: "as dead as a nail in a
door."
[4] This was formerly the usual punishment of suicides. There
is a pun in the last line on a s t a k e of wood and a b e a f s t e a k.

fessions. Mr. Barham was a royal chaplain and a minor canon of St. Paul's, and no man was more assiduous or earnest in the discharge of his clerical duties, but this nowise detracted from the pleasure he took in the society of Theodore Hook, the elder Charles Matthews, and the other wits and literary celebrities of the day. Nor is this an isolated example. Dr. South, Sterne, Swift, Churchill, Sydney Smith, Whately, were all, like Barham, men distinguished for wit and humour, and all were clergymen of the Church of England. Mr. Barham has left us a novel, entitled *My Cousin Nicholas;* but his reputation is based on his inimitable *Ingoldsby Legends*, which he contributed to *Bentley's Miscellany*, under the signature of *Thomas Ingoldsby.* These legends, a number of which are in prose, are in part humorous versions of old stories, and in part the invention of the author. One of the most amusing, founded on a legend existing among the Cistercian monks, is called

THE JACKDAW OF RHEIMS.[1])

The Jackdaw sat on the Cardinal's chair!
Bishop and abbot and prior were there!
    Many a monk and many a friar,
    Many a knight and many a squire
With a great many more of lesser degree,
In sooth a goodly company;
And they served the Lord Primate on bended knee.
    Never, I ween,
    Was a prouder seen,
Read of in books, or dreamt of in dreams,
Than the Cardinal Lord Archbishop of Rheims!

    In and out
    Through the motley rout,
That little Jackdaw kept hopping about;
    Here and there,
    Like a dog at a fair,

---

[1]) Tunc miser Corvus adeo conscientiae stimulis compunctus fuit, et execratio eum tantopere excarneficavit, ut exinde tabescere inciperet, nec amplius crocitaret. . . . . . Tunc abbas sacerdotibus mandavit ut rursus furem absolverent; quo facto, Corvus, omnibus mirantibus, propediem convaluit, et pristinam sanitatem recuperavit. — *De Illust. Ord. Cisterc.*

Over comfits and cates,
And dishes and plates,
Cowl and cope, and rochet and pall,
Mitre and crosier! he hopp'd upon all!
With saucy air,
He perch'd on the chair
Where, in state the great Lord Cardinal sat,
In the great Lord Cardinal's great red hat;
And he peer'd in the face
Of his Lordship's grace,
With a satisfied look, as if he would say,
"We two are the greatest folks here to-day!"
And the priests with awe,
As such freaks they saw,
Said, "the Devil must be in that little Jackdaw!"

The feast was over, the board was clear'd,
The flawns and the custards had all disappear'd,
And six nice little singing-boys — dear little souls!
In nice clean faces, and nice white stoles,
Came, in order due,
Two by two,
Marching that grand refectory through!
A nice little boy held a golden ewer,
Emboss'd and fill'd with water, as pure
As any that flows between Rheims and Namur,
Which a nice little boy stood ready to catch
In a fine golden hand-basin made to match.
Two nice little boys, rather more grown,
Carried lavender-water and eau-de-Cologne;
And a nice little boy had a nice cake of soap,
Worthy of washing the hands of the Pope.

The great Lord Cardinal turns at the sight
Of these nice little boys dress'd all in white:
From his finger he draws
His costly turquoise;
And, not thinking at all about little Jackdaws,
Deposits it straight
By the side of his plate,
While the nice little boys on his Eminence wait;
Till, when nobody's dreaming of any such thing,
That little Jackdaw hops off with the ring!

There's a cry and a shout,
And a deuce of a rout,
And nobody seems to know what they're about,
But the monks have their pockets all turn'd inside out.
The friars are kneeling,
And hunting, and feeling

The carpet, the floor, and the walls, and the ceiling.
 The Cardinal drew
 Off each plum-colour'd shoe,
And left his red stockings exposed to the view;
 He peeps, and he feels
 In the toes and the heels;
They turn up the dishes — they turn up the plates —
They take up the poker and poke out the grates.
 They turn up the rugs,
 They examine the mugs:
 But, no! — no such thing; —
 They can't find *the Ring!*

The Cardinal rose with a dignified look,
He call'd for his candle, his bell, and his book!
 In holy anger, and pious grief,
 He solemnly cursed that rascally thief!
 He cursed him at board, he cursed him in bed;
 From the sole of his foot to the crown of his head;
 He cursed him in sleeping, that every night
 He should dream of the devil, and wake in a fright;
 He cursed him in eating, he cursed him in drinking,
 He cursed him in coughing, in sneezing, in winking;
 He cursed him in sitting, in standing, in lying;
 He cursed him in walking, in riding, in flying;
Never was heard such a terrible curse!
 But what gave rise
 To no little surprise,
Nobody seem'd one penny the worse!

 The day was gone,
 The night came on,
The monks and the friars they search'd till dawn;
 When the Sacristan saw,
 On crumpled claw,
Come limping a poor little lame Jackdaw!
 No longer gay,
 As on yesterday;
His feathers all seemed to be turn'd the wrong way; —
His pinions droop'd — he could hardly stand, —
His head was as bald as the palm of your hand;
 His eye so dim,
 So wasted each limb,
That, heedless of grammar, they all cried, "That's him!
That's the scamp that has done this scandalous thing!
That's the thief that has got my Lord Cardinal's ring!"
 The poor little Jackdaw,
 When the monks he saw,
Feebly gave vent to the ghost of a caw;
And turn'd his bald head, as much as to say,
"Pray, be so good as to walk this way!"

Slower and slower
He limp'd on before,
Till they came to the back of the belfry door.
Where the first thing they saw,
Midst the sticks and the straw,
Was the ring in the nest of that little Jackdaw!

Then the great Lord Cardinal call'd for his book,
And off that terrible curse he took;
The mute expression
Served in lieu of confession,
And, being thus coupled with full restitution,
The Jackdaw got plenary absolution!
When these words were heard,
That poor little bird,
Was so changed in a moment, 'twas really absurd.
He grew sleek and fat;
In addition to that,
A fresh crop of feathers came thick as a mat!
His tail waggled more
Even than before;
But no longer it wagg'd with an impudent air,
No longer he perch'd on the Cardinal's chair.
He hopp'd now about
With a gait devout;
At Matins, at Vespers, he never was out;
And, so far from any more pilfering deeds,
He always seem'd telling the Confessor's beads.
If any one lied — or if any one swore —
Or slumber'd in prayer-time and happen'd to snore,
That good Jackdaw
Would give a great "Caw!"
As much as to say, Don't do so any more!
While many remark'd, as his manners they saw,
That they never had known such a pious Jackdaw!
He long lived, the pride
Of that country side,
And at last in the odour of sanctity died.

Mr. Barham possessed such a fund of drollery, that
even his ordinary correspondence overflowed with it. On
one occasion he sent his friend, Dr Wilmot of Ashford,
an invitation to dinner in four stanzas, forming an exact
counterpart to Dr Percy's ballad, "O Nancy, wilt thou
go with me?" Dr Percy's first stanza is:

O Nancy, wilt thou go with me,
Nor sigh to leave the flaunting town?
Can silent glens have charms for thee,
The lowly cot and russet gown?

No longer drest in silken sheen,
        No longer decked with jewels rare,
Say, can'st thou quit each courtly scene,
        Where thou wert fairest of the fair?

Barham's imitation is:

O Doctor! wilt thou dine with me,
        And drive on Tuesday morning down?
Can ribs of beef have charms for thee —
        The fat, the lean, the luscious brown?
No longer dress'd in silken sheen,
        Nor deck'd with rings and brooches rare,
Say, wilt thou come in velveteen,
        Or corduroys that never tear?

Nothing gave this genial humorist more amusement than to read aloud, in a circle of friends, some serious verses ending with an *attrappe*, which left his auditors staring at the reader in blank amazement. One of these pieces he calls

THE CONFESSION.

There's something on my breast, father,
        There's something on my breast!
The livelong day I sigh, father,
        And at night I cannot rest.
I cannot take my rest, father,
        Though I would fain do so;
A weary weight oppresseth me —
        This weary weight of woe!

'Tis not the lack of gold, father,
        Nor want of wordly gear;
My lands are broad and fair to see,
        My friends are kind and dear.
My kin are leal and true, father,
        They mourn to see my grief;
But oh! tis not a kinsman's hand
        Can give my heart relief!

'Tis not that Janet's false, father,
        'Tis not that she's unkind;
Tho' busy flatterers swarm around,
        I know her constant mind.

'Tis not her coldness, father,
    That chills my labouring breast.
It's that confounded cucumber
    I've eat and can't digest.

A memoir of the Rev. Richard Harris Barham has been written by his son.

H. Coleridge.

Samuel T. Coleridge's three children, *Hartley, Derwent* and *Sara Coleridge*, all distinguished themselves as writers. Hartley, the eldest (1796—1849), was not only a poet, but an essayist, a critic and a biographer. His poetry, as might be expected, is of the school of Wordsworth, or to use the popular designation, the "Lake School." It is very sad that all the efforts of this talented man to gain a position in society were frustrated by his fatal propensity to intemperance. He gained a fellowship at Oxford, but soon lost it in consequence of his irregularities, and his career as a schoolmaster at Ambleside was equally brief. Of Hartley Coleridge's graceful poetry the following lines will give a good idea:

ADDRESS TO CERTAIN GOLD-FISHES.

Restless forms of living light,
Quivering on your lucid wings,
Cheating still the curious sight
With a thousand shadowings;
Various as the tints of even,
Gorgeous as the hues of heaven,
Reflected on your native streams
In flitting, flashing, billowy gleams!
Harmless warriors, clad in mail
Of silver breastplate, golden scale;
Mail of Nature's own bestowing,
With peaceful radiance mildly glowing —
Fleet are ye as fleetest galley
Or pirate rover sent from Sallee;
Keener than the Tartar's arrow,
Sport ye in your sea so narrow.

Was the sun himself your sire?
Were ye born of vital fire?

Or of the shade of golden flowers,
Such as we fetch from eastern bowers,
To mock this murky clime of ours?
Upwards, downwards now ye glance,
Weaving many a mazy dance,
Seeming still to grow in size
When ye would elude our eyes —
Pretty creatures! we might deem
Ye were happy as ye seem —
As gay, as gamesome, and as blithe,
As light, as loving, and as lithe,
As gladly earnest in your play,
As when ye gleamed in far Cathay.

And, yet, since on this hapless earth
There's small sincerity in mirth,
And laughter oft is but an art
To drown the outcry of the heart;
It may be that your ceaseless gambols,
Your wheelings, dartings, divings, rambles,
Your restless roving round and round
The circuit of your crystal bound —
Is but the task of weary pain,
An endless labour, dull and vain;
And while your forms are gaily shining,
Your little lives are inly pining!
Nay — but still I fain would dream
That ye are happy as ye seem.

Derwent Coleridge entered the church, and for some time instructed a small number of boys, among whom was young Charles Kingsley, the future poet and novelist. Besides writing a memoir of his brother Hartley, and a series of sermons, he annotated some of his father's works. His sister Sara published a fairy tale called *Phantasmion*, and some other instructive works for the young. She married her cousin, Henry Nelson Coleridge, a Chancery barrister, and died in 1852.

William Wordsworth.

William Wordsworth (1770—1850) was born at Cockermouth in Cumberland. In 1798 he published the *Lyrical Ballads* in conjunction with Coleridge; in 1814 he produced his principal poem, *the Excursion;* and in the next year *the White Doe of Rylstone*, which was soon followed by *Peter Bell*, and other poems. All these, however, were coldly received, and it was only between 1830 and 1840 that his poetry began to be generally relished. On the death of Southey in 1843, he was made Poet-Laureate, and from that time he rose so rapidly and so high in public estimation, that he gave a tone to all the serious poetry that appeared till Swinburne published his *Atalanta*. The aim and plan of the present volume forbid us to enter into a disquisition on the merits and demerits of Wordsworth, which have been amply canvassed in many other works; hence we shall merely quote a few of what we consider his happiest or his most characteristic verses:

THE RAINBOW.

My heart leaps up when I behold
    A rainbow in the sky:
So was it when my life began;
So is it now I am a man;
So be it when I shall grow old,
    Or let me die!
The child is father of the man;
And I could wish my days to be
Bound each to each by natural piety.

EARLY MORNING IN LONDON.

Earth has not anything to show more fair:
Dull would he be of soul who could pass by
A sight so touching in its majesty:
This city now doth like a garment wear
The beauty of the morning; silent, bare,
Ships, towers, domes, theatres, and temples lie
Open unto the fields and to the sky.

All bright and glittering in the smokeless air,
Never did sun more beautifully steep,
In his first splendour, valley, rock, or hill;
Ne'er saw I, never felt, a calm so deep!
The river glideth at his own sweet will:
Dear God! The very houses seem asleep;
And all that mighty heart is lying still!

PRISON THOUGHTS OF MARY STUART.

As the cold aspect of a sunless way
Strikes through the traveller's frame with deadlier chill,
Oft as appears a grove, or obvious hill,
Glistening with unparticipated ray,
Or shining slope where he must never stray;
So joys, remembered without wish or will,
Sharpen the keenest edge of present ill, —
On the crushed heart a heavier burthen lay.

Just Heaven, contract the compass of my mind
To fit proportion with my altered state!
Quench those felicities whose light I find
Reflected in my bosom all too late! —
Oh, be my spirit, like my thraldom, strait;
And, like mine eyes that stream with sorrow, blind!

MILTON.

Milton! thou shouldst be living at this hour.
England hath need of thee; she is a fen
Of stagnant waters; altar, sword, and pen,
Fireside, the heroic wealth of hall and bower
Have forfeited their ancient English dower
Of inward happiness. We are selfish men;
Oh, raise us up, return to us again;
And give us manners, virtue, freedom, power.
Thy soul was like a star, and dwelt apart;
Thou hadst a voice whose sound was like the sea;
Pure as the naked heavens — majestic, free,
So didst thou travel on life's common way
In cheerful godliness; and yet thy heart
The lowliest duties on herself did lay.

EARLY SPRING.

I heard a thousand blended notes,
    While in a grove I sate reclined,
In that sweet mood when pleasant thoughts
    Bring sad thoughts to the mind.

To her fair works did Nature link
    The human soul that through me ran;
And much it grieved my heart to think
    What man has made of man.

Through primrose tufts, in that green bower,
    The periwinkle trailed its wreaths.
And 'tis my faith that every flower
    Enjoys the air it breathes.

The birds around me hopped and played,
    Their thoughts I cannot measure: —
But the least motion which they made,
    It seemed a thrill of pleasure.

The budding twigs spread out their fan,
    To catch the breezy air;
And I must think, do all I can,
    That there was pleasure there.

If this belief from heaven be sent,
    If such be Nature's holy plan,
Have I not reason to lament
    What man has made of man?

James Montgomery.

The highly esteemed poet, *James Montgomery*, the author of *the World before the Flood, Greenland,* and *Pelican Island,* was born at Irvine, in Ayrshire, in the year 1771, and he survived till 1854. He was the son of a clergyman and missionary, and all he has written is pervaded by a deep but happy and hopeful religious conviction. We subjoin his beautiful description of the Nautilus in *Pelican Island:*

Light as a flake of foam upon the wind,
Keel-upward from the deep emerged a shell,
Shaped like the moon ere half her horn is filled;
Fraught with young life, it righted as it rose,
And moved at will along the yielding water.
The native pilot of this little bark
Put out a tier of oars on either side,
Spread to the wafting breeze a twofold sail,
And mounted up and glided down the billow.

In happy freedom, pleased to feel the air,
And wander in the luxury of light,
Worth all the dead creation, in that hour,
To me appeared this lonely Nautilus,
My fellow-being, like myself alive.
Entranced in contemplation, vague yet sweet,
I watched its vagrant course and rippling wake,
Till I forgot the sun amidst the heavens.

His picture of the eternal ice-fields and the stupendous icebergs in the Arctic regions, in his fine poem of *Greenland,* is equally correct and still more majestic:

Piled on a hundred arches, ridge by ridge,
O'er fixed and fluids strides the alpine bridge,
Whose blocks of sapphire seem to mortal eye
Hewn from cerulean quarries in the sky;
With glacier battlements that crowd the spheres,
The slow creation of six thousand years,
Amidst immensity it towers sublime,
Winter's eternal palace, built by Time:
All human structures by his touch are borne
Down to the dust; mountains themselves are worn
With his light footsteps; here for ever grows,
Amid the region of unmelting snows,
A monument; where every flake that falls
Gives adamantine firmness to the walls.
The sun beholds no mirror in his race
That shows a brighter image of his face;
The stars, in their nocturnal vigils, rest
Like signal-fires on its illumined crest;
The gliding moon around the ramparts wheels,
And all its magic lights and shades reveals.

Montgomery's verses on *Night* have been often
quoted, and are justly admired:

NIGHT.

Night is the time for rest;
    How sweet, when labours close,
To gather round an aching breast
    The curtain of repose,
Stretch the tired limbs, and lay the head
Upon our own delightful bed!

Night is the time for dreams;
    The gay romance of life,
When truth that is and truth that seems
    Blend in fantastic strife;
Ah! visions less beguiling far
Than waking dreams by daylight are!

Night is the time for toil;
    To plough the classic field,
Intent to find the buried spoil
    Its wealthy furrows yield;
Till all is ours that sages taught,
That poets sang or heroes wrought.

Night is the time to weep;
    To wet with unseen tears
Those graves of memory where sleep
    The joys of other years;

Hopes that were angels in their birth,
But perished young like things on earth.

Night is the time to watch,
  On Ocean's dark expanse
To hail the Pleiades, or catch
  The full moon's earliest glance,
That brings unto the home-sick mind
All we have loved and left behind.

Night is the time for death;
  When all around is peace,
Calmly to yield the weary breath,
  From sin and suffering cease:
Think of heaven's bliss, and give the sign
To parting friends — such death be mine!

Professor Wilson.

John Wilson (1785—1854) was born at Paisley, in Scotland, and studied at Glasgow and Magdalene College, Oxford. He afterwards purchased some property on the beautiful banks of Lake Windermere, in Lancashire, where he resided for four years, but having experienced a reverse of fortune, he became a candidate for, and obtained the chair of moral philosophy in Edinburgh University. Wilson's principal poetical works are the *Isle of Palms,* and a dramatic poem, *the City of the Plague.* His poetry is characterized in general by softness and sweetness, and the *Isle of Palms* has been adduced as one of the best specimens of the "beautiful sublime", but he occasionally shows great force and vigour, as in his fine picture of the shipwreck in the same poem. Perhaps nothing he wrote has been so much read as his lines, *A sleeping Child,* suggested, it is said, by one of the sculptor Chantrey's two sleeping children in Lichfield Cathedral. It suited the poet's purpose better, however, to transform the child of marble into one of flesh and blood, so as to enable him to paint successively the tranquil slumber and the joyous waking of infancy.

A SLEEPING CHILD.

Art thou a thing of mortal birth,
Whose happy home is on our earth?
Does human blood with life imbue
Those wandering veins of heavenly blue
That stray along thy forehead fair,
Lost 'mid a gleam of golden hair?
Oh, can that light and airy breath
Steal from a being doomed to death;
Those features to the grave be sent
In sleep thus mutely eloquent?
Or art thou, what thy form would seem,
The phantom of a blessed dream?

Oh! that my spirit's eye could see
Whence burst those gleams of ecstasy!
That light of dreaming soul appears
To play from thoughts above thy years.
Thou smil'st as if thy soul were soaring
To heaven, and heaven's God adoring!
And who can tell what visions high
May bless an infant's sleeping eye!
What brighter throne can brightness find
To reign on than an infant's mind,
Ere sin destroy or error dim
The glory of the seraphim?

Oh! vision fair! that I could be
Again as young, as pure as thee!
Vain wish! the rainbow's radiant form
May view, but cannot brave the storm:
Years can bedim the gorgeous dyes
That paint the bird of Paradise.
And years, so fate hath ordered, roll
Clouds o'er the summer of the soul.
Fair was that face as break of dawn,
When o'er its beauty sleep was drawn
Like a thin veil that half concealed
The light of soul, and half revealed.

While thy hushed heart with visions wrought,
Each trembling eyelash moved with thought,
And things we dream, but ne'er can speak
Like clouds came floating o'er thy cheek,
Such summer-clouds as travel light,
When the soul's heaven lies calm and bright;
Till thou awok'st — then to thine eye
Thy whole heart leapt in ecstasy!

And lovely is that heart of thine,
Or sure these eyes could never shine
With such a wild, yet bashful glee,
Gay, half-o'ercome timidity!

Mrs. Southey.

Mrs. Southey (1787—1854), when still Miss Caroline Bowles, made herself favourably known to the public by the publication of the *Widow's Tale* and other poems. In 1839 she became the second wife of the then poet laureate, Robert Southey, though quite aware that his reason had already begun to totter, and devoted herself to her husband, in his terrible and incurable malady, with exemplary fortitude and patience, up to the time of his death in 1843. Miss Bowles and Southey, many years before their marriage, had projected a poem on the subject of *Robin Hood*, but the idea was only partially carried out, and after Southey's death, the work was given to the world as a fragment by the widow. Of Mrs. Southey's numerous minor poems we present to our readers, as one of the most characteristic, the lines entitled, *Once upon a Time.*

I mind me of a pleasant time,
    A season long ago;
The pleasantest I've ever known,
    Or ever now shall know.
Bees, birds, and little tinkling rills,
    So merrily did chime;
The year was in its sweet spring-tide,
    And I was in my prime.

I've never heard such music since,
    From every bending spray;
I've never plucked such primroses,
    Set thick on bank and brae.
I've never smelt such violets
    As all that pleasant time
I found by every hawthorn-root —
    When I was in my prime.

Yon moory down, so black and bare,
    Was gorgeous then and gay
With golden gorse — bright blossoming —
    As none blooms now-a-day.

The blackbird sings but seldom now
    Up there in the old lime,
Where hours and hours he used to sing
    When I was in my prime.

And blackberries — so mawkish now —
    Were finely flavoured then;
And nuts — such reddening clusters ripe
    I ne'er shall pull again.
Nor strawberries blushing bright as rich
    As fruits of sunniest clime;
How all is altered for the worse
    Since I was in my prime!

Thomas Noon Talfourd (1795—1854).

The distinguished dramatist, *Mr. Talfourd*, sergeant-at-law, was a native of Reading, in Berkshire. Of his numerous poetical effusions, nothing pleases us so much as his verses on the death of one of his children, named after his friend, the poet and essayist Charles Lamb, who died at Brighton a year after his gifted and genial godfather.

THE POET AND THE CHILD.

Our gentle Charles[1]) has pass'd away,
    From earth's short bondage free,
And left to us its leaden day
    And mist-enshrouded sea.

Here by the ocean's terraced side,
    Sweet hours of hope were known,
When first the triumph of its tide
    Seem'd presage of our own.

That eager joy the sea-breeze gave,
    When first it raised his hair,
Sunk with each day's retiring wave,
    Beyond the reach of prayer.

The sun-blink that through drizzling mist,
    To flickering hope akin,
Lone waves with feeble fondness kiss'd,
    No smile as faint can win;

---

[1]) The first seven stanzas refer exclusively to the child.

Yet not in vain with radiance weak
    The heavenly stranger gleams —
Not of the world it lights to speak,
    But that from whence it streams.

That world our patient sufferer sought,
    Serene with pitying eyes,
As if his mounting spirit caught
    The wisdom of the skies.

With boundless love it look'd abroad
    For one bright moment given,
Shone with a loveliness that awed,
    And quiver'd into Heaven.

A year made slow by care and toil
    Has paced its weary round,
Since death enrich'd with kindred spoil
    The snow-clad, frost-ribb'd ground.

Then *Lamb*, with whose enduring name
    Our boy we proudly graced,
Shrank from the warmth of sweeter fame
    Than ever bard embraced.

Still 'twas a mournful joy to think
    Our darling might supply
For years to us a living link
    With name that cannot die.

And though such fancy gleam no more
    On earthly sorrow's night,
Truth's nobler torch unveils the shore
    Which lends to both its light.

The nurseling there that hand may take
    None ever grasp'd in vain,
And smiles of well-known sweetness wake
    Without their tinge of pain.

Though, 'twixt the child and childlike bard
    Late seem'd distinction wide,
They now may trace, in Heaven's regard,
    How near they were allied.

Within the infant's ample brow
    Blythe fancies lay unfurl'd,
Which all uncrush'd may open now
    To charm a sinless world.

Though the soft spirit of those eyes
    Might ne'er with *Lamb's* compete —
Ne'er sparkle with a wit so wise,
    Or melt in tears as sweet —

The nurseling's unforgotten look
    A kindred love reveals
With his who never friend forsook,
    Or hurt a thing that feels.

In thought profound, in wildest glee,
    In sorrow's lengthening range,
His guileless soul of infancy
    Endured no spot or change.

From traits of each our love receives
    For comfort nobler scope;
While light which childlike genius leaves
    Confirms the infant's hope:

And in that hope, with sweetness fraught,
    Be aching hearts beguiled
To blend in one delighful thought
    The Poet and the Child.

Lord Macaulay.

Had *Lord Macaulay* devoted himself more to the service of the Muse, it is doubtful if he would ever have reached that proud eminence which he has attained as a critic, essayist, and historian, but we may safely assume, that he would have held no mean position among the poets of the Age. His four *Lays of ancient Rome,* with which he surprised the world in 1842, prove at once his intimate acquaintance with the old Roman writers and his capacity for writing poetry of the highest order. The *Songs of the Huguenots* and of the *Civil War,* which belong to his earliest poetical efforts, are full of energy and martial fire, and it seems almost incredible to us, that they were the productions of inexperienced youth. In reading *Naseby Battle*, whatever our religious opinions or political leanings may be, we are carried away in spite of ourselves by the stream of rushing words, that seem to re-echo the rolling of the drums, the clang of the trumpet, and the clash of encountering swords.

NASEBY BATTLE.

(June 14, 1645.)

Oh! wherefore come ye forth, in triumph from the North,
  With your hands and your feet and your raiment all red?
And wherefore doth your rout send forth a joyous shout?
  And whence be the grapes of the wine-press which ye tread?

Oh! evil was the root, and bitter was the fruit,
  And crimson was the juice of the vintage that we trod;
For we trampled on the throng of the haughty and the strong,
  Who sate in the high places and slew the saints of God.

It was about the noon of a glorious day in June,
  That we saw their banners dance, and their cuirasses shine;
And the Man of Blood[1]) was there, with his long essenced hair,
  And Astley, and Sir Marmaduke, and Rupert of the Rhine.

Like a servant of the Lord, with his Bible and his sword,
  The General[2]) rode along us to form us for the fight,
When a murmuring sound broke out, and swell'd into a shout,
  Among the godless horsemen upon the tyrant's right.

And hark! like the roar of the billows on the shore,
  The cry of battle rises along their charging line,
"For God! for the Cause! for the Church! for the Laws!
  For Charles, King of England, and Rupert of the Rhine!"

The furious German comes, with his clarions and his drums,
  His bravoes of Alsatia and pages of Whitehall:
They are bursting on our flanks. Grasp your pikes! close your ranks!
  For Rupert never comes but to conquer or to fall.

They are here — they rush on. We are broken — we are gone —
  Our left is borne before them, like stubble on the blast.
O Lord, put forth thy might! O Lord, defend the right!
  Stand back to back, in God's name, and fight it to the last.

Stout Skippon hath a wound: — the centre hath given ground: —
  Hark! hark! what means the trampling of horsemen in our rear?
Whose banner do I see, boys? 'Tis he, thank God, 'tis he;
  Bear up another minute. Brave Oliver[3]) is here.

Their heads all stooping low, their points all in a row,
  Like a whirlwind on the trees, like a deluge on the dyke,
Our cuirassiers have burst on the ranks of the Accurst,
  And at a shock have scattered the forest of his pikes.

---

  [1]) Charles I.
  [2]) Fairfax.
  [3]) Cromwell.

Fast, fast the gallants ride, in some safe nook to hide
    Their coward heads, predestined to rot on Temple-Bar.
And he — he turns, he flies — shame on those cruel eyes,
    That bore to look on torture, and dared not look on war.

Fools, your doublets shone with gold, and your hearts were gay and bold,
    When you kissed your lily hands to your lemans[1]) to-day,
And to-morrow shall the fox, from her chambers in the rocks,
    Lead forth her tawny cubs to howl above the prey.

And she of the seven hills shall moan her children's ills,
    And tremble when she thinks on the edge of England's sword,
And the kings of earth in fear shall shudder when they hear
    What the Hand of God hath wrought for the Houses and the Word!

As a worthy pendant to this fine lyric, we give
Ivry, in a slightly abbreviated form:

The king[2]) is come to marshal us, all in his armour drest;
And he has bound a snow-white plume upon his gallant crest.
He looked upon his people, and a tear was in his eye;
He looked upon the traitors, and his glance was stern and high.
Right graciously he smiled on us, as rolled from wing to wing,
Down all our line, a deafening shout, "God save our lord the King."
"And if my standard-bearer fall, as fall full well he may —
For never saw I promise yet of such a bloody fray —
Press where ye see my white plume shine, amidst the ranks of war,
And be your oriflamme to day the helmet of Navarre."

Hurrah! the foes are moving! Hark to the mingled din
Of fife, and steed, and trump, and drum, and roaring culverin.
The fiery Duke[3]) is pricking fast across Saint André's plain,
With all the hireling chivalry of Guelders and Almayne.
Now by the lips of those ye love, fair gentlemen of France,
Charge for the golden lilies — upon them with the lance!
A thousand spurs are striking deep — a thousand spears in rest,
A thousand knights are pressing close behind the snow-white crest,
And in they burst, and on they rushed, while, like a guiding star,
Amidst the thickest carnage blazed the helmet of Navarre!

Now God be praised, the day is ours! Mayenne hath turned his rein.
D'Aumale hath cried for quarter. The Flemish Count[4]) is slain.
Their ranks are breaking like thin clouds before a Biscay gale;
The field is heaped with bleeding steeds, and flags, and cloven mail.

---

[1]) Corresponds to the German *Liebchen*.
[2]) Henry IV.
[3]) Mayenne.
[4]) Count Egmont.

And then we thought on vengeance, and all along our van
"Remember St. Bartholomew!" was passed from man to man;
But out spake gentle Henry: "No Frenchman is my foe:
Down, down with every foreigner, but let your brethren go."
Oh! was there ever such a knight, in friendship or in war,
As our sovereign lord, King Henry, the soldier of Navarre!

Thomas Babington Macaulay, though belonging by his father's side to an old Highland family, was born in the year 1800 at Rothley Temple, Leicestershire. His father, Zachary Macaulay, a native of Scotland, had settled in England, and married the daughter of a Bristol bookseller, Miss Selina Mills, who became the mother of the distinguished writer. Young Macaulay studied at Cambridge, wrote for the *Edinburgh Review,* was called to the bar, and in 1830 entered parliament as member for the borough of Calne. Having obtained the post of legal adviser to the Supreme Court of Calcutta, he resigned his seat in Parliament, and went to India. After returning to England, he was elected member for Edinburgh in 1839, and again in 1852. In 1857 he was raised to the peerage as Baron Macaulay of Rothley Temple. He died in 1859.

A. Smith.

Mr. *Albert Smith* (1816—1860), the popular lecturer, besides many humorous sketches in prose, wrote a good deal of comic poetry. Perhaps his most amusing pleasantry in rhyme is his account of the alarm and flight of those merry sprites, the fairies, at the advent of Science.

SCIENCE AND THE FAIRIES.

When Father Time was in his prime,
   Some thousand years ago,
Ere his beard was long, or his pinions strong,
   Or his locks as white as snow,

In our merry land there dwelt a band
   Of tiny joyous elves,
Who owned no order or command
   From any but themselves.

And each one lived in a cottage orné
    Of these elfen gamesome things,
By the tiger-moth thatched with his plume so gay,
    And glazed with a dragon-fly's wings.

They danced all night in the moonbeams bright,
    And quaffed their cowslip wine;
Then hid their heads in their moth-down beds
    Ere day began to shine.

And they revelled long, with their dance and song,
    Till a strange gigantic dame
A visit paid to their forest glade,
    And Science was her name.

Her lungs were air-pumps of monstrous size;
    Her breath blew forth a steam,
And with oxyhydrogen her eyes [1])
    Like meteor sparks did gleam.

With triple cranks and rackwork neat, [2])
    Her limbs and joints did move;
And her vital powers were raised to heat
    With a Dr. Arnott's stove. [3])

The fairies gazed on this fearful sight,
    Then swift through the summer air,
In a dreadful fright they all took flight
    To the realms of my lord knows where. [4])

They have gone for aye, for since that day
    They no longer in England dwell;
Lone is the glade, and the leafy shade,
    And forsaken each quiet dell.

And Science still her march keeps on;
    But since that epoch dread,
Our legends old to their graves have gone,
    And Romance herself has fled.

In a poetical epistle, addressed to a lady in Chamouni, a clerk in the Foreign Office, in Downing Street,

---

[1]) A reference to the oxyhydrogen, or Drummond light (Siderallicht).

[2]) Crank and rackwork, in German, Kurbel and Zahnstange mit Rad.

[3]) Dr. Neill Arnott, physician-in-ordinary to Queen Victoria, obtained the Rumford Medal, in 1854, for an improved stove.

[4]) The Lord knows where, is a popular expression, equivalent to Wer weiss wohin?

complains that in consequence of the Crimean War he is obliged to remain in London, while his friends are travelling and solely occupied with sight-seeing:

> Confound the telegraphs and war,
>   And letters sent off wet!
> Confound the Russians and their Czar!
>   Confound the whole "Gazette!"
> I thought at last upon the Alps
>   That you and I should meet;
> But n o w you are at Chamouni,
>   And I'm in Downing Street.
>
> I made my plans, I fixed the day,
>   I got some thick-soled shoes
> To "do the Alps;" and on the way
>   I meant to buy a blouse.
> I lost myself in visions bright,
>   Day-dreaming of the treat
> To be with you at Chamouni,
>   . Away from Downing Street.
>
> I thought of those dark pine-tree woods,
>   Those fern-clad granite cells,
> Those channels of the glacier floods,
>   Those sweet-toned cattle bells.
> That milk, these girls, those f r a i s e s d u b o i s —
>   In fact, those things you meet
> At every turn in Chamouni,
>   But not in Downing Street.
>
> And, Annie dear, I thought of you —
>   A poet would say "thee" —
> In that "unclouded weather blue"
>   (That's Tennyson, not me,
> Or rather "I"), but all my wits
>   Have beaten a retreat,
> Whilst thinking you're at Chamouni,
>   And I'm in Downing Street.

It is worthy of remark, that though a good-natured drollery is the principal feature in Mr. Albert Smith's verses, in prose he occasionally rises into the region of true poetry. What could surpass the following description of evening on the *Grands Mulets*, in his *Ascent of Mont Blanc?*

"The sun at length went down behind the Aiguille du Goûté, and then, for two hours. a scene of such

wild and wondrous beauty — of such inconceivable
and unearthly splendour — burst upon me, that, spell-
bound and almost trembling with the emotion its magni-
ficence called forth — with every sense, and feeling,
and thought absorbed by its brilliancy, I saw far more
than the realization of the most gorgeous visions that
opium or *hasheesh* could evoke, accomplished. At first,
every thing about us — above, around, below — the
sky, the mountain, and the lower peaks — appeared
one uniform creation of burnished gold so brightly
dazzling that, now our veils were removed, the eye
could scarcely bear the splendour. As the twilight
gradually crept over the lower world, the glow became
still more vivid; and presently, as the blue mists rose
in the valleys, the tops of the higher mountains looked
like islands rising from a filmy ocean — an archipelago
of gold. By degrees this metallic lustre was softened
into tints, — first orange, and then bright, transparent
crimson, along the horizon, rising through the different
hues, with prismatic regularity, until, immediately above
us, the sky was a deep pure blue, merging towards
the east into glowing violet. ... These beautiful hues
grew brighter as the twilight below increased in depth;
and it now came marching up the valley of the glaciers
until it reached our resting-place. Higher and higher
still, it drove the lovely glory of the sunlight before
it, until at last the vast Dôme du Goûté and the
summit itself stood out, icelike and grim, in the cold
evening air, although the horizon still gleamed with
a belt of rosy light. ... The stars had come out, and
looking over the plateau, I soon saw the moonlight
lying cold and silvery on the summit, stealing slowly
down the very track by which the sunset glories had
passed upward and away. ... In such close communion
with Nature in her grandest aspect, with no trace of
the actual living world beyond the mere speck that
our little party formed, the mind was carried far away
from its ordinary trains of thought — a solemn emotion
of mingled awe and delight, and yet self-perception of
abject nothingness, alone rose above every other feeling.

A vast untrodden region of cold, and silence, and death,
stretched out, far and away from us, on every side;
but above, heaven, with its countless, watchful eyes,
was over all!"

Mr. A. H. Clough.

Arthur Hugh Clough (1819—1861) is a philosophic
and satirical poet, who is little read. and was never
popular. His best-known poem is *the Bothie of Tober-
na-Vuolich*, (1848) which, being written in hexameter
metre, is somewhat heavy reading, in spite of the
rich vein of comedy pervading it through and through.
In one of his best poems, *Easter Day,* he presents us
with a curious doubleness of view, a fantastic combi-
nation of the doubts of the sceptic with the faith of
the believer; though he finally teaches us, that

> Hope conquers cowardice, joy grief;
> Or, at the least, faith unbelief.
> Though dead, not dead;
> Not gone, though fled;
> Not lost, though vanquished:
> In the great Gospel and true creed,
> He is yet risen indeed;
> Christ is yet risen.

Mr. Clough, at his death, left an unfinished set of
poems, called *Mari Magno,* which have been compared
by critics to the stern but strikingly truthful sketches
of nature and character given us by Crabbe. These
poems differ widely in style from his earlier pieces.
As a good specimen of his satirical and ironical vein,
we subjoin *the latest Decalogue,* a new version of the
ten commandments, which Clough recommends as
better adapted than the old one to the present state
of society:

> Thou shalt have one God only; who
> Would be at the expense of two?
> No graven images may be
> Worshipped, except the currency:
> Swear not at all; for, for thy curse
> Thine enemy is none the worse:

At Church on Sunday to attend
Will serve to keep the world thy friend:
Honour thy parents; that is, all
From whom advaucement may befall:
Thou shalt not kill; but need'st not strive
Officiously to keep alive:
Do not adultery commit;
Advantage rarely comes of it:
Thou shalt not steal; an empty feat,
When it's so lucrative to cheat:
Bear not false witness; let the lie
Have time on its own wings to fly:
Thou shalt not covet; but tradition
Approves all forms of competition.

W. M. Thackeray.

Though *William Makepeace Thackeray* (1811—1863) never advanced any pretensions to be considered a poet, we may find, scattered through his novels and miscellaneous works, verses replete with humour or pathos, which show what he was capable of doing, had he seriously devoted himself to writing poetry. Few readers will peruse without emotion the following lines on Napoleon the First in *the Chronicle of the Drum*:

He captured many thousand guns;
   He wrote "the Great" before his name;
And dying, only left his sons
   The recollection of his shame.

Though more than half the world was his,
   He died without a rood his own;
And borrowed from his enemies
   Six foot of ground to rest upon.

He fought a thousand glorious wars,
   And more than half the world was his,
And somewhere, now, in yonder stars,
   Can tell, mayhap, what greatness is.

Of Thackeray's humorous style of writing in verse we can scarcely give a better sample than the verses with the title, *Peg of Limavaddy*, in the *Irish Sketch-Book*.

PEG OF LIMAVADDY.[1])

Riding from Coleraine
  (Famed for lovely Kitty[2])
Came a Cockney bound
  Unto Derry city.
Weary was his soul, ·
  Shivering and sad he
Bumped along the road
  Leads to Limavaddy.

*   *   *

Limavaddy's inn's
  But a humble baithouse,
Where you may procure
  Whiskey and potatoes;
Landlord at the door
  Gives a smiling welcome
To the shivering wights
  Who to his hotel come.
Landlady within
  Sits and knits a stocking.
With a wary foot
  Baby's cradle rocking.

To the chimney nook
  Having found admittance,
There I watch a pup
  Playing with two kittens;
(Playing round the fire,
  Which of blazing turf is,
Roaring to the pot
  Which bubbles with the murphies;[3])
And the cradled babe
  Fond the mother nursed it!
Singing it a song
  As she twists the worsted!

Up and down the stair
  Two more young ones patter
(Twins were never seen
  Dirtier nor fatter);
Both have mottled legs,
  Both have snubby noses,
Both have — here the Host
  Kindly interposes;

---

[1]) Limavaddy (the Dog's Leap) is a small town in the north
of Ireland, on the river Bush.
[2]) An allusion to the popular song, Kitty of Coleraine.
[3]) Popular name for potatoes in Ireland.

"Sure you must be froze
  With the sleet and hail, sir;
So will you have some punch,
  Or will you have some ale, sir?"

Presently a maid
  Enters with the liquor,
(Half a pint of ale
  Frothing in a beaker).
Gods! I didn't know
  What my beating heart meant
Hebe's self I thought
  Entered the apartment.
As she came she smiled,
  And the smile bewitching,
On my word and honour,
  Lighted all the kitchen!

With a curtsey neat
  Greeting the new-comer,
Lovely, smiling Peg
  Offers me the rummer;
But my trembling hand
  Up the beaker tilted,
And the glass of ale
  Every drop I spilt it:
Spilt it every drop
  (Dames, who read my volumes,
Pardon such a word,)
  On my what-d'ye-call'ems!

Witnessing the sight
  Of that dire disaster,
Out began to laugh
  Missis, maid, and master;
Such a merry peal,
  Specially Miss Peg's was,
(As the glass of ale
  Trickling down my legs was),
That the joyful sound
  Of that ringing laughter
Echoed in my ears
  Many a long day after.

Such a silver peal!
  In the meadows listening,
You who've heard the bells
  Ringing to a christening;
You who ever heard
  Caradori pretty,

Smiling like an angel,
  Singing "Giovinetti,"
Fancy Peggy's laugh,
  Sweet, and clear, and cheerful,
At my pantaloons
  With half a pint of beer full!

When the laugh was done,
  Peg. the pretty hussy,
Moved about the room
  Wonderfully busy;
Now she looks to see
  If the kettle keep hot,
Now she rubs the spoons,
  Now she cleans the teapot;
Now she sets the cups
  Trimly and secure,
Now she scours a pot,
  And so it was I drew her.

Thus it was I drew her,
  Scouring of a kettle,
(Faith! her blushing cheeks,
  Redden'd on the metal!)
Ah! but 'tis in vain
  That I try to sketch it;
The pot perhaps is like,
  But Peggy's face is wretched.
No: the best of lead,
  And of Indian-rubber,
Never could depict
  That sweet kettle-scrubber!

See her as she moves!
  Scarce the ground she touches,
Airy as a fay,
  Graceful as a duchess.
Bare her rounded arm,
  Bare her little leg is,
Vestris never show'd
  Ankles like to Peggy's:
Braided is her hair,
  Soft her look and modest,
Slim her little waist
  Comfortably boddiced.

This I do declare,
  Happy is the laddy
Who the heart can share
  Of Peg of Limavaddy;

Married if she were,
  Blest would be the daddy
Of the children fair
  Of Peg of Limavaddy;
Beauty is not rare
  In the land of Paddy,
Fair beyond compare
  Is Peg of Limavaddy.

Citizen or squire
  Tory, Whig, or Radi-
cal would all desire
  Peg of Limavaddy.
Had I Homer's fire,
  Or that of Sergeant Taddy,
Meetly I'd admire
  Peg of Limavaddy.
And till I expire,
  Or till I grow mad, I
Will sing unto my lyre
  Peg of Limavaddy!

Samuel Lover.

Among the successful song-writers of the Victorian Age must be mentioned *Samuel Lover* (1797—1868). This highly talented man, a native of Dublin, was a poet, musician, painter and novelist. He occasionally gave public entertainments, reciting his own sketches of Irish life, and singing his own songs, and always succeeded in delighting his audience, not only in Ireland and England, but in America. Lover's principal songs are, *the Angels' Whisper, the low-backed Car, Molly Bawn, the Land of the West,* and *the Four-leaved Shamrock.*

THE LAND OF THE WEST.

Oh, come to the West, love — oh, come there with me;
'Tis a sweet land of verdure that springs from the sea,
Where fair Plenty smiles from her emerald throne;
Oh, come to the West, and I'll make thee mine own!
I'll guard thee, I'll tend thee, I'll love thee the best,
And you'll say there's no land like the land of the West!

The South has its roses and bright skies of blue,
But ours are more sweet with love's own changeful hue —

Half sunshine, half tears, like the girl I love best; —
Oh! what is the South to the beautiful West!
Then come to the West, and the rose on thy mouth
Will be sweeter to me than the flow'rs of the South!

The North has its snow-tow'rs of dazzling array,
All sparkling with gems in the ne'er-setting day;
There the Storm-king may dwell in the halls he loves best,
But the soft-breathing zephyr he plays in the West.
Then come there with me, where no cold wind doth blow,
And thy neck will seem fairer to me than the snow.

The Sun in the gorgeous East chaseth the night
When he riseth, refresh'd, in his glory and might!
But where doth he go when he seeks his sweet rest?
Oh! doth he not haste to the beautiful West?
Then come there with me; 'tis the land I love best,
'Tis the land of my sires! — 'tis my own darling West.

W. Carleton.

William Carleton (1798—1869), the well-known
author of *Traits and Stories of the Irish Peasantry*, has,
like Thackeray, interspersed his prose-works with oc-
casional verses and short poems. His most remarkable
poetical effort is called *Sir Turlough, or, the Church-
yard Bride*, a poem which has some resemblance to
Goethe's *Bride of Corinth*, and is founded on an ancient
and curious Irish superstition. It is believed, among
the Irish peasantry, that if a man at a funeral loiters
in the churchyard after the departure of the other
mourners, he meets with a lady of surpassing beauty,
who casts such a spell over him, that he pledges him-
self by a kiss to meet her again in the same place on
that day month. With this embrace, however, a deadly
poison diffuses itself through his whole frame, and from
that moment he begins to waste away, so that when
the appointed day arrives, it is his dead body that is
borne to the trysting-place. In Carleton's poem the
constantly recurring chorus: "Killeevy, O Killeevy!"
is intended to represent the *keen*, or wailing of the
hired mourners, as it is still practised in some remote
districts of Ireland.

SIR TURLOUGH, OR, THE CHURCHYARD BRIDE.

The bride she bound her golden hair,
    Killeevy, O Killeevy!
And her step was light as the breezy air,
When it bends the morning flowers so fair
    By the bonnie green woods of Killeevy.

The bridegroom is come with youthful brow,
    Killeevy, O Killeevy!
To receive from his Eva her virgin vow.
"Why tarries the bride of my bosom now?"
    By the bonnie green woods of Killeevy.

A cry! a cry! 'twas her maidens spoke,
    Killeevy, O Killeevy!
"Your bride is asleep — she has not awoke;
And the sleep she sleeps will never be broke,"
    By the bonnie green woods of Killeevy.

Sir Turlough sank down with a heavy moan,
    Killeevy, O Killeevy!
And his cheek became like the marble stone —
"Oh, the pulse of my heart is for ever gone!"
    By the bonnie green woods of Killeevy.

The keen is loud, it comes again,
    Killeevy, O Killeevy!
And rises sad from the funeral train,
As in sorrow it winds along the plain,
    By the bonnie green woods of Killeevy.

There is a voice that but one can hear,
    Killeevy, O Killeevy!
And it softly pours from behind the bier
Its notes of death on Sir Turlough's ear,
    By the bonnie green woods of Killeevy.

The keen is loud, but that voice is low,
    Killeevy, O Killeevy!
And it sings its song of sorrow slow,
And names young Turlough's name with woe,
    By the bonnie green woods of Killeevy.

Now the grave is closed, and the mass is said,
    Killeevy, O Killeevy!
And the bride she sleeps in her lonely bed,
The fairest corpse among the dead
    By the bonnie green woods of Killeevy.

"Oh, go not yet — not yet away,
    Killeevy, O Killeevy!
Let us feel that life is near our clay,"
The long-departed seem to say,
    By the bonnie green woods of Killeevy.

But the tramp and voices of life are gone,
    Killeevy, O Killeevy!
And beneath each cold forgotten stone,
The mouldering dead sleep all alone,
    By the bonnie green woods of Killeevy.

But who is he who lingereth yet?
    Killeevy, O Killeevy!
The fresh green sod with his tears is wet,
And his heart in the bridal grave is set,
    By the bonnie green woods of Killeevy.

Oh, who but Sir Turlough, the young and brave,
    Killeevy, O Killeevy!
Should bend him o'er that bridal grave,
And to his death-bound Eva rave,
    By the bonnie green woods of Killeevy.

"Weep not, weep not," said a lady fair,
    Killeevy, O Killeevy!
"Should youth and valour thus despair,
And pour their vows to the empty air?"
    By the bonnie green woods of Killeevy.

There's charmed music upon her tongue,
    Killeevy, O Killeevy!
Such beauty — bright and warm and young —
Was never seen the maids among,
    By the bonnie green woods of Killeevy.

The charm is strong upon Turlough's eye,
    Killeevy, O Killeevy!
His faithless tears are already dry,
And his yielding heart has ceased to sigh,
    By the bonnie green woods of Killeevy.

"The maid for whom thy salt tears fall,
    Killeevy, O Killeevy!
Thy grief or love can ne'er recall;
She rests beneath that grassy pall,
    By the bonnie green woods of Killeevy.

"My heart it strangely cleaves to thee,
    Killeevy, O Killeevy!
And now that thy plighted love is free,
Give its unbroken pledge to me,"
    By the bonnie green woods of Killeevy.

"To thee," the charmed chief replied,
    Killeevy, O Killeevy!
"I pledge that love o'er my buried bride;
Oh! come, and in Turlough's hall abide,"
    By the bonnie green woods of Killeevy.

Again the funeral voice came o'er,
    Killeevy, O Killeevy!
The passing breeze, as it wailed before,
And streams of mournful music bore,
    By the bonnie green woods of Killeevy.

"If I to thy youthful heart am dear,
    Killeevy, O Killeevy!
One month from hence thou wilt meet me here,
Where lay thy bridal Eva's bier,"
    By the bonnie green woods of Killeevy.

He pressed her lips as the words were spoken,
    Killeevy, O Killeevy!
And his banshee's[1]) wail — now far and broken —
Murmur'd "Death," as he gave the token,
    By the bonnie green woods of Killeevy.

"Adieu, adieu!" said this lady bright,
    Killeevy, O Killeevy!
And she slowly passed like a thing of light,
Or a morning cloud, from Sir Turlough's sight,
    By the bonnie green woods of Killeevy.

Now Sir Turlough has death in every vein,
    Killeevy, O Killeevy!
And there's fear and grief o'er his wide domain,
And gold for those who will calm his brain,
    By the bonnie green woods of Killeevy.

---

[1]) What rank the b a n s h e e holds in the scale of spiritual
beings, it is not easy to determine; but her favourite occupation
seems to be that of foretelling the death of the different branches
of the families over which she presided, by the most plaintive cries.
— M i s s B a l f o u r.

"Come, haste thee, leech, right swiftly ride,
     Killeevy, O Killeevy!
Sir Turlough the brave, green Truagh's pride,
Has pledged his love to the churchyard bride."
     By the bonnie green woods of Killeevy.

The leech groaned aloud, "Come, tell me this,
     Killeevy, O Killeevy!
By all thy hopes of weal and bliss,
Has Sir Turlough given the fatal kiss?"
     By the bonnie green woods of Killeevy.

"The banshee's cry is loud and long,
     Killeevy, O Killeevy!
At eve she weeps her funeral song,
And it floats on the twilight breeze along,"
     By the bonnie green woods of Killeevy.

"Then the fatal kiss is given — the last
     Killeevy, O Killeevy!
Of Turlough's race and name is past,
His doom is sealed, his die is cast,"
     By the bonnie green woods of Killeevy.

The leech has failed, and the hoary priest,
     Killeevy, O Killeevy!
With pious shrift his soul releas'd,
And the smoke is high of his funeral feast,
     By the bonnie green woods of Killeevy.

The shanachies[1]) now are assembled all,
     Killeevy, O Killeevy!
And the songs of praise, in Sir Turlough's hall,
To the sorrowing harp's dark music fall
     By the bonnie green woods of Killeevy.

The month is closed, and green Truagh's pride,
     Killeevy, O Killeevy!
Is married to death — and side by side,
He slumbers now with his churchyard bride,
     By the bonnie green woods of Killeevy.

From Carleton's story, *Owen M'Carthy,* we extract another specimen of his poetry, in a different style, and on a widely different subject:

---

[1]) The bards.

THE NATIVE GLENS.

Take, proud ambition, take thy fill
    Of pleasures, won through toil or crime;
Go, learning, climb thy rugged hill,
    And give thy name to future time;
Philosophy, be keen to see
    Whate'er is just, or false, or vain;
Take each thy meed; but oh! give me
    To range my mountain glens again.

Pure was the breeze that fann'd my cheek,
    As o'er Knockmany's brow I went;
When every lonely dell could speak,
    In airy music, vision sent: —
False world, I hate thy cares and thee;
    I hate the treacherous haunts of men;
Give back my early heart to me,
    Give back to me my mountain glen.

How bright my youthful visions shone,
    When spann'd by fancy's radiant form;
But now her glitt'ring bow is gone,
    And leaves me but the cloud and storm;
With wasted form and cheek all pale —
    With heart long sear'd by grief and pain.
Dunroe, I'll seek thy native gale —
    I'll tread thy mountain glens again.

Thy breeze once more may fan my blood —
    Thy valleys all are lovely still;
And I may stand where oft I stood,
    In lonely musings on thy hill:
But ah! the spell is gone; — no art,
    In crowded town or native plain,
Can teach a crushed and breaking heart
    To pipe the song of youth again!

William Carleton was the son of a small farmer in the County Tyrone, Ireland, and being designed for the church, received the education of a priest; but he declined to take orders, and resolved to support himself by his pen. He rendered his country most important services by his Irish tales, in which he exposed the oppression practised by greedy landlords and agents, and his writings have exercised a salutary influence on recent parliamentary legislation. Though an Irishman and a Roman Catholic, he palliates neither the faults of the peasantry nor those of their spiritual guides, the priests. For several years before his death, Carleton enjoyed a pension of L. 200 from the literary fund.

Rev. **Francis Mahony** (Father Prout.)

The *Rev. Francis Mahony*, an Irish Roman Catholic priest, born in 1805, and educated in France, contributed to *Fraser's Magazine*, in 1834, a series of witty papers, as the *Reliques of Father Prout, late parish priest of Watergrass-hill, in the County of Cork, Ireland.* These papers are remarkable for the singular skill of their author in the production of comic rhymes, as well as for the unrivalled facility he displays in turning verse from one language into another. By the latter talent he was enabled to play off a practical joke on his countryman, Thomas Moore, which annoyed the poet not a little. Having translated a number of the *Irish Melodies* into Latin and French, he gravely maintained in one of these contributions to *Fraser,* that Moore had stolen them from French and Latin originals. Thus the lines:

> Lesbia hath a beaming eye,
>   But no one knows for whom it beameth;
> Right and left its arrows fly,
>   But what they're aimed at no one dreameth,

he maintained, were merely a translation of

> Lesbia semper hinc et inde
>   Oculorum tela movit;
> Captat omnes, sed deinde
>   Quis ameter nemo novit.

In like manner he gave the pretended French original of "Go where glory waits thee;" which he attributed to a French countess who lived in the first half of the sixteenth century. Perhaps Moore was the only reader of this paper who did not enjoy the joke. As a specimen of Mahony's powers in a different style of writing, we quote his lines on the flight of the swallows at the end of autumn:

Down comes rain-drop, bubble follows:
   On the house-top one by one
Flock the synagogue of swallows,
   Met to vote that autumn's gone.

There are hundreds of them sitting,
   Met to vote in unison;
They resolve on general flitting,
   "I'm for Athens off," says one.

"Every year my place is filled in
   Plinth of pillared Parthenon,
Where a ball has struck the building,
   Shot from Turk's besieging gun."

"As for me, I've got my chamber
   O'er a Smyrna coffee-shop,
Where his beadroll, made of amber
   Hadji¹) counts, and sips a drop."

"I prefer Palmyra's scantlings,²)
   Architraves of lone Baalbec,
Perched on which I feed my bantlings
   As they ope their bonnie beak."

While the last, to tell her plan says,
   "On the second cataract
I've a statue of old Ramses,
   And his neck is nicely crack'd."

A complete edition of Mahony's works appeared in 1870, not long after his death.

Lord Lytton (Edward Lytton Bulwer Lytton).

The celebrity of *Lord Lytton* (1805—1872) as a novelist has made many readers forget that he began his literary career as a poet; and, in fact it can hardly be said that he ever altogether gave up verse-making. His earliest effusions, especially *O'Neil or the Rebel,* he indirectly confesses, in his preface to the *Siamese Twins,* were imitations of Byron, but he frames

---

¹) General name for a Mahometan pilgrim to Mecca.
²) Properly speaking, timber cut small for building purposes; but likewise, the general form or outline of an object.

for himself an ingenious excuse. He says: "While the public, fascinated by the brilliancy of a bold and uncommon genius, grow wedded to his style — even to his faults — they resent with peculiar contempt any resemblance to the object of an admiration which they affect to preserve as an exclusive worship. And yet how few can escape from *a seeming imitation,* which in reality is nothing more than the tone of the age in which they live; and though more emphatically noted in the most popular poet than in his less fortunate contemporaries, *he* also was *influenced by,* instead of *creating.*" Of his more matured poetical efforts one of the best is *Milton,* which, as he informs us, "is founded upon the well-known, though unauthenticated tradition of the Italian lady seeing Milton asleep under a tree, and leaving some verses beside him, descriptive of her admiration of his beauty." Lord Lytton makes the young poet awake in time to distinguish the lady's features, and he is no less struck with her beauty than she is with his.

> O'er him she leant enamour'd, and her sigh
> Breath'd near and nearer to his silent mouth,
> Rich with the hoarded odours of the south.
> Did her locks touch his cheek? or did he feel
> Her breath like music o'er his spirit steal?
> I know not — but the spell of sleep was broke;
> He started — faintly murmur'd — and awoke!
>
> He woke as Moslems wake from death, to see
> The Houris of their heaven; and reverently,
> He look'd the transport of his soul's amaze:
> And their eyes met! — the deep, deep love supprest
> For years, and treasur'd in each secret breast
> Waken'd, and glow'd, and center'd in their gaze.
> And their eyes met — one moment and no more!

Young Milton, after some time has elapsed, meets with the lady, who is called Zoe, in Rome, and they become declared lovers; but they are at last forced to part, and Milton returns to England, to aid in upholding the menaced cause of liberty. Years pass over. The poet becomes blind and old, and sinks gradually into the grave.

Beneath a church's chancel there were laid
A great man's bones — and when the crowd was gone,
An aged woman, in black robes arrayed,
Lingered and wept beside the holy stone.
None knew her name, or land; her voice was sweet
With the strange music of a foreign tongue:

Thrice on that spot her bending form they meet,
Thrice on that stone are freshest garlands hung.
On the fourth day she came not; and the wreath
Look'd dim and withered from its odorous breath;
And if I err not wholly, on that day,
A soul that loved till death had passed away!

The *Siamese Twins* is a satirical poem, in four books. It purports to contain the history of the Siamese brothers, Ching and Chang, but is full of hard hits at English society, as it existed in 1831. Many of these have now lost their point; even the ironical compliments, in the dedication to the great traveller and champion of the English aristocracy, Captain Basil Hall, will be hardly understood by many readers. Another satire of Lord Lytton's, the *New Timon,* is really an admirable production, not unworthy of Byron or Pope, but the author has marred its effect a good deal, not only by the undiscriminating praise or blame which he lavishes on nearly all the leading men of the day, but also by encumbering it with an improbable romantic story, which he would have done better to omit. It is in the *New Timon,* the first part of which appeared in December 1845, that the sarcastic allusion to Tennyson occurred, which drew on Lord Lytton a severe castigation from the laureate. The obnoxious lines were:

Not mine, not mine (O Muse forbid!) the boon
Of borrow'd notes, the mock-bird's modish tune,
The jingling medley of purloined conceits,
Out-babying Wordsworth and out-glittering Keats;
Where all the airs of patch-work pastoral chime
To drown the ears in Tennysonian rhyme!

Let school-miss Alfred vent her chaste delight
On "darling little rooms so warm and light;"
Chant "I'm a-weary" in infectious strain,
And catch "the blue fly singing i' the pane;"

> Tho' praised by critics and adored by Blues,
> Tho' Peel with pudding plump the puling muse,
> Tho' Theban taste the Saxon purse controls,
> And pensions Tennyson while starves a Knowles.[1])

Among Lord Lytton's more important poetical works, we have still to mention *Eva, the Ill-omened Marriage,* which appeared, in conjunction with some other pieces, in 1842; and *King Arthur,* a legendary, allegorical, satirical and serio-comic poem in twelve books, imitated from Spenser and Ariosto, but too long to sustain the interest and avoid tediousness, in spite of its many keen allusions to modern public personages. The first part of this poem was published in 1848, not long after the February revolution in Paris, the remainder in the following year; and many of the characters may be easily identified as actors in that great political drama. Thus, Guizot, under the name of Astutio, is presented to us as a man who

> Took souls for wares, and conscience for a till; [2])
> And damned his fame to serve his master's will.

In the volume previously mentioned (Eva), there are some good verses. The ingenious illustration of the difference between genius and mere talent is familiar to every educated Englishman:

> Genius, the sudden Iris of the skies,
> On cloud itself reflects its wondrous dyes:
> And, to the earth, in tears and glory given,
> Clasps in its airy arch the pomp of Heaven!
> Talent gives all that vulgar critics need —
> From its plain horn-book learn the dull to read:
> Genius, the Pythian of the beautiful,
> Leaves its large truths a riddle to the dull —
> From eyes profane a veil the Isis screens,
> And fools on fools still ask — "What Hamlet means?"

---

[1]) Sir Robert Peel had granted Tennyson a pension of £ 200 a-year. Mr. Knowles finally obtained a pension to the same amount.

[2]) A money-box in a shop.

Of Lord Lytton's shorter poems we give a few specimens:

SONG.

Ah, let us love while yet we may:
　Our summer is decaying;
And woe to hearts which in their gray
　December go a-maying.

Ah, let us love, while of the fire
　Time hath not yet bereft us:
With years our warmer thoughts expire,
　Till only ice is left us.

We'll fly the bleak world's bitter air —
　A brighter home shall win us;
And if our hearts grow weary there,
　We'll find a world within us.

They preach that passion fades each hour,
　That nought will pall like pleasure:
My bee, if life's so frail a flower,
　Oh, haste to hive its treasure!

Wait not the hour when all the mind
　Shall to the crowd be given;
For links which to the m i l l i o n bind
　Shall from the o n e be riven.

But let us love while yet we may:
　Our summer is decaying;
And woe to hearts which in their gray
　December go a-maying.

THE FLOWER GIRL BY THE CROSSING.

By the muddy crossing in the crowded streets
　Stands a little maid with her basket full of posies,
Proffering all who pass her choice of knitted sweets,
　Tempting Age with heart's-ease, courting Youth with roses.
　　Age disdains the heart's-ease,
　　　Love rejects the roses;
　　London life is busy —
　　　Who can stop for posies?

One man is too grave, another is too gay —
　This man has his hothouse, that man not a penny;
Flowerets too are common in the month of May,
　And the things most common least attract the many.
　　Ill on London crossings
　　　Fares the sale of posies;
　　Age disdains the heart's-ease,
　　　Youth rejects the roses.

KNOWLEDGE.

'Tis midnight! Round the lamp which o'er
    My chamber sheds its lonely beam,
Is widely spread the varied lore
    Which feeds in youth our feverish dream -

The dream — the thirst — the wild desire,
    Delirious yet divine — to k n o w ;
Around to roam — above aspire —
    And drink the breath of Heaven below!

From Ocean — Earth — the Stars — the Sky,
    To lift mysterious Nature's pall;
And bare before the kindling eye
    In M a n the darkest mist of all!

Alas! what boots the midnight oil?
    The madness of the struggling mind?
Oh, vague the hope, and vain the toil
    Which only leaves us doubly blind!

What learn we from the Past? — the same
    Dull course of glory, guilt and gloom:
I ask'd the Future, and there came
    No voice from its unfathom'd womb.

The Sun was silent, and the Wave;
    The Air but answer'd with its breath;
But Earth was kind; and from the grave
    Arose the eternal answer — D e a t h !

And t h i s was all! We need no sage
    To teach us Nature's only truth.
O fools! o'er Wisdom's idle page
    To waste the hours of golden youth!

In Science wildly do we seek
    What only withering years should bring —
The languid pulse — the feverish cheek —
    The spirits drooping on their wing!

To t h i n k , is but to learn to groan —
    To scorn what all besides adore —
To feel amid the world alone,
    An alien on a desert shore;

To lose the only ties which seem
    To idler gaze in mercy given! —
To find love, faith, and hope, a dream,
    And turn to dark despair from heaven!

We close our remarks on Lord Lytton's poetry by quoting Tennyson's stinging reply to Lord Lytton's attack on him in the *New Timon*. To thoroughly appreciate the force of the retort, it is necessary to know, that Lord Lytton. a very dressy man, was suspected by the public of resorting to certain means, for the adornment of his person. which may be excusable in women, but are generally looked on as ridiculous in a man. The verses, which originally appeared in 1846 in the *London Punch*, are here given in full:

THE NEW TIMON AND THE POET.

We know him out of Shakespeare's art,
    And those full curses which he spoke;
The old Timon, with his noble heart,
    That strongly loathing, greatly broke.

So died the Old; here comes the New.
    Regard him; a familiar face;
I thought we knew him: What, it's you,
    The padded man that wears the stays;

Who killed the girls, and thrilled the boys
    With dandy pathos when you wrote;
O Lion! you that made a noise,
    And shook a mane en papillotes,

And once you tried the Muses too, —
    You failed, Sir; therefore now you turn;
You fall on those who are to you
    As captain is to subaltern[1]).

But men of long-enduring hopes,
    And careless what the hour may bring,
Can pardon little would-be Popes[2])
    And Brummels[3]) when they try to sting.

An artist, Sir, should rest in Art,
    And waive a little of his claim;
To have a great poetic heart
    Is more than all poetic fame.

---

[1]) The self-assertion in these two lines somewhat impairs the effect of the retort.

[2]) Alexander Pope.

[3]) The reference is to Beau Brummel, a famous dandy in the latter part of George the Third's reign.

> But you, Sir, you are hard to please,
>   You never look but half content,
> Nor like a gentleman at ease,
>   With moral breadth of temperament.
>
> And what with spites and what with fears,
>   You cannot let a body be;
> It's always ringing in your.ears —
>   They call this man as great as me.
>
> What profits now to understand
>   The merits of a spotless shirt —
> A dapper boot — a little hand —
>   If half the little soul is dirt?
>
> You talk of tinsel! Why, we see
>   Old marks of rouge upon your cheeks.
> You prate of Nature! Y o u are he
>   That spilt his life upon the cliques.
>
> A Timon you! Nay, nay, for shame;
>   It looks too arrogant a jest —
> The fierce old man to take h i s name —
>   You bandbox! Off, and let him rest.

We should greatly hesitate to certify the accuracy and justice of everything in these lines, but Lord Lytton certainly gave the provocation.

Rev. **Charles Kingsley.**

The *Rev. Charles Kingsley* (1819—1875), sometime Regius Professor of Modern History at Cambridge, and afterwards Canon of Westminster, has written some good poetry, though he is best known to the general public by his novels and other works in prose. In 1847 he published a dramatic poem, called *the Saint's Tragedy,* based on the story of St. Elizabeth of Hungary; and he afterwards wrote *Andromeda,* and a number of minor poetical effusions. Two specimens of Kingsley's poetry are subjoined:

THREE FISHERS.

> Three fishers went sailing out into the west,
>   Out into the west, as the sun went down;
> Each thought on the woman who loved him best,
>   And the children stood watching them out of the town.

For men must work and women must weep,
And there's little to earn, and many to keep,
Though the harbour be moaning.

Three wives sat up in the light-house tower,
And they trimmed the lamps as the sun went down;
They looked at the squall, and they looked at the shower,
And the night-rack came rolling up ragged and brown.
But men must work and women must weep,
Though storms be sudden and waters deep,
And the harbour be moaning.

Three corpses lay out on the shining sands
In the morning gleam as the tide went down,
And the women are weeping and wringing their hands
For those who will never come back to the town.
For men must work and women must weep,
And the sooner it's over the sooner to sleep,
And good-bye to the bar and its moaning.

THE DAY OF THE LORD.

The day of the Lord is at hand, at hand!
Its storms roll up the sky:
The nations sleep starving on heaps of gold;
All dreamers toss and sigh;
The night is darkest before the morn;
When the pain is sorest the child is born,
And the day of the Lord is at hand.

Gather you, gather you, angels of God —
Freedom, and Mercy, and Truth;
Come! for the Earth is grown coward and old;
Come down and renew us her youth.
Wisdom, Self-Sacrifice, Daring, and Love,
Haste to the battle-field, stoop from above,
To the day of the Lord at hand.

In these lines "the day of the Lord" is not used in a religious, but in a social and political sense; and refers to that moral and intellectual elevation which Kingsley believed the human race capable of attaining.

Lord Houghton.

Richard Moncton Milnes, later *Lord Houghton* (1808—1885), published four volumes of poems between 1840 and 1844, the first of which was called, *Poetry for the People.* In 1848 he produced the *Life and Remains of Keats.* Of his pleasing, graceful, and thoughtful style the following verses will serve as a specimen:

LONG-AGO.

On that deep-retiring shore
  Frequent pearls of beauty lie,
Where the passion-waves of yore
  Fiercely beat and mounted high:
Sorrows that are sorrows still
  Lose the bitter taste of woe;
Nothing's altogether ill
  In the griefs of Long-ago.

Tombs where lonely love repines,
  Ghastly tenements of tears,
Wear the look of happy shrines
  Through the golden mists of years:
Death to those who trust in good,
  Vindicates his hardest blow;
Oh! we would not, if we could,
  Wake the sleep of Long-ago!

Though the doom of swift decay
  Shocks the soul where life is strong,
Though for frailer hearts the day
  Lingers sad and overlong —
Still the weight will find a leaven,
  Still the spoiler's hand is slow,
While the future has its heaven,
  And the past its Long-ago.

THE HOWITTS.

William and *Mary Howitt* published a great deal of both prose and poetry, under their joint names, from the year of their marriage (1823) up to the time of Mr. Howitt's death (1879). Of kindred tastes, they spent many long happy years together in literary labour and fellowship. The following stanzas in their earliest published volume, *the Forest Minstrel,* place before us an attractive picture of the felicity of so well assorted a union as theirs:

Away with the pleasure that is not partaken!
  There is no enjoyment by one only ta'en:
I love in my mirth to see gladness awaken
  On lips, and in eyes, that reflect it again.

When we sit by the fire that so cheerily blazes
   On our cozy hearthstone, with its innocent glee,
Oh! how my soul warms, while my eye fondly gazes,
   To see my delight is partaken by thee!

And when, as how often, I eagerly listen
   To stories thou read'st of the dear olden day,
How delightful to see our eyes mutually glisten,
   And feel that affection has sweetened the lay.
Yes, love, and when wandering at even or morning,
   Through forest or wild, or by waves foaming white,
I have fancied new beauties the landscape adorning
   Because I have seen thou wast glad in the sight.

And how often in crowds, where a whisper offendeth,
   And we fain would express what there might not be said;
How dear is the glance that none else comprehendeth,
   And how sweet is the thought that is secretly read!
Then away with the pleasure that is not partaken!
   There is no enjoyment by one only ta'en:
I love in my mirth to see gladness awaken
   On lips, and in eyes, that reflect it again.

Mrs. Howitt possessed more of the poetic faculty than her husband. The subjoined lines have appeared under her own name:

Alas! what secret tears are shed,
   What wounded spirits bleed;
What loving hearts are sundered,
   And yet man takes no heed!
He goeth in his daily course,
   Made fat with oil and wine;
And pitieth not the weary souls,
   That in his bondage pine.

To him they are but as the stones
   Beneath his feet that lie,
It entereth not his thoughts that they
   From him claim sympathy;
It entereth not his thoughts that God
   Heareth the sufferer's groan,
That, in his righteous eye, their life
   Is precious as his own.

Mr. Howitt is the author of an interesting work entitled *Student Life in Germany*. Mrs. Howitt has translated Frederika Bremer's principal tales from the Swedish into English. Both husband and wife were brought up as members of the Society of Friends, or, as they are popularly called, "the Quakers."

Mr. A. A. Watts.

Alaric Alexander Watts (not to be confounded with Dr. Isaac Watts), born in London in 1799, was many years connected, as editor or contributor, with the newspaper press. He likewise originated or edited several of those collections of tales and poetry, known by the generic name of annuals, which were once so popular in England. His *Poetical Sketches* were published in 1822, and another volume of poetry, *the Lyrics of the Heart*, appeared in 1850; but most of his best pieces were written for the *Literary Souvenir*, and some other periodical works of the same class. Mr. Watts writes with taste and elegance. His beautiful verses, *Ten Years Ago*, were addressed, as will be readily surmised, to his wife, a daughter of William and Mary Howitt, who died 24th July, 1884. Mr. Watts quite recently resigned his secretaryship in the Inland Revenue Office, and retired into private life.

> Ten years ago, ten years ago,
> Life was to us a fairy scene,
> And the keen blasts of worldly woe
> Had seared not then its pathway green.
> Youth and its thousand dreams were ours,
> Feelings we ne'er can know again,
> Unwithered hopes, unwasted powers,
> And frames unworn by mortal pain:
> Such was the bright and genial flow
> Of life with us — ten years ago!
>
> Time has not blanched a single hair
> That clusters round thy forehead now;
> Nor hath the cankering touch of care
> Left even one furrow on thy brow.
> Thine eyes are blue as when we met,
> In love's deep truth, in earlier years;
> Thy cheek of rose is blooming yet,
> Though sometimes stained by secret tears;
> But where, oh! where's the spirit's glow
> That shone through all ten years ago!

I, too, am changed — I scarce know why —
  Can feel each flagging pulse decay;
And youth and health, and visions high,
  Melt like a wreath of snow away;
Time cannot sure have wrought the ill;
  Though worn in this world's sickening strife,
In soul and form, I linger still
  In the first summer month of life;
Yet journey on my path below,
  Oh! how unlike — ten years ago!

But look not thus: I would not give
  The wreck of hopes that thou must share,
To bid those joyous hours revive
  When all around me seemed so fair.
We've wandered on in sunny weather,
  When winds were low, and flowers in bloom,
And hand in hand have kept together,
  And still will keep 'mid storm and gloom;
Endeared by ties we could not know
  When life was young — ten years ago!

Has fortune frowned? Her frowns were vain,
  For hearts like ours she could not chill;
Have friends proved false? Their love might wane,
  But ours grew fonder, firmer still.
Twin barks on this world's changing wave,
  Steadfast in calms, in tempests tried;
In concert still our fate we'll brave,
  Together cleave life's fitful tide;
Nor mourn, whatever winds may blow,
  Youth's first wild dreams — ten years ago!

Have we not knelt beside his bed,
  And watched our first-born blossom die?
Hoped till the shade of hope had fled,
  Then wept till feeling's fount was dry?
Was it not sweet, in that dark hour,
  To think, 'mid mutual tears and sighs,
Our bud had left its earthly bower,
  And burst to bloom in Paradise?
What to the thought that soothed that woe
  Were heartless joys — ten years ago?

Yes, it is sweet, when heaven is bright,
  To share its sunny beams with thee;
But sweeter far, 'mid clouds and blight
  To have thee near to weep with me.

Then dry those tears — though something changed
  From what we were in earlier youth,
Time, that hath hopes and friends estranged,
  Hath left us love in all its truth,
Sweet feelings we would not forego
For life's best joys — ten years ago.

P. J. Bailey.

Philip James Bailey, born in 1816 at Nottingham, is a philosophical poet, who between 1839 and 1858 produced four poems, entitled respectively *Festus, the Angel World, the Mystic,* and *the Age,* the first three in blank verse, the last, which is a satire in the style of Cowper's *Table Talk,* in verse. The most successful of these poems by far is *Festus,* in which the writer depicts the upward soaring of a purified soul towards the universal source of life. In the first edition, this poem consisted of only about one thousand lines, but it has been gradually expanded by the author, at the expense of its popularity as we believe, till in the tenth edition the number of lines can be hardly less than thirty to forty thousand. When it first appeared, the influence of *Festus* on the thinking world was electrical, and its readers maintained that it stilled a craving which neither philosophy nor theology had till then been able to satisfy. Though we cannot accept this excessive laudation, we readily admit, that the poem abounds in admirable 'passages. Let us take as an example the lines in which Festus dwells on the transitory nature of beauty, and the common lot of humanity?

Festus.   Who doth not
Believe that that he loveth cannot die?
There is no mote of death in thine eye's beams
To hint of dust, or darkness, or decay;
Eclipse upon eclipse, and death on death;
No! immortality sits mirrored there,
Like a fair face long looking on itself;
Yet shalt thou lie in death's angelic garb,
As in a dream of dress, my beautiful:
The worm shall trail across thine unsunned sweets,
And feast him on the heart men pined to death for;
Yea, have a happier knowledge of thy beauties
Than best-loved lover's dream e'er duped him with.

In another fine passage he maintains the necessity
of faith for the poet.

> The world is full of glorious likenesses.
> The poet's power is to sort them out;
> And to make music from the common strings
> With which the world is strung; to make the dumb
> Earth utter heavenly harmony, and draw
> Life clear, and sweet, and harmless as spring water
> Welling its way through flowers. Without faith,
> Illimitable faith, strong as a state's
> In its own might, in God, no bard can be.

Mr. Bailey's similes are always happily chosen:

> Some peaceful spot where we might dwell unknown;
> Where home-born joys might nestle round our hearts
> As swallows round our roofs.

> Just when the stars falter forth one by one,
> Like the first words of love from a maiden's lips.

> I said we were to part, but she said nothing;
> There was no discord — it was music ceased.

Eleven years after *Festus,* appeared the *Angel World,*
but readers complained, that the execution was inferior
to the boldness of the conception, and that they missed
in it nearly all the qualities that had charmed then
in the earlier poem. Disappointed and chagrined at
this verdict, which Mr. Bailey refused to accept, he
incorporated the whole of the **Angel World** into the
next edition of *Festus,* a hazardous, and not a very
successful experiment.

Hon. Mrs. Norton.

The *Hon. Mrs. Norton,* called by a writer in the
Quarterly Review "the Byron of our modern poetesses,"
is the daughter of Thomas, the only son of Richard
Brinsley Sheridan, and was born in 1808. When hardly
seventeen, Caroline Sheridan wrote a pathetic village
tale in verse, called *the Sorrows of Rosalie,* which was
followed in 1831 by *the Undying One,* founded on the
old legend of the Wandering Jew, and in 1845 by the
Child of the Islands, a poem designed to interest the

young Prince of Wales in the privations and sufferings
of the humbler classes. In 1827 she was married to
the Hon. George Chapple Norton, but the union was
dissolved in 1840, under circumstances peculiarly painful
for the lady. The persecution to which at that time
she was subjected, has lent a tinge of melancholy and
bitterness to most of her later poetry. Mrs. Norton has
written a number of ballads, which are highly popular,
particularly *Love not!* (from *the Sorrows of Rosalie*),
My Childhood's Home, I remember thy Voice, and *We have
been Friends together*.

LOVE NOT!

Love not! Love not! ye hapless sons of clay,
    Hope's gayest wreaths are made of earthly. flow'rs;
Things that are made to fade and fall away
    Ere they have blossom'd for a few short hours.
        Love not! Love not!

Love not! Love not! the thing you love may die,
    May perish from the gay and gladsome earth;
The silent stars, the blue and smiling sky
    Beam on its grave, as once upon its birth.
        Love not! Love not!

Love not! Love not! the thing you love may change
    The rosy lip may cease to smile on you;
The kindly beaming eye grow cold and strange,
    The heart yet warmly beat, but not be true.
        Love not! Love not!

Love not! Love not! oh, warning vainly said!
    In present hours, as in years gone by,
Love flings a halo round the dear one's head,
    Faultless, immortal, till they change or die.
        Love not! Love not!

In all her trials, in good report as in bad report,
Mrs. Norton found a firm friend in the Duchess of
Sutherland, to whom she addressed the following ele-
gant lines:

Thou, then, when cowards lied away my name,
    And scoffed to see me feebly stem the tide;
When some were kind on whom I had no claim,
    And some forsook on whom my love relied,
And some, who might have battled for my sake
Stood off in doubt to see what turn the world would take.

> Thou gav'st me that the poor do give the poor,
>> Kind words and holy wishes, and true tears;
> The loved, the near of kin could do no more,
>> Who changed not with the gloom of varying years,
> But clung the closer when I stood forlorn,
> And blunted Slander's dart with their indignant scorn.

Like Byron, Mrs. Norton felt a genuine admiration and warm friendship for the banker-poet Rogers, the author of the *Pleasures of Memory,* and one of the few who remained faithful to her grandfather in sickness and adversity. Rogers's unwavering fidelity to Sheridan, after that unfortunate genius had been abandoned by his former patron, the Prince Regent (afterwards George IV.), is touchingly referred to by Mrs. Norton:

> And when at length he laid his dying head
> On the hard rest of his neglected bed,
> He found (though few or none around him came
> Whom he had toiled for in his hour of fame —
> Though by his prince unroyally forgot
> And left to struggle with his altered lot),
> By sorrow weakened, by disease unnerved —
> Faithful at least the friend he had n o t served:
> For the same voice essayed that hour to cheer,
> Which now sounds welcome to his grandchild's ear;
> And the same hand, to aid that life's decline,
> Whose gentle grasp so late was linked in mine.

It was this desertion of Sheridan, in poverty and disease, by his royal patron that suggested to Thomas Moore the ingenious but acrimonious simile:

> In the woods of the north there are insects that prey
>> On the brain of the elk, till his very last sigh;
> O Genius, thy patrons, more cruel than they,
>> First feed on thy brains, and then leave thee to die!

In the prose-writings of Mrs. Norton, we find the same covert but continual allusions to the wrongs of her wedded life as in her poetry. Her three-volume novel, *Stuart of Dunleath,* gives us an interesting but sombre picture of social life, the prevailing gloom of which is hardly relieved by occasional flashes of sarcastic humour. In *Lost and Saved,* the tone is equally sad, and the incidents, till we reach the last two chapters, of the most harrowing description. The heroine, Beatrice Brooke, deceived by a false marriage, becomes the victim of a designing and heartless man; her former friends desert her, refusing to believe in her innocence; she sinks into the most wretched poverty. and contemplates suicide, but is finally saved.

These incidents give Mrs. Norton occasion to make some observations on self-murder, so striking and original that we are tempted to deviate so far from the plan of the present work as to reproduce them here:

On the fascination of suicide volumes might be written, but all reasoning on that mystery resolves itself into the fact, too little noticed, that it is rather a physical than a mental temptation. A man does not debate on self-murder; or if he does, he for that time avoids the act. It is not the Hamlet who stands with folded arms, arguing the "To be or not to be", who is most in danger of seeking his quietus with a bare bodkin. It is he who has to endure a sensation of helpless weariness in the soul, analogous to the helpless weariness sometimes felt in the body. A man no more says. "I will endure so much, and then I will commit suicide," than he says, "I will walk so many miles, and then I shall be so exhausted, I shall fling myself upon the earth and rest." But in his walk he suddenly pauses and says, "I can no more," like a soldier on a march he cannot make. And so the soul, taxed beyond the powers given, feels suddenly, it "can no more," and drops from the battle-field of life to the rest of death!

After life's fitful fever, he sleeps well —
is the sort of language which the great master of German literature puts into the mouth of Wallenstein, when lamenting his young and passionate friend, Max Piccolomini. The idea that predominates — even in the very freshness of the great sorrow that is crushing the heart of the tormented hero — is the p e a c e attained by the sharer of his troubled victories and warlike struggles: the silence that for ever surrounds him: a silence in which "no evil-boding hour can knell again!"

Having spoken of Mrs. Norton's sarcastic humour, we believe it will not be out of place to quote the following specimen from one of her novels. The vain and selfish elderly Marchioness of Updown, while daily expecting the news of her aged uncle's death, learns that one of her nephews has suddenly died, and being greatly perplexed to know what sort of mourning she should order, writes to request the opinion of her sister Eudocia, who, by the way. is the defunct nephew's mother-in-law:

I wish you would write and tell me about uncle Caerlaverock — when we may expect his death. I suppose. one mourning will do for both; at least, I can't conceive why there should be any difference, as one is a nephew and the other an uncle, but perhaps an uncle is deepest. But to be sure, y o u r puzzle will be, that though he's only a nephew, he married Sara; but then, that won't rule my mourning, you know. I do hate mourning altogether; and they've got dyes now that all come off. I'm sure I had to wash my hands twenty times a-day the last time I was in black, and I hate it. Do you think, whatever y o u do, that I need put on any crape? Madame Troisballous thinks lace will do just as well, and she has covered my dress with a new sort of lace, all worked in little round black beads, which I thought looked extremely well; and indeed, it was the first thing for a long time that has put me in spirits. I wish, Eudocia, you would try and pick me up some of that heavy black Genoese lace, like the Maltese, only finer. You say you don't like executing my commissions, because I never repay you. but that is really only because you never ask me when I have got any money.

Miss Cook.

The popular poetess, *Miss Eliza Cook*, is a native of London, and was born in 1818. When twenty years of age she published a volume, with the title, *Melaia and other poems*. After contributing for a time to several magazines. she began a periodical, in 1849, called *Eliza Cook's Journal*, which was very successful. Miss Cook's poetry, while quite original, has at one and the same time something of the character of Miss Landon's verses, without their melancholy, and something of Mrs. Hemans's warmth of feeling, tempered by reflexion. Her subjects she generally finds in home and the domestic circle, and she dwells with a fond but quiet enthusiasm on such themes as *Old Songs, Christmas*, and *My old Arm-Chair*. Her lines, *Love on!* in reply to Mrs. Norton's *Love not!* have been set to music by Mr. John Blockley. We quote three of her shorter poems:

CHRISTMAS.

Once again, once again,
 Christmas wreaths are twining;
Once again, once again,
 Mistletoe is shining.

Time is marching through the land,
　Deck'd with leaf and berry;
He leads the Old Year in his hand,
　But both the churls are merry.

He speaketh in the clanging bells,
　He shouts at every portal;
God speed the tidings that he tells —
　"Goodwill and peace to mortal."

Gladly welcome shall he be,
　Even though he traces
Silver threads upon our heads
　And wrinkles on our faces.

For once again, once again,
　He brings the happy meeting;
When cynic lips may preach in vain
　That life is sad and fleeting.

Christmas logs should beacon back
　The wanderer from his roving;
Leave, oh! leave the world's wide track
　And join the loved and loving.

Spirits that have dwelt apart,
　Cold with pride and folly;
Bring olive in your hand and heart,
　To weave with Christmas holly.

Breathe a name above the cup,
　And leave no drop remaining;
When Truth and Feeling fill it up,
　'Tis always worth the draining.

Though few and short the flashes are
　That break on Care's dull story;
Yet, like the midnight shooting star,
　Those moments pass in glory.

Then once again, once again,
　We'll tap the brimming barrel;
"Goodwill and peace" shall never cease
　To be a wise man's carol.

All, all we love!—a health to those!
　A bumper!—who won't fill it?
A health to brave and open foes,
　A bumper!—who would spill it!

And here's to him who guards our right
  Upon the distant billow!
And him who sleeps in watch fire-light
  Upon his knapsack pillow!

If changing fate has frown'd of late,
  And some of joys bereft us,
Still, let us "gang a gleesome gait,"
  And prize the blessings left us.

Wisdom's helmet strapped too tight
  Wearies in the bearing;
And Folly's bells on Christmas night
  Are always pleasant wearing.

Then once again, once again,
  Let holly crown each portal;
And echo round the welcome sound—
  "Goodwill and peace to mortal!"

THE WELCOME BACK.

Sweet is the hour that brings us home,
  Where all will spring to meet us;
Where hands are striving as we come
  To be the first to greet us.
      Oh! joyfully dear is the homeward track
      When we're sure of a welcome back.

When the world hath spent its frowns and wrath,
  And care been sorely pressing,
'Tis sweet to leave our roving path,
  And find a fireside blessing.
      Oh! joyfully dear is the homeward track
      When we're sure of a welcome back.

What do we reck on a dreary way,
  Though lonely and benighted,
If we know there are lips to chide our stay,
  And eyes that beam love-lighted.
      Oh! joyfully dear is the homeward track
      When we're sure of a welcome back.

THE HAPPY MIND.

Oh! out upon the calf, I say,
Who turns his grumbling head away,
And quarrels with his feed of hay,
      Because it is not clover.

Give to me the happy mind.
That will ever seek and find
Something fair and something kind
    All the wide world over.

Give me the heart that spreads its wings,
Like the free bird that soars and sings,
And sees the bright side of all things,
    From Behring's Straits to Dover.

'Tis a bank that never breaks,
'Tis a store thief never takes,
'Tis a rock that never shakes,
    All the wide world over.

Miss F. Brown.

Miss Frances Brown is a striking example of genius forcing its way, in spite of the most adverse circumstances. Born in the year 1816, in the small village of Stranorlar, in the north-west of Ireland, and blind from her earliest infancy, she managed to educate herself by getting friends and relatives to read her such books as she could obtain in that remote locality. She soon began to contribute short pieces to the *Dublin Penny Journal*, and in 1841 at last ventured to send some small poems to the *Athenaeum*. These offerings were so favourably received by the public, that she was encouraged to publish a volume of poems in 1844, and a second in 1847. Miss Brown is, we think, most successful in lyrical poetry. She has also furnished the magazines with some short tales, which, though not of the highest class, are surprising productions for a blind lady. One of these, we recollect, was called *the Kendal Illumination.* As a sample of her poetry, we quote a couple of stanzas from a piece called *the last Friends*, in which an Irish exile returns to see once more the hills of his country, all his other friends being gone.

I come to my country, but not with the hope
    That brightened my youth like the cloud-lighting bow,
For the vigour of soul that seemed mighty to cope
    With time and with fortune hath fled from me now;

And love, that illumined my wand'rings of yore,
  Hath perished, and left but a weary regret
For the star that can rise on my midnight no more—
  But the hills of my country they welcome me yet!

The hue of their verdure was fresh with me still,
  When my path was afar by the Tanais' lone track;
From the wide-spreading deserts and ruins, that fill
  The lands of old story, they summoned me back;
They rose on my dreams through the shades of the west,
  They breathed upon sands which the dew never wet,
For the echoes were hushed in the home I loved best—
  But I knew that the mountains would welcome me yet!

Lord Tennyson.

Alfred Tennyson is generally considered to be the greatest poet of the Victorian Age, and at least he is by far the most read of them all. The son of a clergyman in Lincolnshire, he was born at Somersby, near Spilsby, in 1810; and studied at Cambridge, where, while still an undergraduate, he published his first volume of poems, chiefly lyrical, in 1830. At that time his two brothers, Charles and Septimus, were his rivals in poetry, but he very soon outstripped them both. This first volume contained, among other short poems, *Claribel, Oriana, the Merman,* and *Mariana,* but though a promising book for a young author, it met with rather a chilly reception. It must be admitted that the subjects were mostly wanting in human interest; and even in one of the best pieces, *Mariana,* the lone and desolate woman, sitting in a crazy old house, in such a bleak and sterile landscape as the poet Crabbe has so wonderfully painted, and continually repeating to herself: "My life is dreary," and "I am aweary, aweary, I would that I were dead" is not an agreeable picture to dwell upon. Three years later Tennyson re-published this volume with omissions, alterations and decided improvements, but still it did not satisfy the critics, and Tennyson, mortified, remained silent for nine years. In 1842 he again appeared before the public with two volumes of poems; and it was quite evident that he had made a great advance in poetical power since 1833. Some of the poems in this third series were reprints of his older verses, altered and polished, but many of them, such as the *Morte d'Arthur, Godiva,* and *Locksley Hall*, were new. Tennyson now began to find favour with the reviews, and was soon quite as much praised as he had previously been ridiculed. It was already whispered, too, that the Queen and Prince Albert were among his admirers, and this not a little contributed to procure him readers among the general public. In 1847 appeared *the Princess,* which, when first announced, gave room to all sorts of conjectures, as it was generally though quite erroneously believed, that it was some way or other connected with the royal family. In 1850 appeared *In Memoriam,* a series of short poems or sonnets in memory of his friend, Arthur H. Hallam, son of the historian; and on the death of Wordsworth, in the same year, Tennyson succeeded to the laureateship. The great London exhibition was opened the next year, and it was generally expected that the new laureate would hail it with a poetical greeting: but Thackeray forestalled him with an admirable ode, which appeared in the *Times*, and Tennyson lost his chance till the opening of the second London exhibition in 1862. When the Duke of Wellington died, however, in 1852, he wrote some verses on his funeral which he has never since surpassed. Three years later he published *Maud,* a poem which, as we learn from some of his friends, he regards as the best thing he ever wrote; but authors often err in their judgment of their own compositions. In 1859 he returned to the Arthurian legends, and produced the *Idylls of the King,* which were completed by the successive addition of the *Holy Grail, Pelleas and Ettarre*, the *Coming of Arthur,* the *Last Tournament,* and finally *Gareth and Lynette,* which appeared in 1872, *Enoch Arden* he had already published in 1864.

Tennyson's *Morte d'Arthur* is given as a fragment of an unfinished poem, read aloud by a young poet, Everard Hall, to a cheerful company assembled

At Francis Allen's on the Christmas-eve.

The incidents are much the same as in the old French poem. of which we have an English version in the *Percy Reliques*. After a disastrous battle. in which

> King Arthur's table, man by man
> Had fallen in Lyonness about their Lord,

the King, mortally wounded, is borne by Sir Bedivere to a place of safety, but feeling the approach of death he bids the knight cast his famous sword. Excalibur — the gift of the Lady of the Lake — into the neighbouring mere, and bring him word what he sees. Sir Bedivere twice attempts to deceive the King by a false report. and retain the sword for himself, but at last, stung by Arthur's reproaches, he throws it far out into the water:

> The great brand
> Made lightnings in the splendour of the moon,
> And flashing round and round, and whirled in an arch,
> Shot like a streamer of the northern morn,
> Seen where the moving isles of winter shock
> By night, with noises of the northern sea :
> So flashed and fell the brand Excalibur.

On returning to the King, the knight finds him dying, and in obedience to the request:

> Make broad thy shoulders to receive my weight,

he bears him tenderly to the edge of the mere, where a dusky bark, manned by black-hooded phantoms, among whom stand three queens with crowns of gold, now lies. The ladies receive the dying monarch:

> But she that rose the tallest of them all,
> And fairest, laid his head upon her lap,
> And loosed the shatter'd casque, and chafed his hands,
> And call'd him by his name, complaining loud.

The mysterious crew join in the lamentation:

> — from them rose
> A cry that shiver'd to the tingling stars ;

and the barge moves slowly off on its way to the happy island-valley of Avilion,

Where falls not rain, or hail, or any snow,
Nor ever wind blows loudly; but it lies
Deep-meadowed, happy, fair with orchard-lawns
And bowery hollows crowned with summer sea.

Sir Bedivere is the last survivor of the knights of the Round Table — the last representative of the old order of things. A new epoch is about to begin.

In the *Gardener's Daughter*, the hero relates how he wooed and won the gentle Rose. The poem abounds in beautiful descriptions of English scenery. In fact, it was written shortly after Tennyson had turned his back on the fens of Lincolnshire, and fixed his residence at Farringford in the Isle of Wight. "The fields dewy-fresh, browsed by deep-uddered kine", are not common in Lincolnshire; where the eye more frequently rests on the "long gray fields", "the oat-grass and the sword-grass and the bulrush in the pool," or the "tangled water-courses" and "the willow over the river" of the *May-Queen* and his other early poems. At the end of the *Gardener's Daughter*, the narrator represents himself as a widower, and seated with his eyes fixed on the portrait of his lost wife:

> Behold her there
> As I beheld her ere she knew my heart,
> My first, last love: the idol of my youth,
> The darling of my manhood, and alas!
> Now the most blessed memory of mine age.

In the *Miller's Daughter*, a husband recalls to his wife the history of their courtship and marriage, and repeats a song he had given her on her wedding-day:

> It is the miller's daughter,
>   And she is grown so dear, so dear,
> That I would be the jewel
>   That trembles at her ear;
> For hid in ringlets day and night,
>   I'd touch her neck so warm and white.
>
> And I would be the girdle
>   About her dainty, dainty waist,
> And her heart would beat against me,
>   In sorrow and in rest:

And I should know if it beat right,
  I'd clasp it round so close and tight.

And I would be the necklace,
  And all day long to fall and rise
Upon her balmy bosom,
  With her laughter or her sighs,
And I would lie so light, so light,
  I scarce should be unclasp'd at night.

Another of these early poems, *the Brook*, tells us
of a lovers' quarrel and reconciliation, followed by
emigration to Australia and return to England; while
all this time the Brook, the work of the eternal God,
still sweetly murmured its unchanging lay. We quote
the verses that more immediately refer to the stream:

I come from haunts of coot and hern,
  I make a sudden sally
And sparkle out among the fern,
  To bicker down a valley.

By thirty hills I hurry down,
  Or slip between the ridges,
By twenty thorps, a little town,
  And half a hundred bridges.

Till last by Philip's farm I flow
  To join the brimming river,
For men may come and men may go,
  But I go on for ever.

I chatter over stony ways,
  In little sharps and trebles,
I bubble into eddying bays,
  I babble on the pebbles.

With many a curve my banks I fret
  By many a field and fallow,
And many a fairy foreland set
  With willow-weed and mallow.

I chatter, chatter, as I flow
  To join the brimming river,
For men may come and men may go,
  But I go on for ever.

I wind about, and in and out,
　With here a blossom sailing.
And here and there a lusty trout.
　And here and there a grayling,

And here and there a foamy flake
　Upon me, as I travel
With many a silvery waterbreak·
　Above the golden gravel.

And draw them all along, and flow
　To join the brimming river,
For men may come and men may go,
　But I go on for ever.

I steal by lawns and grassy plots,
　I slide by hazel-covers;
I move the sweet forget-me-nots
　That grow for happy lovers.

I skip, I slide, I gloom, I glance,
　Among my skimming swallows;
I make the netted sunbeam dance
　Against my sandy shallows.

I murmur under moon and stars
　In brambly wildernesses;
I linger by my shingly bars;
　I loiter round my cresses;

And out again I curve and flow
　To join the brimming river,
For men may come and men may go.
　But I go on for ever.

The *Talking Oak* is a graceful poem, with a somewhat fantastic subject. A lover converses with the oak on the charms of a certain Olivia, and the tree relates, with what rapture the lady, on visiting the park, had read her name carved on its trunk by the hand of the lover. Hereupon, the youth, who is likewise a poet, vows he will make the tree no less famous than its historical brother oak,

　　Wherein the younger Charles abode
　　　Till all the paths were dim;
　　And far below the Roundhead rode,
　　　And humm'd a surly hymn.

For descriptive force, the last two lines are perhaps unrivalled.

Godiva is the well-known legend of Coventry. Her husband, the Lord of Mercia, having laid a very heavy tax upon the then poor town, Lady Godiva remonstrates with him; but he will only consent to rescind his resolution on terms which he believes she cannot accept:

> She sought her lord, and found him where he stood
> About the hall, among his dogs alone.
>   She told him of their tears,
> And prayed him: "If they pay this tax, they starve."
> Whereat he stared, replying, half amazed,
> "You would not let your little finger ache
> For such as these." "But I would die," said she.
> He laughed, and swore by Peter and by Paul,
> Then fillipped at the diamond in her ear:
> "Oh ay, Oh ay, you talk!" "Alas!" she said,
> "But prove me what it is I would not do."
> And from a heart as rough as Esau's hand,
> He answered: "Ride you naked through the town,
> And I repeal it;" and nodding as in scorn,
> He parted.

The lady takes him at his word. On learning this, the authorities of the town decree that

>   — as they loved her well,
> From then till noon no foot should pace the street,
> No eye look down, she passing; but that all
> Should keep within, door shut, and window barred.

This order being strictly obeyed by the citizens, Lady Godiva "rode forth, clothed on with chastity," through all the town, and back to the castle. Only one irreverent and inquisitive wight, the "Peeping Tom" of the popular legend, disobeyed the prohibition, and met with a signal punishment:

> One low churl, compact of thankless earth,
> The fatal byword of all years to come,
> Boring a little auger-hole in fear,
> Peeped; but his eyes, before they had their will,
> Were shrivelled into darkness in his head,
> And dropped before him. So the powers who wait
> On noble deeds cancelled a sense misused.

None of Tennyson's poems has been more praised than *Locksley Hall*. It is the complaint of an unfortunate lover, who has first been encouraged, and then jilted, by his cousin Amy. Tennyson is fond of making his principal personages tell their own story. After dwelling upon the happy past, when "Love took up the glass of Time, and turned it in his glowing hands;" when for him every thing was bright in nature, even the most uninviting landscape — for Amy was there beside him — he turns with bitterness of soul to the present, when every illusion is gone, and he exclaims: "O the dreary, dreary moorland! O the barren, barren shore!" Not only has Amy forsaken him, but she is "mated with a clown," one who regards her as "Something better than his dog, a little dearer than his horse." He continues:

Drug thy memories, lest thou learn it, lest thy heart be put to proof,
In the dead, unhappy night, and when the rain is on the roof.
Like a dog, he hunts in dreams. and thou art staring at the wall,
Where the dying night-lamp flickers, and the shadows rise and fall.
Then a hand shall pass before thee, pointing to his drunken sleep,
To thy widowed marriage-pillows, to the tears that thou wilt weep.
Thou shalt hear the Never, never, whispered by the phantom years,
And the song from out the distance in the ringing of thine ears.
And an eye shall vex thee looking ancient kindness on thy pain:
Turn thee, turn thee, on thy pillow, get thee to thy rest again.

In his disappointment and despair, he forms several wild projects for the future. Among others, he proposes to wander:

On from island unto island at the gateways of the day;

and there to seek a compensation for what he has lost in Europe:

I will take some savage woman; she shall rear my dusky race.

But on reflexion he abandons this insensate scheme:

Better fifty years of Europe than a cycle of Cathay;

and he resolves to grieve no longer for the faithless Amy, but to go among his fellow-men, who have achieved great things, and yet consider "that which they have done but earnest of the things that they shall do."

The often-quoted complaint of the Latin poet:

Eheu! quam infortunii miserrimum est fuisse felicem,

has been repeated both by Dante and by Tennyson in Locksley Hall. The Italian poet's version is,

Nessun maggior dolore
Che ricordarsi del tempo felice
Nella miseria!

George Eliot gives the preference to Tennyson's rendering of the same idea:

This is truth the poet sings,
That a sorrow's crown of sorrow is remembering happier things.

In the following lines, Tennyson shows a keen and truly poetical appreciation of the beauty of the southern heavens:

Many a night from yonder ivied casement, ere I went to rest,
Did I look on great Orion sloping slowly to the West.
Many a night I saw the Pleiads, rising through the mellow shade,
Glitter like a swarm of fire-flies tangled in a silver braid.

In the *Lotos-Eaters,* we are introduced to an ideal world — to the imaginary region in northern Africa, where Homer locates that dreamy, tranquilly happy race of men. About the design of the poem opinions are divided. While some look on it as merely a paraphrase of a passage in the ninth book of the Odyssey, others find in it a warning against wasting our lives in inglorious repose. The poem opens with the arrival of a crew of wearied seamen in this pleasant land:

"Courage!" he said, and pointed towards the land,
"This mounting wave will roll us shoreward soon."
In the afternoon they came unto a land,
In which it seemed always afternoon.
All round the coasts the languid air did swoon,
Breathing like one that hath a weary dream.
Full-faced above the valley shone the moon;
And like a downward smoke the slender stream
Along the cliff to fall and pause and fall did seem.
A land of streams! some, like a downward smoke,
Slow-dropping veils of thinnest lawn, did go;
And some thro' wavering lights and shadows broke,
Rolling a slumberous sheet of foam below.

They saw the gleaming river seaward flow
From the inner land: far off, three mountain tops,
Three silent pinnacles of aged snow,
Stood sunset-flush'd: and dew'd with showery drops.
Up-clomb the shadowy pine above the woven copse.

The charmed sunset linger'd low adown
In the red West: thro' mountain clefts the dale
Was seen far inland, and the yellow down
Border'd with palm, and many a winding vale
And meadow, set with slender galingale;
A land where all things always seem'd the same!
And round about the keel with faces pale,
Dark faces pale against that rosy flame
The mild-eyed melancholy Lotos-eaters came.

Branches they bore of that enchanted stem,
Laden with flower and fruit, whereof they gave
To each, but whoso did receive of them,
And taste, to him the gushing of the wave
Far, far away did seem to mourn and rave
On alien shores; and if his fellow spake,
His voice was thin, as voices from the grave;
And deep-asleep he seem'd, yet all awake,
And music in his ears his beating heart did make.

The seamen then burst into a Choric Song, expressive of the charms of an existence in this enchanted land, and their resolution to live and die there.

Hateful is the dark-blue sky
Vaulted o'er the dark-blue sea.
Death is the end of life; ah, why
Should life all labour be?

* * *

How sweet it were, hearing the downward stream,
With half-shut eyes ever to seem
Falling asleep in a half-dream!
To dream and dream, like yonder amber light
Which will not leave the myrrh-bush on the height;
To hear each other's whisper'd speech;
Eating the Lotos day by day,
To watch the crisping ripples on the beach,
And tender curving lines of creamy spray;
To lend our hearts and spirits wholly
To the influence of mild-minded melancholy!
To muse and brood and live again in memory,
With those old faces of our infancy,
Heap'd over with a mound of grass,
Two handfuls of white dust, shut in an urn of brass!

No reader of Thomson can fail to notice the strong resemblance of the *Lotos-Eaters* to the *Castle of Indolence*.

It is no easy matter to characterize *the Princess*. Tennyson calls it a *medley*, and as it is a strange mixture of the serious and the grotesque, the romantic and the prosaic, we may admit the accuracy of the designation. It was evidently written to cast ridicule on the sticklers for the pretended "rights of women," but it is disappointing, and owes any popularity it possesses to two beautiful lyrics, which are incidentally introduced. The story is incongruous, not to say, absurd. The Princess Ida. who has been betrothed in infancy to a Prince she has never seen, is no sooner of marriageable age than she takes refuge in a palace given her by her father King Gama, and with the aid of two widow ladies, Lady Psyche and Lady Blanche, founds there a blue-stocking university, from which men are to be rigorously excluded. The poet observes *à propos* of this singular academy:

> Pretty were the sight
> If our old halls could change their sex, and flaunt
> With prudes for proctors, dowagers for deans,
> And sweet girl-graduates in their golden hair.
> I think they. should not wear our rusty gowns.

The betrothed Prince, chagrined at the flight of the Princess, persuades two friends, Florian and Cyril, to accompany him to the university, all three being disguised as women. They are admitted as students, but soon detected through the indiscretion of Cyril. After a number of minor incidents of no great importance, Arac, the Princess's valiant brother, challenges the Prince to meet him in mortal combat. There are to be fifty combatants on each side, and the lists are prepared. Ida watches the combat with composure from a tower, but when the Prince at last falls dangerously wounded, her real or assumed indifference is overcome. She stanches the blood of her all but lifeless lover, tends him till his recovery, and comes to the conviction that the sphere of woman in life is quite different from what she had supposed:

For woman is not undevelopt man,
But diverse: could we make her as the man,
Sweet love were slain: his dearest bond is this,
Not like to like, but like in difference.
Yet in the long years liker must they grow;
The man be more of woman, she of man;
He gain in sweetness and in moral height,
Nor lose the wrestling thews that throw the world:
She mental breadth, nor fail in childward care,
Nor lose the childlike in the larger mind;
Till at the last she set herself to man,
Like perfect music unto noble words.

We subjoin the two lyrics already mentioned:

I.

The splendour falls on castle walls,
   And snowy summits old in story;
The long light shakes across the lakes,
   And the wild cataract leaps in glory.
Blow, bugle, blow, set the wild echoes flying;
Blow, bugle; answer, echoes, dying, dying, dying.

O hark, O hear! How thin and clear,
   And thinner, clearer, farther going;
O sweet and far, from cliff and scar,
   The horns of Elfland faintly blowing!
Blow, let us hear the purple glens replying;
Blow, bugle; answer, echoes, dying, dying, dying.

O love, they die in yon rich sky,
   They faint on hill, or field, or river;
Our echoes roll from soul to soul,
   And grow for ever and for ever.
Blow, bugle, blow; set the wild echoes flying;
And answer, echoes, answer, dying, dying, dying.

II.

Home they brought her warrior dead:
   She nor swooned, nor uttered cry:
All her maidens, watching, said,
   She must weep or she will die.

Then they praised him, soft and low,
   Called him worthy to be loved,
Truest friend and noblest foe;
   Yet she neither spoke nor moved.

Stole a maiden from her place,
  Lightly to the warrior stept,
Took the face-cloth from the face;
  Yet she neither moved nor wept.

Rose a nurse of ninety years,
  Set his child upon her knee—
Like summer-tempest came her tears—
  Sweet my child, I'll live for thee!

The most characteristic of all Tennyson's poems is *In Memoriam,* which overflows with the tenderness that is the prominent feature of the poet's character. Passion Tennyson seldom attempts to depict. His friend, Arthur Hallam, died at Vienna in 1833, and his remains were brought to England by way of Trieste, and interred in a spot overlooking Bristol Channel:

Fair ship, that from the Italian shore
  Sailest the placid ocean plains
  With my lost Arthur's loved remains,
Spread thy full wings and waft them o'er.

So draw him home to those that mourn
  In vain: a favourable speed
  Ruffle thy mirrored mast, and lead
Through prosperous floods his holy urn.

*   *

The Danube to the Severn gave
  The darkened heart that beats no more;
  They laid him by the pleasant shore,
And in the hearing of the wave.

*   *

The path by which we twain did go,
  Which led by tracts that pleased us well,
  Through four sweet years arose and fell,
From flower to flower, from snow to snow:

But where the path we walked began
  To slant the fifth autumnal slope,
  As we descended, following hope,
There sat the Shadow feared of man;

Who broke our fair companionship,
  And spread his mantle dark and cold;
  And wrapt thee formless in the fold,
And dulled the murmur on thy lip;

And bore thee where I could not see
  Nor follow, though I walk in haste;
  And think that, somewhere in the waste,
The Shadow sits and waits for me.

      *   *   *

Calm is the morn, without a sound,
  Calm as to suit a calmer grief,
  And only through the faded leaf
The chestnut pattering to the ground:

Calm and deep peace on this high wold,
  And on these dews that drench the furze,
  And all the silver gossamers
That twinkle into green and gold;

Calm and deep peace in this wide air,
  These leaves that redden to the fall;
  And in my heart, if calm at all,
If any calm, a calm despair:

Calm on the seas, and silver sleep,
  And waves that sway themselves in rest,
  And dead calm in that noble breast,
Which heaves but with the heaving deep.

The last line of course refers to the motion of the ship at sea. In this fine poem we find occasional obscurities, arising sometimes from the want of close connexion between the sonnets of which it is composed, and sometimes from over-polish, for Tennyson kept the manuscript many years by him before sending it to the press. The following verses, however, welcoming in the new year, leave nothing to be desired in point of clearness:

Ring out, wild bells, to the wild sky,
  The flying cloud, the frosty light:
  The year is dying in the night;
Ring out, wild bells, and let him die.

Ring out the old, ring in the new,
  Ring, happy bells, across the snow:
  The year is going, let him go;
Ring out the false, ring in the true.

Ring out the grief that saps the mind,
  For those that here we see no more;
  Ring out the feud of rich and poor,
Ring in redress to all mankind.

> Ring out a slowly dying cause,
>   And ancient forms of party strife;
>   Ring in the nobler modes of life,
> With sweeter manners, purer laws.
>
> Ring out the want, the care, the sin,
>   The faithless coldness of the times;
>   Ring out, ring out my mournful rhymes,
> But ring the fuller minstrel in.
>
> Ring out false pride in place and blood,
>   The civic slander and the spite;
>   Ring in the love of truth and right,
> Ring in the common love of good.
>
> Ring out old shapes of foul disease,
>   Ring out the narrowing lust of gold;
>   Ring out the thousand wars of old,
> Ring in the thousand years of peace.
>
> Ring in the valiant man and free,
>   The larger heart, the kindlier hand;
>   Ring out the darkness of the land;
> Ring in the Christ that is to be!

In *Maud,* we again find a hapless suitor, who this time has been rejected by the maiden's family, in favour of a wealthier lover, a new-made lord. While the father is entertaining a number of political friends at. dinner — "a gathering of the Tory" — the lover seeks an interview with the daughter:

> Come into the garden, Maud,
>   For the black bat, night, has flown.
> Come into the garden, Maud,
>   I am here at the gate alone;
> And the woodbine spices are wafted abroad,
>   And the musk of the roses blown.
>
> For a breeze of morning moves,
>   And the planet of Love is on high
> Beginning to faint in the light that she loves
>   On a bed of daffodil sky,
> To faint in the light of the sun that she loves,
>   To faint in his light and to die.

The concluding lines of the invocation, though a little hyperbolical, possess great beauty:

> She is coming, my own, my sweet;
>   Were it ever so airy a tread,
> My heart would hear her and beat.
>   Were it earth in an earthy bed;

> My dust would hear her and beat,
> Had I lain for a century dead;
> Would start and tremble under her feet,
> And blossom in purple and red.

Maud obeys the summons, but their interview is rudely interrupted by the lady's brother, who favours the lordly wooer. A duel ensues, in which the intrusive brother falls, and the lover is obliged to take refuge in France. Here he depicts the sad condition to which he has been reduced by unmerited misfortune:

> Half the night I waste in sighs,
> Half in dreams I sorrow after
> The delight of early skies;
> In a wakeful doze I sorrow
> For the hand, the lips, the eyes,
> For the meeting of the morrow,
> The delight of happy laughter,
> The delight of low replies.

Remorse, and the pangs of an eternal separation, at last drive him mad, and we are startled by the strange delusion under which he labours, that he is dead and buried

> Dead, long dead,
> Long dead!
> And my heart is a handful of dust,
> And the wheels go over my head,
> And my bones are shaken with pain,
> For into a shallow grave they are thrust,
> Only a yard beneath the street,
> And the hoofs of the horses beat, beat,
> And the hoofs of the horses beat,
> Beat into my scalp and brain!

Fortunately, while in this deplorable state, he hears that England and France have declared war with Russia. These tidings arouse him from his lethargy;

> "It is time, it is time, O passionate heart," said I—
> For I cleaved to a cause that I felt to be pure and true—
> "It is time, O passionate heart and morbid eye,
> That old hysterical mock-disease should die;"

and he goes to enrol himself as a volunteer in the ranks of his countrymen. We have already observed, that Tennyson thought very highly of *Maud;* but none of his poems has been so rigorously judged by the reviews, nor has it ever been a favourite with the English public.

Tennyson's most ambitious poem, *the Idylls of the King*, as published in 1859, contains four books, of which the first three are entitled *Enid*, *Vivien*, and *Elaine*, the names of three ladies at King Arthur's court, the companions, or favourite attendants of Queen Guinevere. The last book is devoted to the Queen herself. In the first of these Idylls, the gentle Enid, daughter of Earl Yniol. who had been won from many rivals and wedded by Geraint, Prince of Devon, at the first report of Queen Guinevere's guilty love for Lancelot du Lake, withdraws with her husband from the Court. Geraint, who loves her tenderly, misinterpreting some disconnected words that had fallen from her, comes precipitately to the conclusion that he has some way or other lost her love, and being desirous of convincing her that he is not unworthy of it, rides forth to seek chivalrous adventures, taking Enid with him. On this expedition Enid's fidelity is put to nearly as many and as cruel tests as that of Chaucer's patient Griselda. At length, in an encounter with the formidable and gigantic Earl Doorm, "the Bull", Geraint is struck bleeding and senseless to the ground. The Earl, who believes him to be dead, struck with Enid's beauty, as she sitting weeping beside her lord, "propping his head, and chafing his faint hands", vainly invites her to eat and drink with him. Nowise dismayed by a first repulse, he offers her his hand in marriage, and when the lady refuses him point-blank, he commits the un-knightly offence of smiting her on the cheek:

> Then Enid, in her utter helplessness,
> And since she thought he had not dared to do it,
> Except he surely knew my lord was dead,
> Sent forth a sudden sharp and bitter cry
> As of a wild thing taken in a trap.

Geraint, however, has recovered from his swoon in time to hear the Earl's proposal, and witness the insult; and starting up he puts an end to Doorm's matrimonial projects by striking off his head at a single blow. Being now convinced of Enid's continued affection for him, he leads her home in triumph, and they enjoy all imaginable domestic felicity, till

> —he crown'd
> A happy life with a fair death, and fell
> Against the heathen of the Northern Sea
> In battle, fighting for the blameless King.

Vivien, the heroine of the second Idyll, is a beautiful, but worthless woman, who by the power of her personal charms fascinates the great enchanter Merlin, the ideal representative of intellect and knowledge; and having drawn from him the secret of his most powerful spells, seeks an opportunity of turning them against himself. One day, when she is conversing with him, this chance occurs. A thunderstorm comes on, and

> —out of heaven a bolt
> (For now the storm was close above them) struck
> Furrowing a giant oak, and javelining
> With darted spikes and splinters of the wood
> The dark earth round.

The fair, though ungrateful sorceress, now employs a sort of mesmerism against her instructor in magic, for we are told, she

> —put forth the charm
> Of woven paces and of waving hands;

and when he has fallen into a deep sleep, she imprisons him in the tree; so that

> In the hollow oak he lay as dead,
> And lost to life and use, and name and fame.

How many Viviens, since the days of Merlin, have taken the most gifted and the most distinguished in their toils, the history of nations can tell! The subject of the third Idyll is the unrequited love of *Elaine*, "the lily maid of Astolat" for Lancelot. She first sees him at the annual tournament in Camelot, where desiring to remain unknown, he intrusts his shield to her care, and agrees, in return, to wear her colours. When the tournament is over, King Arthur returns home, and relates unsuspiciously to the Queen how Lancelot had worn

> —against his wont, upon his helm
> A sleeve of scarlet, broidered with great pearls,
> Some gentle maiden's gift.

This awakens the jealousy of Guinevere. Turning, to hide her emotion, she

> Moved to her chamber, and there flung herself
> Down on the great king's couch, and writhed upon it,
> And clench'd her fingers till they bit the palm,
> And shriek'd out Traitor to the unhearing wall,
> Then flash'd into wild tears, and rose again,
> And mov'd about her palace, proud and pale.

Lancelot, victorious but grievously wounded, has in the mean time been watched over and healed by the devoted Elaine; but he has no love to give her, and as soon as he feels himself strong enough, he sets out for the court, to lay his prizes at the feet of Queen Guinevere. This breaks Elaine's heart; and on her death-bed she desires that her corpse, dressed in her richest robes, should be placed in a black barge; and rowed down the river to the palace of the queen. Lancelot's fidelity to Queen Guinevere is ill rewarded, for she rejects his peace-offering, and dismisses him with contumely.

> Then, while Sir Lancelot leant, in half disgust
> At love, life, all things on the window-ledge,
> Close underneath his eyes, and right across
> Where these had fallen, slowly past the barge,
> Whereon the lily maid of Astolat
> Lay smiling, like a star in blackest night.

In the last of the Idylls, Guinevere's guilt has been discovered. Lancelot has withdrawn from the court; and the Queen, under a false name, has taken refuge with the nuns of Almesbury. Arthur, "the blameless King", imagines at first that she has fled with Lancelot, and, after appointing Sir Mordred regent in his absence, pursues her vainly, but finally discovers where she is, and wends his way thither; not to reproach her, but to bid her farewell for ever. Before he reaches the convent, he learns that Sir Mordred has rebelled, and that he must collect his forces, and march against the traitor forthwith. It is with a presentiment that he is going to his last of fields that Arthur addresses his parting words to Guinevere:

> Yet think not that I come to urge thy crimes;
> I did not come to curse thee, Guinevere,
> I whose vast pity almost makes me die
> To see thee laying there thy golden head,
> My pride in happier summers, at my feet.
>
> * * *
>
> Lo! I forgive thee, as Eternal God
> Forgives: do thou for thine own soul the rest.
> But how to take last leave of all I loved?
> O golden hair! With which I used to play
> Not knowing! O imperial-moulded form,
> And beauty such as woman never wore,
> Until it came a kingdom's curse with thee.
>
> * * *
>
> Perchance, and so thou purify thy soul,
> And so thou lean on our fair father Christ,
> We two may meet before high God, and thou
> Wilt spring to me, and claim me thine, and know
> I am thy husband.

The order in which Tennyson has taken up the Arthurian legends is not a little bewildering; for he began with the end, and ended with the middle: but they have been re-issued by the publishers in their correct chronological order, and with some alterations in the titles. In their completed form, they now stand as follows: *the Coming of Arthur, Gareth and Lynette, Geraint and Enid, Merlin and Vivien, Lancelot and Elaine, the Holy Grail, Pelleas and Ettarre, the Last Tournament, Guinevere, the Passing of Arthur.* Of these, *the Coming of Arthur,* "the approach to the edifice", as it has been called, relates how young Arthur came to the court of King Leodogran, where he so greatly distinguished himself in every knightly accomplishment that he gained the heart and hand of the King's fair daughter, Guinevere. **The Holy Grail** treats of the successful quest of the sacred vessel, out of which our Lord had eaten the Last Supper with his disciples, by the stainless knight, Sir Galahad, to whom and the saintly Sir Percivale it is exclusively vouchsafed to view the object itself; while the less irreproachable knights, Sir Lancelot included, have to withdraw baffled from the enterprise. It is, however, a nun as holy as beautiful, Sir Percivale's sister, who incites Sir Galahad, and the other knights of the Round Table, to undertake the quest, by her relation of a blessed vision accorded her through the special favour of Heaven. This is the most exquisite passage in the poem:

> Sweet brother, I have seen the Holy Grail:
> For, waked at dead of night, I heard a sound
> As of a silver horn from o'er the hills
> Blown, and I thought— "It is not Arthur's use
> To hunt by moonlight," and the slender sound
> As from a distance beyond distance grew,
> Coming upon me. Oh, never harp, nor horn,
> Nor aught we blow with breath, or touch with hand,
> Was like that music as it came; and then
> Stream'd through my cell a cold and silver beam,
> And down the long beam stole the Holy Grail,
> Rose-red, with beatings in it, as if alive,
> Till all the white walls of my cell were dyed
> With rosy colours leaping on the wall;
> And then the music faded, and the Grail
> Pass'd and the beam decay'd, and from the walls
> The rosy quiverings died into the night.

The whole tone of this poem is austere and ascetic. *Pelleas and Ettarre* is a trivial episode. Pelleas, one of those who received the honour of knighthood to fill up the gap in the Round Table left by the quest of the Holy Grail. when on his way to Caerleon meets with Ettarre in the forest, and chooses her as the lady of his love. He distinguishes himself in the *Tournament of Youth;* but after a time, Sir Gawain, the "gay Lothario" of Arthur's court, presents himself to Ettarre, and pretending that he has killed Pelleas in single combat, supplants him in her favour. The lady, it is true, on discovering the deception, experiences a revulsion of feeling in favour of Pelleas, but the disgusted knight seeks an honourable but disastrous encounter with Lancelot. Thus the end is sad. Still sadder is the entire tone of *the Last Tournament,* which serves to prepare us for the coming catastrophe. The scene is the royal residence, Camelot, and Lancelot presides at the joustings, the King having undertaken an expedition to punish some robbers in the North. On the occasion the first prizes are borne away by the famous Sir Tristram of the Woods, who had married Isolt the White in Brittany, and was now on his last and fateful journey to behold once more the other Isolt, the lady with the "black-blue Irish hair and Irish eyes", whom some time before he had fetched from Ireland to be the bride of his jealous uncle, King Mark, "in lonely Tintagil". *The Passing of Arthur,* as may be guessed, is the former *Morte d'Arthur. Gareth and Lynette* differs in many respects from the other Idylls, and the character of the heroine is as peculiar as her personal appearance is singular. Gareth was "the last tall son of Lot and Bellicent", and consequently King Arthur's nephew, for his mother, Queen Bellicent of Orkney, was the King's half-sister. His aged father having sunk into second childhood, and his two brothers being at Arthur's Court, his mother desired to keep Gareth at home, in spite of his continual entreaties to be allowed to join his brothers in Camelot. Wearied at last with his importunity, she gives a reluctant consent, but, hoping to disgust him with the Court, makes it a condition that he shall go there disguised as a peasant, and "serve for meats and drinks among the scullions and the kitchen-knaves". Gareth accepts these hard conditions, and on reaching his destination is engaged as a scullion by Sir Kay, the seneschal of the palace, but he soon finds an opportunity of making himself known to the King, who secretly dubs him a knight, and promises him the first quest. On this he has not long to wait, for

> That same day there past into the hall
> A damsel of high lineage, and a brow
> May-blossom, and a cheek of apple-blossom,
> Hawk-eyes; and lightly was her slender-nose
> Tip-tilted like the petal of a flower.

The young lady. who announces herself as Lynette, has come to crave the aid of the brave Sir Lancelot for the rescue of her sister. the Lady Lyonors, just then besieged by certain ruffian knights in Castle Perilous. Gareth reminds the King of his promise, and to the great disgust of Sir Kay, demands the quest:

> "Yea, King, thou knowest thy kitchen knave am I,
> "And mighty thro' thy meats and drinks am I,
> "And I can topple over a hundred such.
> "Thy promise, King;" and Arthur, glancing at him,
> Brought down a momentary brow. "Rough, sudden,
> "And pardonable, worthy to be knight—
> "Go, therefore," and all hearers were amazed.

Gareth looses his cloak, and reveals himself fully equipped as a knight. A horse alone is wanting, and this he obtains from Lancelot. But Lynette feels herself at first disappointed and insulted, when Gareth presents himself to her as her champion:

> She thereat, as one
> That smells a foul-flesh'd agaric in the holt,
> And deems it carrion of some woodland thing,
> Or shrew, or weasel, nipt her slender nose
> With petulant thumb and finger. shrilling "Hence!
> Avoid, thou smellest all of kitchen grease."

As Sir Gareth, however, successively conquers the three hostile knights, who call themselves respectively "the Morning Star", "the Sun", and "the Evening Star", she confesses that the smell of the kitchen grows more faint; her heart melts, and she sings:

> O morning star, that smilest in the blue,
> O star. my morning dream hath proven true,
> Smile sweetly, thou! my love hath smiled on me.
>
> O sun, that wakenest all to bliss or pain;
> O moon, that layest all to sleep again,
> Shine sweetly; twice my love hath smiled on me.
>
> O dewy flowers that open to the sun,
> O dewy flowers that close when day is done,
> Blow sweetly; twice my love hath smiled on me.

O birds that warble to the morning sky,
O birds that warble as the day goes by,
Sing sweetly; twice my love hath smiled on me.

O trefoil, sparkling on the rainy plain,
O rainbow, with three colours after rain,
Shine sweetly; thrice my love hath smiled on me.

At the conclusion, we learn that Gareth, according to some, married the Lady Lyonors, but according to others, who seem better informed, his bride was Lynette.

The *Idylls of the King*, with all their merits, are somewhat too long and diffuse, and we cannot help thinking that the poem would have gained, as a whole, by the omission of some of the less interesting episodes. We have still to say something about another poem, to which no such objections can be made. We mean *Enoch Arden;* which, as the *Quarterly Review* observes, "bears evident marks of being a cherished work, perfected by untiring and affectionate care." It is a simple story. The hero, "a rough sailor's lad", the miller's son Philip Ray, and Annie Lee, were playmates in childhood; and Annie was "little wife" to both the boys; but in maturer years, when Annie had to make a choice, she gave her hand to Enoch. For some years all went well, but then came unforeseen misfortunes, and Enoch, first a fisherman but in time a skilful sailor, was induced to embark as boatswain aboard a ship "China-board." The voyage out was prosperous, but the ship when homewards bound was wrecked on a rocky island, and only three of the crew, including Enoch, escaped to land. The island was beautiful and fruitful, but one of the survivors, who had been hurt in the shipwreck, soon after died, another "fell sun-stricken", and Arden was left alone. Here he passed many years in solitude, while all at home supposed him to have perished with the ship. Of that tropical paradise, and Enoch's life there, we have the following exquisite description:

The mountain wooded to the peak, the lawns
And winding glades high up like ways to Heaven,
The slender coco's drooping crown of plumes,
The lightning flash of insect and of bird,

The lustre of the long convolvuluses
That coil'd around the stately stems, and ran
Ev'n to the limit of the land, the glows
And glories of the broad belt of the world,
All these he saw; but what he fain had seen
He could not see, the kindly human face,
Nor ever hear a kindly voice, but heard
The myriad shriek of wheeling ocean-fowl,
The league-long roller thundering on the reef,
The moving whisper of huge trees that branch'd
And blossom'd in the zenith, or the sweep
Of some precipitous rivulet to the wave,
As down the shore he ranged, or all day long
Sat often in the seaward-gazing gorge,
A shipwreck'd sailor, waiting for a sail:
No sail from day to day, but every day
The sunrise broken into scarlet shafts
Among the palms and ferns and precipices;
The blaze upon the waters to the east;
The blaze upon his island overhead;
The blaze upon the waters to the west;
Then the great stars that globed themselves in Heaven,
The hollower-bellowing ocean, and again
The scarlet shafts of sunrise— but no sail!

A ship at last touches at the island, and the wedded wanderer is enabled, after many years' absence, to return to his native land and his native place. He first seeks a tavern he had known of old, kept by an old woman called Miriam Lane, who does not recognise him, but in reply to his inquiries, tells him how Enoch Arden was lost at sea, how Annie had bravely battled with

—her growing poverty,
How Philip put her little ones to school,
And kept them in it;

and then proceeds to recount

—his long wooing her,
Her slow consent and marriage, and the birth
Of Philip's child.

Enoch Arden with a strong effort suppresses his feelings; he directs his steps to Philip's house; conceals himself behind a yew-tree in the small garden, and sees the happy family seated at the hearth:

Philip, the slighted suitor of old times,
Stout, rosy, with his babe across his knees;
And o'er her second father stoopt a girl,
A later but a loftier Annie Lee,

> Fair-hair'd and tall, and from her lifted hand
> Dangled a length of ribbon and a ring
> To tempt the babe, who rear'd his creasy arms,
> Caught it and ever miss'd it, and they laugh'd:
> And on the left side of the hearth he saw
> The mother glancing often toward her babe.

At this sight, the returned sailor feels what misery his re-appearance must cause these dear ones; and he nobly resolves to sacrifice himself; to withdraw unseen, and to live alone and unknown for the brief space of time he may still linger on earth, with his broken heart and shattered frame.

> He therefore turning softly like a thief,
> Lest the harsh shingle should grate underfoot,
> And feeling all along the garden-wall,
> Lest he should swoon, and tumble, and be found,
> Crept to the gate, and open'd it, and closed,
> As lightly as a sick man's chamber-door,
> Behind him, and came out upon the waste.
>
>   *   *   *
>
> He was not all unhappy. His resolve
> Upbore him, and firm faith, and evermore
> Prayer from a living source within the will,
> And beating up thro' all the bitter world,
> Like fountains of sweet water in the sea,
> Kept him a living soul.

He finds employment, for "almost to all things he could turn his hand", but it was "work without hope"; and when a year has slowly passed away

>   —a languor came
> Upon him, gentle sickness, gradually
> Weakening the man till he could do no more,
> But kept the house, his chair, and last his bed.

And thus he dies, after revealing his secret to Miriam Lane, and blessing his wife, his children, and Philip.

Whatever may be the defects of Tennyson's earlier poetry, however insipidly sweet the stanzas addressed to the Adelines, Isabels, Lilians, or Claribels, no candid critic will deny the power and vigour of his later productions. Even among these earlier efforts, which have been sneeringly styled "mere drawing-room verses", we may find some short poems, like that here subjoined, which proved that a new poet of no ordinary rank had arisen in England.

LADY CLARA VERE DE VERE.

Lady Clara Vere de Vere,
  Of me you shall not win renown:
You thought to break a country heart
  For pastime, ere you went to town.
At me you smiled, but unbeguiled
  I saw the snare, and I retired:
The daughter of a hundred Earls,
  You are not one to be desired.

Lady Clara Vere de Vere,
  I know you proud to bear your name,
Your pride is yet no mate for mine,
  Too proud to care from whence I came.
Nor would I break for your sweet sake
  A heart that doats on truer charms.
A simple maiden in her flower
  Is worth a hundred coats of arms.

Lady Clara Vere de Vere,
  Some meeker pupil you must find,
For were you queen of all that is,
  I could not stoop to such a mind.
You sought to prove how I could love,
  And my disdain is my reply.
The lion on your old stone gates
  Is not more cold to you than I.

Lady Clara Vere de Vere,
  You put strange memories in my head.
Not thrice your branching limes have blown
  Since I beheld your Laurence dead.
Oh, your sweet eyes, your low replies:
  A great enchantress you may be,
But there was that across his throat
  Which you had hardly cared to see.

Lady Clara Vere de Vere
  When thus he met his mother's view,
She had the passions of her kind,
  She spoke some certain truths of you
Indeed I heard one bitter word
  That scarce is fit for you to hear:
Her manners had not that repose
  Which stamps the caste of Vere de Vere.

Lady Clara Vere de Vere,
  There stands a spectre in your hall:
The guilt of blood is at your door;
  You changed a wholesome heart to gall.
You held your course without remorse
  To make him trust his modest worth,
And, last, you fix'd a vacant stare,
  And slew him with your noble birth.

Trust me, Clara Vere de Vere,
  From yon blue heavens above us bent
The grand old gardener and his wife
  Smile at the claims of long descent.
Howe'er it be, it seems to me
  'Tis only noble to be good.
Kind hearts are more than coronets,
  And simple faith than Norman blood.

I know you, Clara Vere de Vere,
  You pine among your halls and towers:
The languid light of your proud eyes
  Is wearied of the rolling hours.
In glowing health, with boundless wealth,
  But sickening of a vague disease
You know so ill to deal with time,
  You needs must play such pranks as these.

Clara, Clara Vere de Vere,
  If time be heavy on your hands
Are there no beggars at your gate,
  Nor any poor about your lands?
Oh! teach the orphan-boy to read,
  Or teach the orphan-girl to sew
Pray Heaven for a human heart,
  And let the foolish yeoman go.

In 1884, Tennyson was raised to the peerage, with the title of Baron, so that now he is generally spoken of as Lord Tennyson. We shall conclude our notice of the poet and his writings by quoting his spirited lines: *the Charge of the Light Brigade*. During the Crimean war, the Russians attempted, on the morning of Oct. 25, 1854, to surprise the British position in front of Balaclava, by descending in great force, from north to south, the valley between the Causeway Heights and the Fedioukine Hills. On the first-named heights were three redoubts, occupied by Turkish troops, who after a feeble resistance fled, leaving the redoubts in the hands of the Russians, so that the latter, holding as they did the opposite Fedioukine Hills, and having established a twelve-gun battery about an English mile and a quarter to the north of the British position, commanded the valley on both sides, and swept it from north to south with their artillery. The further advance of the Russians was checked by the firmness of the 93rd Highlanders, and a charge of the Heavy Brigade under Brigadier-general Scarlett. In the afternoon of the same day, Lord Lucan, who commanded the Light Brigade, received orders from the commander-in-chief, Lord Raglan, to aid in the recovery of the guns abandoned by the Turks, but unfortunately he misinterpreted the order, and conceived that he was to attempt to take the Russian batteries at the north end of the valley. Lord Cardigan, the second in command, was accordingly dispatched, with the six hundred horsemen of the Light Brigade, on this desperate errand. The small British troop reached and took the Russian battery, sabring the artillerymen at their guns, and then cut their way through a great body of Russian cavalry; but being unable to retain the position they had so valiantly won, they were forced to retreat. Only 198 men returned, and these were rescued by the Heavy Brigade. It was a most daring and brilliant exploit, but a useless sacrifice of life.

THE CHARGE OF THE LIGHT BRIGADE.

Half a league, half a league,
  Half a league onward,
All in the valley of Death
  Rode the six hundred.
"Forward, the Light Brigade!
"Charge for the guns!" he said:
Into the valley of Death
  Rode the six hundred.

"Forward, the Light Brigade!"
Was there a man dismay'd?
Not tho' the soldier knew
  Some one had blunder'd:

Theirs not to make reply,
Theirs not to reason why,
Theirs but to do and die,
Into the valley of Death
  Rode the six hundred.

Cannon to right of them,
Cannon to left of them
Cannon in front of them
  Volley'd and thunder'd;
Storm'd at with shot and shell,
Boldly they rode and well,
Into the jaws of Death,
Into the mouth of Hell
  Rode the six hundred.

Flash'd all their sabres bare,
Flash'd as they turn'd in air,
Sabring the gunners there,
Charging an army, while
  All the world wonder'd:
Plunged in the battery-smoke
Right thro' the line they broke;
  Cossack and Russian
Reel'd from the sabre-stroke
  Shatter'd and sunder'd.
Then they rode back, but not
  Not the six hundred.

Cannon to right of them,
Cannon to left of them,
Cannon behind them
  Volley'd and thunder'd;
Storm'd at with shot and shell,
While horse and hero fell,
They that had fought so well
Came through the jaws of Death
Back from the mouth of Hell,
All that was left of them,
  Left of six hundred.

When can their glory fade?
Oh, the wild charge they made!
  All the world wonder'd.
Honour the charge they made!
Honour the Light Brigade,
  Noble six hundred!

Robert Browning.

Notwithstanding his eccentricity and so frequent obscurity, it cannot be disputed, that Robert Browning is a man of high poetical genius, as well as of extensive though curious and out-of-the-way learning. The obscurity with which he is so often reproached belongs partly to his subjects themselves, and partly to his mode of treating them. He loves to explore the dark nooks of history, to dive into long-forgotten books, and then to contemplate whatever he has brought to light from a standpoint on which no man but himself would have fixed. Some twenty years ago Browning said of himself that the writer and the reader of his books were one and the same; that he himself was all the public he had; but of late years a reaction has taken place; a considerable party have thrown off their allegiance to Tennyson, and declare, that if we can only understand Browning, we must acknowledge him to be the greatest poet and deepest thinker of the present day.

Robert Browning was born in 1812; and his first poetical work *Paracelsus* appeared in 1836. In 1837 he produced a tragedy, *Strafford*, and in 1843 *the Blot on the Scutcheon*, both of which failed, in spite of all the efforts of the great actor Macready. In 1840 he produced *Sordello*; in 1846 *Bells and Pomegranates*, a collection of short poems on various subjects; in 1850 *Christmas Eve* and *Easter Day*; in 1855 *Men and Women*, a series of poems mostly descriptive of Italian scenery and Italian manners; in 1864 his *Dramatis Personae*; and in 1869, in four volumes, the *Ring and the Book*, his longest poem. In 1871 appeared *Prince Hohenstiel-Schwangau, Saviour of Society*, and in 1872 *Fifine at the Fair*.

The subject of the first-named poem is the history of the German-Swiss physician and alchemist, Paracelsus Theophrastus Bombastus von Hohenheim (1493—1541). Browning makes of him a visionary, aspiring to arrive at a knowledge of the principle of life, one who sacrifices love and all the charms of existence to the ambition of becoming, by dint of learning and research. "the greatest and most glorious man on earth." After nine years of labour, study and unfulfilled dreams, he meets with the poet Aprile, who on his side aspires to love "infinitely and be loved." By his intercourse with this man Paracelsus comes to understand that knowledge, to be perfect, must be combined with love for the human race. Renouncing his solitary life, he resolves to teach others what he has himself learned, becomes a professor at Basel, and for a time attracts crowds of auditors. But he dies at last with the conviction, that his life has been purposeless, because he had not understood that *love* should precede *power*. The following lines on lost love are perhaps the finest in the poem:

> 'Tis only when they spring to Heaven, that angels
> Reveal themselves to you; they sit all day
> Beside you, and lie down at night by you,
> Who care not for their presence. Muse or sleep,
> And all at once they leave you, and you know them.
> We are so fool'd and cheated!

Paracelsus is altogether made up of long discussions between the philosopher and his friend Festus or the poet Aprile; and we find him successively at Würzburg, Constantinople, Basel, Colmar, and finally in the Hospital of St. Sebastian at Salzburg, where he is attended in his last moments by the two faithful friends, by whom alone he has been understood and appreciated.

One of Browning's best known, though least popular poems, is *Bishop Blougram*. The Bishop is a sceptic, but produces very plausible reasons for continuing to hold his bishopric. He shows that he cannot be accused of inconsistency; for he has made it a rule through life to consult only his own interest. Browning's grim irony can hardly compensate for the disgust with which the Bishop inspires us. The short poem, *Caliban upon Setebos,* suggested by a passage in Shakespeare's *Tempest:*

> I must obey: his art is of such power,
> It would control my dam's god. Setebos,
> And make a vassal of him.

is the soliloquy of a savage on the Supreme Being, and is designed to show how prone men have been, at all times, to clothe the Deity with human attributes. *Sordello* is the biography of an ambitious Italian poet, who, esteeming of no value the reputation he has already gained, seeks for a more extended influence over his fellow-men for their own good. This poem has been denounced, by most of the critical authorities, as absurd and unintelligible; and in the most favourable criticism we have seen, it is coldly described as "a strange freak of the creative will, which probably no man or woman, except the author, ever understood."

As to the long poem in four volumes, *the Ring and the Book,* it is hard to give even a faint idea of what is so diverse. "It seems", says an enthusiastic reviewer, "to contain everything — the buried wisdom of the ancient world, and the bright but evanescent brilliancy of the intellectual world of the present day." The *Ring* symbolises the main lesson of the poem — that evidence is very difficult to sift, and that hasty judgments on current events are oftener wrong than right. The *Book,* which the author is supposed to have picked up on a Florence book-stall, contains the record of a Roman murder case. Divested of all irrelevant matter, this case of Count Guido Franceschini is but a meagre story, and we are apt to wince with impatience when we find it told over, in the course of the poem, no less than twelve times by different persons.

If the reader inquires, to which of his poems Mr. Browning owes that limited measure of popularity which he enjoys, we shall answer, to a certain number of his simpler and least pretentious productions, in which he shows that he can sometimes write intelligibly. One of these is called: *Pippa passes,* and tells us how the fresh voice of an innocent young girl, a worker in the silk-mills of Asolo, in the Trevisan, who wanders through the streets singing her holiday songs, awakens the slumbering conscience of the wicked, infuses into the artist nobler aspirations, warms the heart of the patriot, and brings the blush of shame to the cheek of the impure. All this, too, is effected by such simple strains as:

> The year's at the spring,
> And day's at the morn.
> Morning's at seven;
> The hill-sides dew-pearled,
> The lark's on the wing.
> The snail's on the thorn;
> God's in his heaven—
> All's right with his world!

Pippa Passes is called a drama by the author; and, being divided ·into scenes, it is at least dramatic in form. Some of scenes are in prose.

Most of Browning's *Dramatic Lyrics* sound somewhat rough and harsh. One of the best is that in which the dying voluptuary, the Bishop of St. Praxed, orders for himself a tomb of purest jasper in St. Praxed's church, glorying in the idea of outshining, even in death, his old rival Gandolf, who lies in "his paltry onion stone", with its inscription in bad Latin. *His* virtues are to be recorded in "choice Latin, picked phrase, Tully's every word"; and here he will

> —lie through centuries,
> And hear the blessed mutter of the mass.

Very similar to this poem is the *Soliloquy of the Spanish Cloister,* in which a monk relates how heartily he abhors Brother Lawrence. *In a Gondola* is a serenade, followed by a dialogue between two lovers, which is abruptly terminated by the assassination of the serenader by a jealous rival. But among all Browning's minor poems, the most interesting to the German reader will probably be *the Pied Piper of Hamelin,* founded on the old familiar legend. The poet begins by telling us how the good burghers of Hameln (or Hamelin, as he writes it) were plagued by the destructive rodents:

> Rats!
> They fought the dogs and killed the cats,
> And bit the babies in the cradles,
> And ate the cheeses out of the vats,
> And licked the soup from the cooks' own ladles,
> Split open the kegs of salted sprats,

> Made nests inside men's Sunday hats,
> And even spoiled the women's chats,
> By drowning their speaking
> With shrieking and squeaking,
> In fifty different sharps and flats.

But a friend in need is at hand; the Pied Piper appears on the scene, and introduces himself to the municipal authorities, assembled in grave consultation in the Town-hall:

> He advanced to the council-table:
> And, "Please your honours," said he, "I'm able
> "By means of a secret charm to draw
> "All creatures living beneath the sun,
> "That creep, or swim, or fly, or run,
> "After me so as you never saw!
> "And I chiefly use my charm
> "On creatures that do people harm —
> "The mole, and toad, and newt, and viper:
> "And people call me the Pied Piper."
> And here they noticed around his neck
> A scarf of red and yellow stripe,
> To match with his coat of the self-same cheque;
> And at the scarf's end hung a pipe.

The Piper offers to clear the town of its unbidden guests, for the consideration of one thousand guilders. The mayor and aldermen jump at the offer, and the Piper goes to work forthwith:

> Into the street the Piper stept,
>   Smiling first a little smile,
> As if he knew what magic slept
>   In his quiet pipe the while;
> Then, like a musical adept,
> To blow the pipe his lips he wrinkled,
> And green and blue his sharp eyes twinkled,
> Like a candle flame where salt is sprinkled;
> And ere three shrill notes the pipe had uttered,
> You heard as if an army muttered;
> And the muttering grew to a grumbling;
> And the grumbling grew to a mighty rumbling;
> And out of the houses the rats came tumbling.
> Great rats, small rats, lean rats, brawny rats,
> Brown rats, black rats, gray rats, tawny rats,
> Grave old plodders, gay young friskers,
>   Fathers, mothers, uncles, cousins,
> Cocking tails and pricking whiskers,
>   Families by tens and dozens,

Brothers, sisters, husbands, wives —
Followed the Piper for their lives.
From street to street he piped advancing,
And step for step they followed dancing,
Until they came to the river Weser,
Wherein all plunged and perished —
Save one, who, stout as Julius Caesar,
Swam across, and lived to carry
(As he the manuscript he cherished)
To Rat-land home his commentary;
Which was: — At the first shrill notes of the pipe,
I heard a sound as of scraping tripe,
And putting apples, wondrous ripe,
Into a cider-press's gripe:
And a moving away of pickle tub-boards,
And a leaving ajar of conserve cupboards
And a drawing the corks of train-oil flasks,
And a breaking the hoops of butter casks,
And it seemed as if a voice
(Sweeter far than by harp or by psaltery
Is breathed) called out: O rats rejoice!
The world is grown to one vast drysaltery!
So munch on, crunch on, take your nuncheon,
Breakfast, supper, dinner, luncheon!
And, just as a bulky sugar-puncheon,
All ready staved, like a great sun shone
Glorious scarce an inch before me,
Just as methought it said: Come, bore me! —
I found the Weser rolling o'er me!

But, when the service was rendered, and the rats all drowned, the conscript fathers of Hameln began to think that one thousand guilders was really too much for such light work as this appeared to be, and they offered the piper fifty; a remuneration which he declined to accept. Finding they were quite resolved to break their faith with him,

Once more he stept into the street,
And to his lips again
Laid his long pipe of smooth straight cane;
And ere he blew three notes (such sweet
Soft notes as yet musician's cunning
Never gave the enraptured air),
There was a rustling that seemed like a bustling
Of merry crowds justling at pitching and hustling.
Small feet were pattering, wooden shoes clattering,
Little hands clapping, and little tongues chattering.

> And, like fowls in a farm-yard when barley is scattering,
> Out came the children running.
> All the little boys and girls
> With rosy cheeks and flaxen curls,
> And sparkling eyes and teeth like pearls,
> Tripping and skipping, ran merrily after
> The wonderful music with shouting and laughter.

The procession marches directly towards the "Koppelberg Hill," and the burghers laugh in their sleeve at the simplicity of the Piper, to think that a troop, which included so many very young children, could climb the mountain. Congratulating themselves on getting rid so cheaply of an importunate creditor, they every moment expect to see the children, who in the mean time have reached the foot of the hill, pause in their march and turn their faces homewards,

> When lo, as they reached the mountain's side,
> A wondrous portal opened wide,
> As if a cavern was suddenly hollowed;
> And the Piper advanced, and the children followed.
> And when all were in, to the very last,
> The door in the mountain-side shut fast.

In the poem, *Prince Hohenstiel-Schwangau*, we have a "Saviour of Society" in the style of the late Emperor of the French. Though not published till 1871, there is internal evidence that it was written soon after the Italian war of 1859, and before the decline of the Second Empire had began. "The poem," observes the *Spectator*, "is not in any sense a portrait, real or ideal, of the personality of the Carbonaro-Conservative, the Imperial adventurer, the star-ruled gambler, the superstitious sceptic, the enthusiastic cynic, though for this we had ventured to hope; it is solely an exposition of the *public* motives, good, bad, and ambiguous — clear, questionable, and confused — which probably asserted themselves in his mind by way of justification of, and criticism on, his own public acts. We are a little disappointed that there is not more of the individual portrait, and less of the general criticism on a policy; but that is perhaps the more in accordance with the conception of the soliloquy — a dream in which the only-in-imagination-dethroned and exiled ruler makes a clean breast of his general designs" to an imaginary sympathetic member of London society. We quote a few striking passages. The position of man in the creation is here defined:

> I'll tell you: all the more I know mankind,
> The more I thank God, like my grandmother,
> For making me a little lower than
> The angels, honour-clothed and glory-crowned.
> This is the honour,—that no thing I know,
> Feel or conceive, but I can make my own
> Somehow, by use of hand or head or heart:
> This is the glory,—that in all conceived,
> Or felt or known, I recognise a mind
> Not mine but like mine,—for the double joy,—
> Making all things for me and me for Him.
> There's folly for you at this time of day!

In the next passage we have a description, too enthusiastic to be altogether truthful, of the French people:

> The people here,
> Earth presses to her heart, nor owns a pride
> Above her pride i' the race all flame and air
> And aspiration to the boundless Great,
> The incommensurably Beautiful—
> Whose very faulterings groundward come of flight
> Urged by a pinion all too passionate
> For heaven and what it holds of gloom and glow:
> Bravest of thinkers, bravest of the brave
> Doers, exalt in Science, rapturous
> In Art, the—more than all—magnetic race
> To fascinate their fellows, mould mankind
> Hohenstiel-Schwangau-fashion.

The following lines evidently refer to the ambiguous language habitually used by the government of the Second Empire; in which professions of an ardent love of peace were neutralized by assurances of readiness for war; and likewise to the policy of keeping the working classes quiet by furnishing them with constant employment at the public cost:

You come i' the happy interval of peace,
The favourable weariness from war:
Prolong it!—artfully, as if intent
On ending peace as soon as possible.
Quietly so increase the sweets of ease
And safety, so employ the multitude,
Put hod and trowel so in idle hands,
So stuff and stop the wagging jaws with bread,
That selfishness shall surreptitiously
Do wisdom's office, whisper in the ear
Of Hohenstiel-Schwangau, there's a pleasant feel
In being gently forced down, pinioned fast
To the easy arm-chair by the pleading arms
O' the world beseeching her to there abide
Content with all the harm done hitherto,
And let herself be petted in return,
Free to re-wage, in speech and prose and verse,
The old unjust wars, nay — in verse and prose
And speech,—to vaunt new victories, as vile
A plague o' the future. — so that words suffice
For present comfort.

Prince Hohenstiel-Schwangau is not over-clear; still
an attentive and patient. reader may generally hope,
with some trouble, to discover the meaning. This is
not so easy with Browning's next poem, *Fifine at the
Fair*. Comparing this production with his enigmatic
Sordello, the *Saturday Review* caustically observed:
"Neither Oedipus nor Daniel could have interpreted
Sordello, unless they had consulted the same books,
whatever they may be, from which Mr. Browning must
have derived his knowledge of an obscure passage in
Italian history; but a reader who should combine the
energy of youth with the tolerance of age, and the
sagacious industry of Scaliger or Bentley with the
microscopic acuteness of a modern German metaphy-
sician, might perhaps after ten readings comprehend
the purpose and the language of *Fifine*." The poem
consists of a Prologue (entitled *Amphibian*), a long
philosophical monologue, or series of reflexions, uttered
by the husband of a certain Elvire, whether for her
edification or simply as a relief to himself is not very
clear, and an Epilogue, called the *Householder*. Fifine,
or Josephine, who has almost nothing to do with the

poem to which she gives a title, is a dancing-girl in a mountebank's show at the fair of Pornic in Brittany, and unwittingly suggests to Elvire's philosopher-husband, either directly or indirectly, that stream of reflexions which he continues to pour out for about two thousand lines. The Prologue, which is much more readable than the rest of the poem, describes a swimmer floating in a tranquil sea, and looking up at a butterfly hovering above him, while he reflects that neither could abide in the other's sphere without something which, like death, should entirely change their being. The sea here represents the region of passion and thought, the true element of the poet, intermediate between earthly and spiritual life, and the butterfly is an emblem of the disembodied soul:

> Can the insect feel the better
>   For watching the uncouth play
> Of limbs that slip the fetter,
>   Pretend as they were not clay?
>
> Undoubtedly I rejoice
>   That the air comports so well
> With a creature which had the choice
>   Of the land once. Who can tell?
>
> What if a certain soul
>   Which early slipped its sheath,
> And has for its home the whole
>   Of heaven, thus look beneath,
>
> Thus watch one who, in the world,
>   Both lives and likes life's way,
> Nor wishes the wings unfurled
>   That sleep in the worm, they say?
>
> But sometimes when the weather
>   Is blue, and warm waves tempt
> To free oneself of tether,
>   And try a life exempt
>
> From worldly noise and dust,
>   In the sphere which overbrims
> With passion and thought,—why, just
>   Unable to fly, one swims!

By passion and thought upborne,
  One smiles to oneself,—"They fare
Scare better, they need not scorn
  Our sea, who live in the air!"

Emancipate through passion
  And thought, with sea for sky,
We substitute, in a fashion,
  For heaven,—poetry:

Which sea, to all intent,
  Gives flesh such noon-disport
As a finer clement
  Affords the spirit-sort.

Whatever they are, we seem:
  Imagine the thing they know;
All deeds they do, we dream;
  Can heaven be else but so?

The whole of the poem (including the Prologue), we are told by a critic, is an illustration of Mr. Browning's text, "that the life of man is a life of error lived by the help of truth, a life of falsehood which implies the need and capacity for reality, a life of illusion grounded and fulfilled in some ultimate perception of true being, a life of endless yearning after that which always eludes and yet always inspires us." Accepting this interpretation, we proceed to add, that Elvire and her husband go forth, arm in arm, to visit the fair, where besides a "chimneyed house on wheels" and such like, they see an

Ape of many years and much adventure, grim
And grey, with pitying fools who find a joke in him.
Or, best, the human beauty, Mimi, Toinette, Fifine,
Tricot fines down if fat, padding plumps up if lean,
Ere shedding petticoat, modesty, and such toys,
They bounce forth, squalid girls transformed to gamesome boys.

Fifine is presented to us as a type of the sensual earthly woman, as Elvire is the impersonation of intellect, refinement, and mortality struggling on to immortality. But Fifine, mean as she is, "the Pariah of the North, the European Nautch", has her place in creation; for just as a grain of sand at a given angle may reflect the rays of the sun,

> No creature's made so mean
> But that some way it boasts, could we investigate
> Its supreme worth.

Fifine's *raison d'être* being thus established. the tolerant philosopher-husband continues:

> Well then, thus much confessed, what wonder if there steal
> Unchallenged to my heart the force of one appeal
> She makes, and justice stamp the sole claim she asserts?
> So absolutely good is truth, truth never hurts
> The teller, whose worst crime gets somehow grace, avowed.
> To me that silent pose and prayer proclaimed aloud
> "Know all of me outside, the rest be emptiness
> For such as you. I call attention to my dress,
> Coiffure, outlandish features, and memorable limbs,
> Piquant entreaty, all that eye-glance overskims.
> Does this much pleasure? Then repay the pleasure—put
> The price i' the tambourine. Do you seek farther? Tut!
> I'm just my instrument—sound hollow, mere smooth skin
> Stretched o'er gilt framework, I rub-dub, nought else within—
> Always for such as you. If I have use elsewhere,
> If certain bells, now mute, can jingle, need you care?
> Be it enough, there's truth i' the pleading, which comports
> With no word spoken out in colleges or courts,
> Since all I plead is, "Pay for just the sight you see,
> And give no credit to another charm in me."

The *Epilogue* to this strange, enigmatical poem is called the *Householder;* and here the house stands for the human body or earthly life. The householder is dispirited and discontented, when a woman - spirit announces herself, and gently rebukes his impatience and petulance. The reader will be surprised to find, that this part of the poem can be regarded as no more than half-serious:

> Savage, I was sitting in my house, late, lone:
>   Dreary, weary with the long day's work:
> Head of me, heart of me, stupid as a stone:
>   Tongue-tied now, now blaspheming like a Turk;
> When, in a moment, just a knock, call, cry,
>   Half a pang and all a rapture, there again were we—
> "What, and is it really you again?" quoth I.
>   "I again; what else did you expect?" quoth She.

> "Never mind, hie away from this old house,
>   Every crumbling brick embrowned with sin and shame.
> Quick, in its corners ere certain shapes arouse—
>   Let them, every devil of the night, lay claim.

Make and mend, rap and rend, for me—Good-bye!
  God be their guard from disturbance at their glee,
Till, crash, comes down the carcase in a heap," quoth I.
  "Nay, but there's a decency required," quoth She.

"Ah, but if you knew how time has dragged, days, nights,
  All the neighbour talk with man and maid—such men!
All the fuss and trouble of street sounds, window sights;
  All the worry of flapping door and echoing roof; and then
All the fancies. . . . Who were they had leave, dared try
  Darker arts that almost struck despair in me!
If you knew but how I dwelt down here!" quoth I.
  "And was I so better off up there?" quoth She.

"Help and get it over! *Reunited to his wife,*
  (How draw up the paper lets the parish people know?)
Lies M. or N. departed from this life,
  Day the this or that, month and year the so and so.
What i' the way of final flourish? Prose, verse? Try!
  Affliction sore long time he bore, or what is it to be?
Till God did please to grant him ease—Do end," quoth I.
  "I end with—Love is all and Death is nought," quoth She.

The study of *Fifine at the Fair* has been recommended by one reviewer as a species of mental gymnastics. "The stimulus to thought", he says, "is in itself valuable, as a difficult or inaccessible Alpine summit furnishes an attraction to mountain climbers."

It is with a deep feeling of relief, that we turn from *Fifine* and *Prince Hohenstiel-Schwangau,* to show what Browning can do as a lyrical poet, when he chooses to descend from his shadowy Pegasus, and adapt himself to the comprehension of ordinary readers:

HOW THEY BROUGHT THE GOOD NEWS') FROM GHENT TO AIX.

I sprang to the stirrup, and Joris, and he,
I galloped, Dirck galloped, we galloped all three:
Good speed! cried the watch, as the gate-bolts undrew;
Speed! echoed the wall to us galloping through;
Behind shut the postern, the lights sank to rest,
And into the midnight we galloped abreast.

') Probably the news of the revolution of 1539.

Not a word to each other; we kept the great pace
Neck by neck, stride by stride, never changing our place:
I turned in my saddle and made its girths tight,
Then shortened each stirrup, and set the pique right,
Rebuckled the cheek-strap, chained slacker the bit,
Nor galloped less steadily Roland a bit.

'Twas sunset at starting; but while we drew near
Lockeren, the cocks crew and twilight dawned clear;
At Boom, a great yellow star came out to see;
At Düffeld, 'twas morning as plain as could be;
And from Mecheln church-steeple we heard the half-chime,
So Joris broke silence with, Yet there is time!

At Aerschot, up leaped of a sudden the sun,
And against him the cattle stood black every one,
To stare thro' the mist at us galloping past,
And I saw my stout galloper Roland, at last,
With resolute shoulders, each butting away
The haze, as some bluff river headland its spray.

And his low head and crest, just one sharp ear bent back
For my voice, and the other pricked out on his track;
And one eye's black intelligence—ever that glance
O'er its white edge at me, his own master, askance!
And the thick heavy spume-flakes which aye and anon
His fierce lips shook upwards in galloping on.

By Hasselt, Dirck groaned; and cried Joris, Stay spur!
Your Roos galloped bravely, the fault's not in her,
We'll remember at Aix:—for one heard the quick wheeze
Of her chest, saw the stretched neck and staggering knees,
And sunk tail, and horrible heave of the flank,
As down on her haunches she shuddered, and sank.

So we were left galloping, Joris and I,
Past Looz and past Tongres, no cloud in the sky;
The broad sun above laughed a pitiless laugh,
'Neath our feet broke the brittle bright stubble like chaff;
Till over by Dalhem a dome-spire sprang white,
And Gallop! gasped Joris, for Aix is in sight!

How they'll greet us—and all in a moment his roan
Rolled neck and croup over, lay dead as a stone;
And there was my Roland to bear the whole weight
Of the news which alone could save Aix from her fate,
With his nostrils like pits full of blood to the brim,
And with circles of red for his eye-socket's rim.

Then I cast loose my buff-coat, each holster let fall,
Shook off both my jack-boots, let go belt and all,
Stood up in the stirrup, leaned, patted his ear,
Called my Roland his pet-name, my horse without peer,
Clapped my hands, laughed and sang, any noise, bad or good: -
Till at length into Aix Roland galloped and stood.

And all I remember is, friends flocking around,
As I sat with his head twixt my knees on the ground,
And no voice but was praising this Roland of mine,
As I poured down his throat our last measure of wine,
Which — the burgesses voted by common consent—
Was no more than his due who brought good news from Ghent.

In 1873 Mr. Browning produced a strange poem, with a still stranger title: *Red Cotton Night-cap Country;* on which our space forbids us to dwell. We have still a few words to say about Mr. Browning's style. Some of his shorter poems, on which he has evidently expended a certain care, are smooth and melodious, but the greater part of what he has written is irregular, jerky and unmusical. A critic in the *Times* lately observed, with a covert allusion to Browning, that the blank verse of the period creates a sensation something like that experienced in a drive over a rutty road. His habitual obscurity we have already to some extent excused, the subjects themselves being often little known, and his mode of handling them being very peculiar. Still, much of that want of perspicuity, of which every reader complains, is chargeable on the unwarrantable liberties which Browning takes with the language. "It is all right, no doubt," ironically observes the above-mentioned critic, "to take any unoffending substantive and enlist it by force in the army of verbs, or, with the addition of one or two letters, in a regiment of adjectives and participles; but just at first the appearance of such a phenomenon is apt to excite prejudice, to provoke an exclamation, as at a sudden shock". Not only does Mr. Browning do this, but he often darkens the riddle by the omission of the article and the sign of the infinitive. A single example will suffice:

What sound out-warbles brook, while at the source it wins
That moss and stone dispart, allow its bubblings breathe?

Here we have *brook*, instead of *a brook; breathe* instead of *to breathe;* and a conjunction is wanting between *dispart* and *allow*. It is nowise surprising that when Douglas Jerrold, on recovering from a dangerous illness, took up Browning's *Sordello*, and found it quite unintelligible, the alarming suspicion should have flashed on him, in regaining his health he had lost his reason; and it was only when Mrs. Jerrold, having read a page or two at his request, threw down the book, exclaiming, "Bother the gibberish!" that he was able to say, with a sigh of relief: "Thank heaven! then I am not an idiot." Of late years Mr. Browning's readers have no doubt increased in number, but in our busy nineteenth century very few have leisure and inclination to search for the clue to these poetical enigmas; and many a reader who opens one of his books from curiosity, will replace it on the shelf, and never again dream of disturbing the dust in which it slumbers.

Mrs. E. B. Browning.

Mrs. *Elizabeth Barrett Browning* was born in London, in the year 1809; and in 1826, when in her seventeenth year, she published a volume anonymously, entitled *An Essay on Mind, and other poems.* In 1833 appeared her translation of the *Prometheus Bound* of Aeschylus; which she afterwards re-published in a greatly improved form, with some fugitive pieces. The *Essay on Mind* was a sort of satire in heroic verse, possessing little merit, and in riper years the author herself judged it so unfavourably that she expressed a hope it "might only be remembered against her by a few of her personal friends." Several of the pieces in the *Prometheus* volume, however, deserved to live, and gave a high promise of future fame. Two of these we subjoin:

A VISION OF LIFE AND DEATH.

Mine ears were deaf to melody,
My lips were dumb to sound:
Where didst thou wander, oh my soul,
When ear and tongue were bound?

"I wander'd by the stream of time,
  Made dark by human tears:
I threw my voice upon the waves,
  And *they* did throw me theirs."

And how did sound the waves, my soul?
  And how did sound the waves?
"Hoarse, hoarse, and wild!—they ever dash'd
  'Gainst ruin'd thrones and graves."

And what sight on the shore, my soul?
  And what sight on the shore?
"Twain beings sate there silently,
  And sit there evermore."

Now tell me fast and true, my soul;
  Now tell me of those twain.
"One was yclothed in mourning vest,
  And one, in trappings vain.

"She, in the trappings vain, was fair,
  And eke fantastical:
A thousand colours dyed her garb;
  A blackness bound them all.

"In part her hair was gaily wreath'd,
  In part was wildly spread:
Her face did change its hue too fast,
  To say 'twas pale or red.

"And when she look'd on earth, I thought
  She smiled for very glee:
But when she look'd to heav'n, I knew
  That tears stood in her ee.

"She held a mirror, there to gaze:
  It could no cheer bestow;
For while her beauty cast the shade,
  Her breath did make it go.

"A harper's harp did lie by her,
  Without the harper's hest;
A monarch's crown did lie by her,
  Wherein an owl had nest:

"A warrior's sword did lie by her,
  Grown rusty since the fight;
A poet's lamp did lie by her:—
  Ah me!—where was its light?"

And what didst *thou* say, O, my soul,
  Unto that mystic dame!
"I ask'd her of her tears, and eke
  I ask'd her of her name.

"She said, she built a prince's throne:
  She said, he ruled the grave;
And that the levelling worm ask'd not
  If he were king or slave.

"She said, she form'd a godlike tongue,
  Which lofty thoughts unsheathed;
Which rolled its thunder round, and purged
  The air the nations breathed.

"She said, that tongue, all eloquent,
  With silent dust did mate;
Whereon false friends betray'd long faith,
  And foes outspat their hate.

"She said, she warm'd a student's heart,
  But heart and brow 'gan fade:
Alas, alas! those Delphic trees
  Do cast an upas shade!

"She said, she lighted happy hearths,
  Whose mirth was all forgot:
She said, she tunèd marriage bells,
  Which rang when love was *not*.

"She said, her name was Life; and then
  Out laugh'd and wept aloud,—
What time the other being strange
  Lifted the veiling shroud.

"Yea! lifted she the veiling shroud,
  And breathed the icy breath;
Whereat, with inward shuddering,
  I knew *her* name was Death.

"Yea! lifted she her calm, calm brow,
  Her clear cold smile on me:
Whereat within my deepness, leap'd
  Mine immortality.

"She told me, it did move her smile,
  To witness how I sigh'd,
Because that what was fragile brake,
  And what was mortal died:

"As if that kings could grasp the earth,
  Who from its dust began;
As if that suns could shine at night,
  Or glory dwell with man.

"She told me, she had freed *his* soul,
  Who aye did freedom love;
Who now reck'd not, were worms below,
  Or ranker worms above!

"She said, the student's heart had beat
  Against its prison dim;
Until she crush'd the bars of flesh,
  And pour'd truth's light on him.

"She said, that they who left the hearth,
  For aye in sunshine dwell;
She said, the funeral tolling brought
  More joy than marriage bell!

"And as she spake, she spake less loud;
  The stream resounded more:
Anon I nothing heard but waves
  That wail'd along the shore."

And what didst thou say, oh my soul,
  Upon that mystic strife?
"I said, that Life was only Death,
  That only Death was Life."

EARTH.

How beautiful is earth! my starry thoughts
Look down on it from their unearthly sphere,
And sing symphonious — Beautiful is earth!
The lights and shadows of her myriad hills;
The branching greenness of her myriad woods;
Her sky-affecting rocks; her zoning sea;
Her rushing, gleaming cataracts; her streams
That race below, the wingèd clouds on high;
Her pleasantness of vale and meadow!—
                              Hush!
Meseemeth through the leafy trees to ring
A chime of bells to falling waters tuned;
Whereat comes heathen Zephyrus, out of breath
With running up the hills, and shakes his hair
From off his gleesome forehead, bold and glad
With keeping blythe Dan Phoebus company;—
And throws him on the grass, though half afraid;
First glancing round, lest tempests should be nigh;
And lays close to the ground his ruddy lips,

And shapes their beauty into sound, and calls
On all the petall'd flowers that sit beneath
In hiding-places from the rain and snow,
To loosen the hard soil and leave their cold
Sad idlesse, and betake them up to him.
They straightway hear his voice —
                    A thought did come,
And press from out my soul the heathen dream.
Mine eyes were purgèd. Straightway did I bind
Round me the garment of my strength, and heard
Nature's death-shrieking — the hereafter cry,
When he o' the lion voice, the rainbow-crown'd,
Shall stand upon the mountains and the sea,
And swear by earth, by heaven's throne, and Him
Who sitteth on the throne, there shall be time
No more, no more! Then, veil'd Eternity
Shall straight unveil her awful countenance
Unto the reeling worlds, and take the place
Of seasons, years, and ages. Aye and aye
Shall be the time of day. The wrinkled heav'n
Shall yield her silent sun, made blind and white
With an exterminating light: the wind,
Unchainèd from the poles, nor having charge
Of cloud or ocean, with a sobbing wail
Shall rush among the stars, and swoon to death.
Yea, the shrunk earth, appearing livid pale
Beneath the red-tongued flame, shall shudder by
From out her ancient place, and leave — a void.
Yet haply by that void the saints redeem'd
May sometimes stray; when memory of sin
Ghost-like shall rise upon their holy souls;
And on their lips shall lie the name of earth
In paleness and in silentness; until
Each looking on his brother, face to face,
And bursting into sudden happy tears
(The only tears undried), shall murmur—"Christ!"

In 1838 and 1839 Mrs. Browning gave to the world
several other poems, including *the Seraphim, the Romant
of the Page,* and *the Drama of Exile.* The subject of
the latter is the fall of man, or rather, to quote her
own words, "the new and strange experience of the
fallen humanity, as it went forth from Paradise into
the wilderness". Of course it is chiefly the dialogues
between the erring first parents of the human race
that awaken our sympathies; but the reader cannot
fail to be struck with the beauty of such passages as

the farewell greeting of the spirits to the hapless
fugitives, as they leave their blissful abode with the
haste of conscious guilt:

> Hark! the Eden trees are stirring
> Soft and solemn in your hearing!
> Oak and linden, palm and fir,
> Tamarisk and juniper,
> Each still throbbing in vibration
> Since that crowning of creation
> When the God-breath spake abroad,
> Let us make man like to God!
> And the pine stood quivering
> As the awful word went by,
> Like a vibrant music string
> Stretched from mountain-peak to sky,
> And the platan did expand
> Slow and gradual, branch and head;
> And the cedar's strong black shade
> Fluttered brokenly and grand.
> Grove and wood were swept aslant
> In emotion jubilant.

* *
 *

> Hearken, oh hearken! ye shall hearken surely
>   For years and years,
> The noise beside you dripping coldly, purely,
>   Of spirit's tears.

* *
 *

> We shall be near you in your poet-languors
>   And wild extremes,
> What time ye vex the desert with vain angers,
>   Or mock with dreams.
> And when upon you, weary after roaming,
>   Death's seal is put,
> By the foregone ye shall discern the coming,
>   Through eyelids shut.

Of Mrs. Browning's minor poems, her beautiful lines
on *Cowper's Grave, Lady Geraldine's Courtship*, the story
of a peasant poet who loves and wins an earl's daughter,
the Cry of the Children, a pathetic pleading for the
children of the poor toiling for their bread in unwhole-
some factories, and *Bertha in the Lane*, are the chief
favourites. In the last-named poem, two orphan sisters
live together; and the elder is happy in the affection
of a lover, till he at length becomes estranged from

her, overcome by the superior charms of the younger girl. The elder sister, mindful of the vow she had made her dying mother, to guard and watch over Bertha, struggles hard to hide her sufferings, but "blood runs faint in womanhood", and the effort undermines her strength and wears her out. On her deathbed she acknowledges all to Bertha, and finds nothing unnatural in the transfer of her lover's affections:

> When he saw thee who art best,
> Past compare, and loveliest,
> He but judged thee as the rest.

Then she makes the touching request:

> And, dear Bertha, let me keep
> On my hand this little ring,
> Which at night, when others sleep,
> I can still see glittering.
> Let me wear it out of sight,
> In the grave — where it will light
> All the dark up, day and night.

The *Sonnets from the Portuguese* are in the style of Shakespeare's sonnets, and passed at first for translations from Camoens; but nothing at all resembling them has been discovered in Portuguese literature.

While engaged in the composition of a large portion of these poems, Miss Barrett — for she was not yet Mrs. Browning — lived as an invalid in a darkened room, and for several years she remained in a highly precarious state of health. Convalescent at last, if not physically strong, she gave her hand to the poet Robert Browning, who took her to Italy to recruit her shattered constitution; and while residing at Florence, in 1848, she was a witness of the revolutionary outbreak in that city. This furnished the subject of her poem, *Casa Guidi Windows,* in which she narrates what she saw from the windows of her residence, and describes the impressions made on her by these stirring popular movements. Every line is instinct with the love of Italy and the passion for political freedom. By an allusion in this poem to her "young Florentine, not two years old", we learn that there was now a new link to unite her at once to her husband, and to the land which they had chosen as their home.

Aurora Leigh (1856) is the most ambitious of Mrs. Browning's poems, and she herself called it "the most mature" of her works. It is the first attempt ever made to write a novel in blank verse — a bold attempt, and only partially successful; for we find in it the poetical and the prosaic so strangely mixed up together that we are often mystified and irritated by the amalgamation. Aurora is the daughter of a learned English father and a Florentine mother; and on the death of the latter, four years after the child's birth, her father becomes her tutor:

> My father taught me what he had learnt the best
> Before he died and left me, — grief and love.
> And, seeing we had books among the hills,
> Strong words of counselling souls confederate
> With vocal pines and waters, — out of books
> He taught me all the ignorance of men,
> And how God laughs in heaven when any man
> Says "Here I'm learned; this, I understand;
> In that, I am never caught at fault or doubt."
> He sent the schools to school, demonstrating
> A fool will pass for such through one mistake,
> While a philosopher will pass for such,
> Through said mistakes being ventured in the gross
> And heaped up to a system.

Her father dies, and she is sent back to England, to her father's sister:

> — (she was not old
> Although my father's elder by a year)
> A nose drawn sharply, yet in delicate lines;
> A close mild mouth, a little soured about
> The ends, through speaking unrequited loves
> Or peradventure niggardly half-truths.

This elderly lady had seen but little of the world, for

> She had lived
> A sort of cage-bird life, born in a cage,
> Accounting that to leap from perch to perch
> Was act and joy enough for any bird.

Under her aunt's care, Aurora receives a curiously assorted education, comprising languages, science, theology,

topography, statistics, drawing, dancing, and needlework:
but at length tired of a formal curriculum, she begins
to read in a desultory and promiscuous way:

> I read books bad and good — some bad and good
> At once; (good aims not always make good books:
> Well-tempered spades turn up ill-smelling soils
> In digging vineyards even) books that prove
> God's being so definitely, that man's doubt
> Grows self-defined the other side the line,
> Made atheist by suggestion; moral books,
> Exasperating to license; genial books,
> Discounting from the human dignity;
> And merry books, which set you weeping when
> The sun shines, — ay, and melancholy books,
> Which make you laugh that any one should weep
> In this disjointed life for one wrong more.

Here she meets with her cousin, Romney Leigh.
a scholar, enthusiast and philanthropist:

> We read, or talked, or quarrelled, as it chanced.
> We were not lovers, nor even friends well-matched.

He thinks that in many respects the world "went
ill", but "his brow would soften", Aurora tells us, when

> — breaking into voluble ecstasy
> I flattered all the beauteous country round
> As poets use, the skies, the clouds, the fields.
> The happy violets hiding from the roads
> The primroses run down to, carrying gold;
> The tangled hedgerows, where the cows push out
> Impatient horns and tolerant churning mouths
> 'Twixt dripping ash-boughs, — hedgerows all alive
> With birds and gnats and large white butterflies
> Which look as if the May-flower had caught life
> And palpitated forth upon the wind;
> Hills, vales, woods, netted in a silver mist,
> Farms, granges, doubled up among the hills;
> And cattle grazing in the watered vales,
> And cottage-chimneys smoking from the woods,
> And cottage-gardens smelling everywhere,
> Confused with smell of orchards . . . .
> And ankle-deep in English grass I leaped
> And clapped my hands, and called all very fair.

This description of an English landscape is, we
believe, the finest passage in the entire poem. Romney
loves his cousin, and would fain make her a fellow-worker

in his great task of ameliorating the condition of the suffering portion of the human race; but Aurora declines the offer, regarding his aims as too frigidly material for a truly poetical soul. She tells him:

> What you love,
> Is not a woman, Romney, but a cause:
> You want a helpmate, not a mistress, sir,
> A wife to help your ends — in her no end.
> Your cause is noble, your ends excellent,
> But I, being most unworthy of these and that,
> Do otherwise conceive of love. Farewell.

Aurora's aunt dies, and she comes to London, with the intention of earning her bread by her pen. While one day seated in her "chamber up three flights of stairs" in Kensington, she receives a visit from Lady Waldemar, the female Mephistopheles of the story, who, after making Aurora the confidant of her love for Romney Leigh, surprises her with the intelligence that the philanthropist is about to marry

> A girl of doubtful life, undoubtful birth,

called Marian Earle, living in St. Margaret's Court. Lady Waldemar's language in this interview is not of the most delicate, as she acknowledges, when she says: "I'm talking garlic." The visitor at length takes her leave; Aurora forthwith resolves she will go to see this Marian Earle; and she finds her lodged in a garret in one of the worst quarters of London. On her way to the house she has to run the gauntlet through a shower of insults and imprecations from the wretches dwelling in the Court. This scene is simply disgusting. Surely, there are two things Mrs. Browning might have known; first, that poor seamstresses do not necessarily live among thieves and burglars; and secondly, that abandoned women are more disposed to slink away from the presence of refined and virtuous women than to vituperate them in the open street. Marian makes a favourable impression on Aurora, and proceeds to relate her brief but sad history: how she had run away from her drunken, poaching father and worthless mother, and after undergoing much suffering was found

by Romney in an hospital. This is the bride the philan-
thropist has chosen.   He says:

> I take my wife
> Directly from the people, — and she comes
> As Austria's daughter to imperial France,
> Betwixt her eagles, blinking not her race,
> From Margaret's Court, at garret height, to meet
> And wed me at St. James's, nor put off
> Her gown of serge for that.

The parallel between Marian Earle and Marie Louise
seems to us singularly infelicitous. The wedding-day
comes; the church is partly filled with elegant wedding-
guests from the aristocratic West-End, partly with the
worst refuse of the metropolis — "half St. Giles in
frieze." The bride has not yet appeared, and the im-
patience of the rabble finds vent in colloquies which
sound very strange in blank verse. A letter from Marian
is at last brought to the impatient bridegroom by a
ragged child; and Romney finds in it the fatal words:

> I never could be happy as your wife,
> I never could be harmless as your friend,
> I never will look more into your face
> Till God says, Look!

Marian has disappeared; she has been deceived
and entrapped by the cunning intriguer, Lady Waldemar,
who has resolved on her ruin, to prevent her from
marrying Romney Leigh. Of this the benevolent philo-
sopher has no suspicion, and he habitually speaks of
Lady Waldemar as "good", an epithet which furnishes
Mrs. Browning with the text of a furious homily:

> In the middle age,
> I think they called malignant fays and imps
> Good people. A good neighbour, even in this,
> Is fatal sometimes, — cuts your morning up
> To mince-meat of the very smallest talk,
> Then helps to sugar her bohea at night
> With your reputation. I have known good wives,
> As chaste, or nearly so, as Potiphar's;
> And good, good mothers, who would use a child
> To better an intrigue, good friends, beside,
> (Very good) who hung succinctly round your neck

And sucked your breath, as cats are fabled to do
By sleeping infants. And we all have known
Good critics who have stamped out poet's hope,
Good statesmen who pulled ruin on the state,
Good patriots who for a theory risked a cause,
Good kings who disembowelled for a tax,
Good popes who brought all good to jeopardy,
Good Christians who sate still in easy chairs
And damned the general world for standing up —
Now may the good God pardon all good men!

Time passes on. Aurora Leigh is in Paris. She has never given up her search for Marian; and one day, when least expecting it, she finds her in the French capital. Marian has again a sad story of treachery and cruelty to tell — the wrong-doer, this time, of course being Lady Waldemar — and Aurora, convinced of the purity of Marian's soul, though she has a baby at her breast, resolves to take her with her to Italy. A railway journey is generally considered a matter prosaic enough, but in Mrs. Browning's hands it acquires a tinge of poetry:

                    I just knew it when we swept
Above the old roofs of Dijon: Lyons dropped
A spark into the night, half trodden out
Unseen. But presently the winding Rhone
Washed out the moonlight large along his banks
Which strained their yielding curves out clear and clean
To hold it, — shadow of town and castle blurred
Upon the hurrying river. Such an air
Blew thence upon the forehead, — half an air
And half a water, — that I leaned and looked,
Then, turning back to Marian, smiled to mark
That she looked only on her child, who slept,
His face toward the moon too.

                         So we passed
The liberal open country and the close,
And shot through tunnels, like a lightning-wedge
By great Thor-hammers driven through the' rock,
Which, quivering through the intestine blackness, splits,
And lets it in at once: the train swept in
Athrob with effort, trembling with resolve,
The fierce denouncing whistle wailing on
And dying off smothered in the shuddering dark,

While we, self-awed, drew troubled breath, oppressed
As other Titans underneath the pile
And nightmare of the mountains. Out, at last,
To catch the dawn afloat upon the land!

In the mean time Romney Leigh has been rewarded for all his benevolent schemes with foul ingratitude. The ruffians he intended to benefit burned down the building he had erected as an asylum and a reformatory; and though he escapes with his life, he loses his eyesight. On learning that Marian has been found, he is still quite willing to marry her; but she resolves to live henceforth only for her child. His heart broken, and his illusions gone, he is just going to take leave of Aurora for ever, when she acknowledges her love for him, and consents to become his wife.

We cannot refrain from quoting a few lines of that very fine passage, which describes Aurora's feelings on revisiting the home of her childhood:

                                I knew the birds
And insects, — which looked fathered by the flowers
And emulous of their hues: I recognised
The moths, with that great overpoise of wings
Which make a mystery of them how at all
They can stop flying: butterflies that bear
Upon their blue wings such red embers round,
They seem to scorch the blue air into holes
Each flight they take: and fire-flies that suspire
In short soft lapses of transported flame
Across the tingling Dark, while overhead
The constant. and inviolable stars
Outburn those light-of-love: melodious owls
(If music had but one note and was sad,
'Twould sound just so); and all the silent swirl
Of bats that seem to follow in the air
Some grand circumference of a shadowy dome
To which we are blind: and then the nightingales,
Which pluck our heart across a garden-wall
(When walking in the town) and carry it
So high into the bowery almond-trees
We tremble and are afraid, and feel as if
The golden flood of moonlight unaware
Dissolved the pillars of the steady earth
And made it less substantial.

By some critics *Aurora Leigh* has been most extravagantly praised. In this poem, declares one writer,
she has proved herself the greatest of English poetesses;
another says, the greatest female poet on record. Coolerheaded judges have found that the poem possesses both
great beauties and serious blemishes. The metaphysical
disquisitions and rambling common-place conversations,
which so largely enter into it, "have more than once
reminded us", says Mr. Robert Chambers, "of the
descriptions of the retreat from Moscow, where the
French soldier might be seen dipping his gold cup into
muddy ponds for drink, or eating the meanest viands
off porcelain and silver." The plot, too, has been by
many authorities pronounced to be unnatural or absurd.
Though intended to be a philosophical poem, it is
written at a passion-heat from beginning to end; and
there is no lack of vehement denunciations, not unfrequently of doubtful justice. With all these defects,
it must be conceded, that *Aurora Leigh* is one of the
most remarkable poems of modern times. The moral
it teaches is succinctly enunciated in these words:

> No earnest work
> Of any honest creature, albeit weak,
> Imperfect, ill-adapted, fails so much,
> It is not gathered as a grain of sand
> To enlarge the sum of human actions used
> For carrying out God's ends.

Mrs. E. B. Browning died in 1861.

Robert Lord Lytton.

Lord Lytton's only son, Robert Lord Lytton, published in 1855, under the name of "Owen Meredith"
Clytemnestra and other Poems, followed by *the Wanderer*
in 1859, and a poetical tale, *Lucile* in 1860. In 1868
appeared, under his own name, his romantic, half-
Byronian *Chronicles and Characters,* and in 1874 his
Fables in Song. On the whole, we rather prefer the
poems of Owen Meredith, which unite fancy with good
sense, and simplicity with smoothness, to those of later

date. With one passage we have been particularly struck. A wife and mother excuses the faults of her sex by reminding us that in love and marriage women have no choice, or, to give her own words: "we women cannot choose our lot:"

> But blame us women not, if some appear
>   Too cold at times; and some too gay and light.
> Some griefs gnaw deep. Some woes are hard to bear.
>   Who knows the past? And who can judge us right?
> Ah, were we judged by what we might have been,
>   And not by what we are, too apt to fall!
> My little child — he sleeps and smiles between
>   These thoughts and me. In heaven we shall know all.

In the *Fables in Song*, the stories, simple as they generally are, show no want of invention, and are well told; but though we have been long accustomed in fables to find birds and beasts, and even trees, conversing freely, it rather takes away our breath to read of the different parts of the engine in a steamboat caballing together against the oil, and by their conspiracy bringing about an explosion. It is likewise our opinion that the following soliloquy is at once too poetical and too philosophical for the solitary eagle who utters it:

> To what end,
> O Time, dost thou from bright to sable turn
> The restless spheres of thy revolving hours?
> Whence slide the silver twilights in between,
> Dreamily shuddering? Say, what is't ye roll,
> Night-wanderers mute, in mystic vapour veil'd,
> That linger laden on the lone hill-tops,
> And pass, like sorrows with a tale untold?
> Who wrought the unimaginable wrong
> Thou callest upon ruin to redress,
> Thou moaning storm that roamest heaven in vain,
> Triumphant never, never long subdued?
> Beautiful anarch! Answer, morn and eve,
> Why to your coming and departing kiss
> Blush, wrapt in rosy joy, the mountains old?
> What happens nighest heaven, and unbeheld,
> To speed thee headlong from thy native haunts,
> Wild torrent cradled in the tranquil cold?

One peculiarity of these fables is a curious blending of different styles, which almost produces the effect of a medley. There are passages which remind us of Tennyson, others of Browning, and the following lines, the reader will perceive, are quite in the early style of Wordsworth:

> A little child, scarce five years old,
>   And blithe as bird on bough;
> A little maiden, bright as gold,
>   And pure as new-fall'n snow.
> Things seen, to her, are things unknown:
>   Things near are far away:
> The neighbouring hamlet, next our own,
>   As distant as Cathay!

It must not, however, be supposed that we do not sometimes meet with fine — we will even say, very fine passages — in the *Fables in Song;* and as an example we will quote from the second volume the description of a sculptor's studio:

> Large was the chamber; bathed with light serene
>   And silence tuned, not troubled, by the sound
> Of one cool fountain tinkling in the green
>   Of laurel groves that girt the porches round.
> And in that chamber the sole dwellers were
>   Ideas, clad in clear and stately shape;
> Save one, a prisoner, huge, uncouth, and bare,
>   Hung fast in fetters, hopeless of escape,
> And broken at the heart, — a Marble Block.
>   Even as a hero, in base ambuscade
> Fallen; so, fall'n, and from his native rock
>   Borne here in chains, the indignant Marble made
> No moan; but round, in dumb remonstrance gazed;
>   And, gazing, saw, surprised, all round him stand
> The images of gods. With right arm raised,
>   Jove launch'd the thunders from his loaded hand:
> A light of undulating lovelinesses,
>   Rose foam-born Venus from the foam; and, dread
> With dismal beauty, by its serpent tresses
>   Did sworded Perseus lift Medusa's head:
> There paused a-tiptoe wing-capp'd Mercury:
>   Apollo, pensive smiling, linger'd here:
> There stately Pallas stood, with brooding eye,
>   Full arm'd, and grasp'd the ægis and the spear.

Besides a number of imitations and free translations from the Italian, Danish, Servian, and other languages, Lord Lytton produced, in 1869, under the name of *Orval; or, the Fool of Time,* a paraphrase of the very remarkable dramatic poem, *the Infernal Comedy,* of the Polish poet, Count Sigismund Krasinski, who, in the early part of 1859, died at Paris. We are informed by Lord Lytton, that he himself had long contemplated a poem, based on the French Revolution, the object of which, however, "was not to depict, in historical detail, any particular series of events, but to give, if possible, imaginative forms to those abstract ideas and general conceptions, from which both the character and occasion of the events of 1789 were derived." In this work he had already made some progress, when, becoming acquainted with Count Krasinski's poem, he was struck with the curious though accidental resemblance, of his own three principal characters to the three leading personages of the Polish poet. In consequence of this discovery, he threw aside his manuscript, and undertook a paraphrase of *the Infernal Comedy;* replacing the Polish names of the three chief actors by the more pronounceable ones of Orval, Veronica, and Muriel. The poem is divided into five epochs, in the first two of which Orval is presented to us as a sort of Faustus, deserting his home and his young wife, Veronica, to seek unholy communion with the world of spirits; in the sequel he becomes a revolutionary chief, but finally falls a victim, together with his son Muriel, to the anarchist insurrection which he has aided in evoking. All through the piece the supernatural accompanies the action, and the spirit of the neglected Veronica, after her decease, continually hovers about her son, till he, in the last scene but one, falls struck by an anarchist ball.

Of the merits of the Polish poem we are not competent to speak; but a couple of extracts from Lord Lytton's paraphrase will show in what a masterly manner his own task has been executed. In the first, Orval, climbing a rugged mountain above a stormy sea, in pursuit of an evil spirit by whose spells he is enthralled, pauses and soliloquizes:

Where am I?

Have they a name for men to know them by,
These desert steeps . . . . . Calpe or Caucasus,
Atlas, or utmost Thule's mountain tops
Mark'd on no mariner's chart? One thing is sure;
That never, even in dream, I trod, before,
The dreadful pavement of this dizzy path
That winds I know not where: never beheld
The broken margent of that savage sea
That in his beachèd basin, far below,
Boils like Hell's caldron; nor yon livid peak
Peering and disappearing through those gaps
Of restless cloud, tormented by the wind.
How horribly the huge stone's solid bulk
Seems hovering in the gust above my head!

. . . .

Already have I cross'd the groaning tract
Of thunder, that with dense blue drench blots all
The blighted plain out. Far beneath me, borne
About these fang'd and crooked crags, I hear
Faint noises only, as ever and anon
Between black sullen shores of gulfy cloud
There runs, and breaks, and falls, a pallid sea
Of momentary fire. Still on! still on!
The few lean firs, and solitary pines,
That struggled, few and fewer, as on I pass'd,
To keep pace with me, all have fallen away
. . . . Nature's self cried "Halt!
I can no further go!" Yet on went I,
And still must on, — still on, while aught is left,
Above me where man's foot may tread. Still on!

The moral degradation of woman — one of the earliest consequences of the anarchist triumph — revolts the mind of Orval, and obtrudes itself on him as a menace and a foretaste of new and ineffable evils. In his despair he exclaims:

O women! women,

Whom we have loved, and honour'd, ay! and served, —
Loved with the loyal heart of honest man,
That fears no falsehood where he trusts all truth!
Honour'd on knightly knee, with tender homage,
Half deified with holy poesies,
And held unsullied in the secretest shrine
Of things divine within us! . . . Served, ah God!

> Served with the soldier's sword, the poet's pen,
> And all the thousand nameless services
> Of silent adoration, that make strong
> The better portion of men's days and deeds!
> Were ye not mothers, daughters, sisters, wives?
> Our mothers, and our daughters, and our sisters?
> And we almost have worship'd you .as angels!

Robert Lord Lytton was Governor-General of India, under Lord Beaconsfield's administration (1874—1880).

A. C. Swinburne.

Algernon Charles Swinburne, born in 1843 at Holmwood in Surrey, belongs to a noble family, his mother being a daughter of Lord Ashburnham, and his uncle a baronet of ancient descent. The poet received his early education in France, and afterwards studied at Eton and Oxford. When at the university, he highly distinguished himself as a Greek scholar. In 1860 he published two plays in verse, the *Queen-Mother* and *Rosamond,* which attracted no attention, but about the same time he became known as the author of some poetical contributions to the London *Spectator*, which were looked on as a sort of protest against the puerilities of the "good boy" school of poetry. It was in the spring of 1865 that he produced his drama, *Atalanta in Calydon,* and, like Byron, he awoke one morning. and found himself famous. The *Athenaeum* said that "no one since Keats could touch him"; the *Saturday Review* declared that "we were listening to one of the contemporaries of Euripides, who sought to copy the manner of Aeschylus"; and the other reviews and journals bestowed on it unstinted praise. *Chastelard,* a tragedy in the style of the Elizabethan school, the subject of which was the passion of the young French poet for the unfortunate Queen of Scots, appeared in the following year, but met with a very different reception from that of the classical *Atalanta.* The warmth of its colouring gave great scandal to sober-minded readers, and it was denounced as "morally repulsive", "licentious", and "overladen with sensuous images." By one section

of the reading public, indeed, who longed for something
beyond feeble imitations of Wordsworth. *Chastelard* was
hailed as the welcome harbinger of a new era of
vigorous and masculine English poetry; but in 1866,
on the appearance of the *Poems and Ballads,* in which
all the faults of Chastelard were repeated in an exag-
gerated form, the apologists were fain to subside into
silence. So loud an outcry was raised against the im-
morality and aggressive atheism ' of the new volume,
that the publishing house of Moxon expunged the book
from their list; and the author had to look for a new
publisher. The London *Punch* changed the name of the
poet into *Swine-born,* and the joke was everywhere
repeated with laughter and applause. Swinburne remon-
strated in his *Notes on Poems and Reviews;* urging that
he did not write for mere boys and girls, but for men;
and that there is a higher class of literature than the
bread-and-butter and pinafore school. In 1867 he gave
vent to his republican sympathies in his *Song of Italy,*
dedicated to Mazzini; and again in 1870, in his *Ode
on the Proclamation of the French Republic,* which he
dedicated to Victor Hugo. In 1871 he gave to the
world his *Songs before Sunrise,* in which, mixed up with
much extravagance, we find some of his finest verses.
His later published productions are: *A Midsummer Holi-
day, Les Casquets,* an incident connected with the light-
house rock off Guernsey, *Ode to Victor Hugo, Cradle
Songs, Five years old,* and *In Sepulcretis,* a poem in
which he castigates those indiscreet admirers of eminent
men, who publish, after their death, what was never
intended to see the light.

Mr. Swinburne is not only a great poetical genius,
notwithstanding all his blemishes, but also no ordinary
prose-writer. In 1872, he and his friend, Mr. Rossetti,
were violently attacked by Mr. Robert Buchanan, the
author of *Napoleon Fallen,* a lyrical drama (1871), in
a magazine article, afterwards reprinted in a separate
form, with the title: *the Fleshly School of Poetry and
other Phenomena of the Day;* to which Mr. Swinburne
wrote his able reply, *Under the Microscope.* This time

the public generally took the side of Swinburne and Rossetti, thinking that a rival poet could hardly be looked on as an impartial critic.

From these observations it may be gathered. that in Swinburne's poetry there is very little which we should feel justified in quoting in such a work as the present. One of his least objectionable pieces, his *Ode to Victor Hugo*, will give some idea of his poetical powers:

Thou art chief of us, and lord;
Thy song is as a sword
Keen-edged and scented in the blade from flowers;
Thou art lord and king; but we
Lift younger eyes, and see
Less of high hope, less light on wandering hours;
Hours that have borne men down so long,
Seen the right fail, and watched uplift the wrong.

But thine imperial soul
As years and ruins roll
To the same end, and all things and all dreams
With the same wreck and roar
Drift on the dim same shore,
Still in the bitter foam and brackish streams
Tracks the fresh water-spring to be
And sudden sweeter fountains in the sea.

In Swinburne, says Mr. Justin M'Carthy, we find everywhere "the same cry of rebellion against established usage, the same hysterical appeal to lawlessness in passion and art."

D. G. Rossetti.

Dante Gabriel Rossetti, the poet and painter, is of Italian origin, but was born in London in 1828. As an artist, he belongs to the pre-Raphaelite school, and in 1857 he supplied the illustrations for an edition of Tennyson's poems. His' principal literary productions are, his *Early Italian Poets, from Civollo d'Alcana to Dante* (1861); his *Translation of Dante's Vita Nuova* (1866); and his *Poems* (1870). Mr. Rossetti's poetry is noted both for sweetness and power, but as has been hinted, it possesses many of the defects, as well as the merits of Swinburne. From his *House of Life* we select some stanzas, which will give an idea of the height and sublimity Mr. Rossetti is capable of reaching:

THE SEA-LIMITS.

Consider the sea's listless chime:
  Time's self it is, made audible, —
  The murmur of the earth's own shell.
Secret continuance sublime
  Is the sea's end: our sight may pass
  No furlong further. Since time was,
This sound hath told the lapse of time.

No quiet, which is death's, — it hath
  The mournfulness of ancient life,
  Enduring always at dull strife.
As the world's heart of rest and wrath,
  Its painful pulse is in the sands.
  Last utterly, the whole sky stands,
Grey and not known, along its path.

Listen alone beside the sea,
  Listen alone among the woods;
  Those voices of twin solitudes
Shall have one sound alike to thee:
  Hark where the murmurs of thronged men
  Surge and sink back and surge again, —
Still the one voice of wave and tree.

Gather a shell from the strown beach
  And listen at its lips: they sigh,
  The same desire and mystery,
The echo of the whole sea's speech,
  And all mankind is thus at heart
  Not anything but what thou art:
And Earth, Sea, Man are all in each.

The Rossettis are a highly gifted family. Gabriele Rossetti, the poet's father, who left Naples and settled in London in the year 1871, was himself a poet and a Dante commentator. Mr. William Michael Rossetti, the poet's brother, translated Dante's *Inferno* into English blank verse. Miss Maria Rossetti, the poet's elder sister, published not long ago an elucidation of the *Divina Commedia;* and Miss Christina Rossetti is the author of *the Prince's Progress, Goblin Market,* and some tales for children. The mother of this talented progeny was an English lady of Italian descent.

W. Morris.

William Morris (born in 1834), is usually classed among the poets of the new or Swinburne school, but his colouring is rarely so vivid, or his language so passionate, as that of Swinburne or Rossetti. His earliest poetical effusion appeared in 1858, under the name, *Defence of Guinevere, and other Poems,* and was followed, in 1867, by his great poem, *the Life and Death of Jason.* In 1868, he published *the Earthly Paradise,* and in 1872 *Love is enough.*

Professor M. Arnold.

Matthew Arnold (born in 1822), Professor of Poetry in the university of Oxford, and son of the late highly popular Dr. Thomas Arnold (1795—1842), Head-master of Rugby School, is a poet who has nothing in common with the Swinburne school. Mr. Arnold published *Cromwell, a prize poem; the Strayed Reveller, and other Poems,* in 1848; *Empedocles on Etna* in 1853; *Poems* in 1854; *Merope, a tragedy* in 1858; besides a great number of prose-works on various subjects. In the following elegant lines, the poet reminds us that man — especially the young man — must be always up and doing, and that life is essentially active and unquiet:

> Ah, no! the bliss youth dreams is one
> For daylight, for the cheerful sun;
> For feeling nerves and living breath —
> Youth.dreams a bliss on this side death!
> It dreams a rest, if not more deep,
> More grateful than this marble sleep.
> It hears a voice within it tell:
> Calm's not life's crown, though calm is well.
> 'Tis all perhaps which man requires,
> But 'tis not what our youth desires.

Mr. Arnold advises young poets to avoid modern innovations in poetic style and diction, and to seek their models in classic antiquity. His own poetical productions all evince a highly cultured taste.

A. Austin.

Alfred Austin began his poetical career by the publication of the satirical poems, *the Season,* and *the Golden Age;* but he is not exclusively a satirist, and he has since then produced *the Human Tragedy, Savonarola, Soliloquies in Song,* and *at the Gate of the Convent.* From one of his later works we extract a few characteristic lines, instinct with a pleasing hopeful feeling:

> I feel no more the snow of years,
>   Sap mounts and pulses bound;
> My eyes are filled with happy tears,
>   My ears with happy sound.
>
> My manhood keeps the dew of morn,
>   And what I have I give;
> Being right glad that I was born,
>   And thankful that I live.

M. F. Tupper.

Martin F. Tupper, born in 1810, the author of *Proverbial Philosophy* and *Geraldine, a sequel to Coleridge's Christabel,* has likewise written *Ballads for the Times,* many of which have been set to music, and they are all recommended by the hopeful and manly sentiments they express. Among the most popular are the following:

HONEST FELLOW, SORE BESET.

> Honest fellow, sore beset,
>   Vexed by troubles quick and keen,
> Thankfully consider yet
>   How much worse it might have been.
>
> Worthily thy faults deserve
>   More than all thine eyes have seen;
> Think thou, then, with sterner nerve,
>   How much worse it might have been.

Though the night be dark and long,
  Morning soon shall break serene;
And the burden of thy song,
  How much worse it might have been.

God, the Good One, calls to us,
  On his Providence to lean,
Shout, then, out, devoutly thus,
  How much worse it might have been.

I LOVE TO LINGER.

I love to linger on the track
  Wherever I have dwelt,
In after years to loiter back,
  And feel as once I felt.

My foot falls lightly on the sward,
  Yet leaves a deathless dint;
With tenderness I still regard
  Its unforgotten print.

Old places have a charm for me
  The new can ne'er attain;
Old faces! how I long to see
  Their kindly looks again!

NEVER GO GLOOMILY.

Never go gloomily, man with a mind,
  Hope is a better companion than fear;
Providence, ever benignant and kind,
  Gives with a smile what you take with a tear.

All will be right, look to the light,
Morning is ever the daughter of night
All that was black will be all that is bright.
Cheerily, cheerily, then cheer up!

Many a foe is a friend in disguise,
  Many a sorrow a blessing most true,
Helping the heart to he happy and wise,
  Bringing true love and joys ever new.

Stand in the van, strive like a man,
This is the bravest and cleverest plan —
Trusting in God while you do what you can:
  Cheerily, cheerily, then cheer up!

Mr. Tupper is certainly not one of the great poets of the Victorian Age, but he is always clear; and possessing the valuable secret of popularity, has a large circle of admirers.

Among the remaining poets of this period we may mention Dr. *C. Mackay (Egeria,* etc.), Mr. *D. F. M'Carthy,* author of *the Poets and Dramatists of Ireland,* and the translator of several of Calderon's dramas; *George Eliot (Spanish Gipsy);* Miss *Procter,* (daughter of B. W. Procter, better known as *Barry Cornwall),* author of *Legends and Lyrics;* Rev. *William Barnes (Poems in the Dorset Dialect);* Rev. *John Keble (the Christian Year, Lyra Innocentium,* etc.*)* Mr. *C. Patmore (the Angel in the House);* Mr. *Charles Swain (Metrical Essays);* Mr. *Francis Davis,* the "Belfast Man" *(Lispings of the Lagan,* etc.); and Mr. *John W. Pitchford (Bramble Cloisters)* from whose *Idyll of the Dawn* we give a brief extract, not unworthy of the author of the *Seasons:*

> Now shoot o'er dewy hedge,
> Through opening woods, the sun's first rays,
> Reddening and warm; and with a thrill of life
> All things awake; the hum of bees is heard
> About the garden hives, and round the elms
> The buzz of darting flies; chirp, twitter, song,
> Glad flit of hasty wing, the upward soar
> Of joyous-throated lark, the blackbird's song,
> Warbled in rounded tones, make sweet the hour.
> Sparkles the hoary dew upon the grass;
> The trailing mists drift from the shining woods,
> From out whose dark blue depths come gentle sounds
> Of cooing doves, happiest of happy birds.
> Cutting and driving through the freshened blue
> Of cloudless heaven, the arrowy swallows dart.
> Ere pale blue wreaths of climbing smoke arise
> Above the garden trees, from cottage roofs,
> The satchelled labourers come, with tools in hand,
> Bound for the hay-fields or the distant woods.

Poet-Translators.

Among the very numerous poet-translators of the present period, it is impossible for us to notice any but the most eminent; and one of the first of these is *Edward Earl of Derby,* the author of an admirable translation of Homer's Iliad, in English blank verse, which appeared in 1864. Of the many existing English translations of the Iliad it is generally considered the most perfect. Chapman's version, in fourteen‑syllable metre and in rhyme, is now out of date, though it was a wonderful work for the Elizabethan age; Pope's celebrated translation, in the English heroic metre, however brilliant and harmonious, is rather a paraphrase than a translation; Cowper's version is accurate, but dull. In Lord Derby's translation we find accuracy and elegance most happily combined; as may be seen by his rendering of the well‑known moonlight scene in Book VIII:

> Full of proud hopes, upon the pass of war
> All night they camped, and frequent blazed their fires:
> As when in heaven around the glittering moon
> The stars shine bright amid the breathless air,
> And every crag and every jutting peak
> Stands boldly forth, and every forest glade.
> E'en to the gates of heaven is opened wide
> The boundless sky; shines each particular star
> Distinct; joy fills the gazing shepherd's heart;
> So bright, so thickly scattered o'er the plain
> Before the walls of Troy, between the ships
> And Xanthus' stream, the Trojans' watchfires blazed.
> A thousand fires burnt brightly, and round each,
> Sat fifty warriors in the ruddy glare;
> With store of provender before them laid,
> Barley and rye, the tethered horses stood
> Beside the cars, and waited for the morn.

The attack of Hector on the Achaean camp, in Book XII., shows us that Lord Derby is as much at home in depicting a warlike scene as a peaceful one:

> Close to the gate he stood, and planting firm
> His foot to give his arm its utmost power,
> Full on the middle dashed the mighty mass.
> The hinges both gave way: the ponderous stone
> Fell inwards: widely gap'd the opening gates;
> Nor might the bars within the blow sustain.
> This way and that the severed portals flew
> Before the crashing missile. Dark as night
> His lowering brow, great Hector sprang within;
> Bright flashed the brazen armour on his breast,
> As through the gates, two jav'lins in his hand,

> He sprang: the gods except, no power might meet
> That onset; blazed his eyes with lurid fire.
> Then to the Trojans turning, to the throng
> He called aloud to scale the lofty wall.

Another translation of the Iliad, not quite so equable, but in other respects hardly inferior to that of Lord Derby, has been made by the philologist, critic and historian, Mr. Wright. We subjoin Mr. Wright's rendering of the indignant rejoinder of Achilles to the taunts of Agamemnon, in Book I.:

> O clothed with insolence, rapacious chief,
> What Greek henceforth will prompt obedience yield,
> March at thy word or strenuous urge the fight?
> I came not to avenge a private wrong.
> I have no quarrel with the Trojans: they
> Ne'er drove away the herds or steeds of mine,
> Nor roamed injurious o'er my fruitful fields
> In fertile Pythia, for between us lie
> For shadowing mountains and the roaring sea.
> Thy cause espousing, and at thy behest
> We came to Troy. O most unblushing chief,
> Not on our own behalf, but to redress
> Wrongs suffered by thy brother and by thee,
> Thou dog in shamelessness.

Mr. *W. E. Gladstone*, the late Premier (author of *Studies on Homer*) has published a translation of the first book of the Iliad in the trochaic measure of Tennyson's *Locksley Hall*. So far as the translation goes, it is pleasant enough reading; but we scarcely think the fifteen-syllable metre could have been maintained without wearisome monotony in so long an epic as the Iliad.

Mr. *Worsley* has undertaken, and very creditably executed, the difficult task of adapting the Odyssey to the English Spenserian stanza.

With regard to most of the other Greek and Roman poets, the English versions of Dryden, Rowe, and Moore are still the best. Dr. William Maginn (1793—1842), the poet and critic, who spoke fluently and wrote in six languages, produced some admirable translations from Lucian, and a series of lays, called *Homeric Ballads*, in the style of Macaulay's *Lays of Ancient Rome*. In modern literature, the translations from the German by Scott, Coleridge, W. Taylor, Carlyle, Lord Lytton, and Professor Blackie, still maintain their reputation. Sir Theodore Martin (born in Edinburgh in 1816), who at the request of Queen Victoria edited *the Life of the Prince Consort,* besides several metrical translations from Horace and Catullus, has published an English version of Dante's *Vita Nuova,* the *Poems and Ballads of Goethe,* and *Faust.* In translating the *Poems and Ballads,* he was aided by his friend, W. E. Aytoun (1813—1865), Professor of Rhetoric in the University of Edinburgh, and author of the *Lays of the Scottish Cavaliers.* Another translation of *Faust,* made by the American writer, Mr. Bayard Taylor, we shall notice hereafter. Most of the French works which of late years have appeared in an English dress are — if we except some of Victor Hugo's poems and Beranger's ballads — novels, comedies and farces. Elegant English versions of the Italian poets have been made by Mr. Leigh Hunt, the two brothers Rossetti, the Rev. H. F. Cary, and Mr. W. S. Rose. To Sir John Bowring we owe many spirited translations from the Russian, Magyar, Polish, and many other languages. One department of literature, long neglected in England, has received in this period extraordinary attention, in consequence of the movement initiated by Byron and some other poets, and since then so ably continued by Frere, Wiffen, Bowring, and Lockhart: we mean the *canciones* or ballad poetry of Spain. Of these graceful versions we give a few specimens. The first is by Mr. Wiffen:

MOUNTAIN SONG.

I ne'er on the border
   Saw girl fair as Rosa,
The charming milk-maiden
   Of sweet Finojosa.

Once making a journey
   To Santa Maria
Of Calatareno,
   From weary desire
Of sleep down a valley
   I strayed, where young Rosa
I saw, the milk-maiden
   Of lone Finojosa.

In a pleasant green meadow
  'Midst roses and grasses,
Her herd she was tending
  With other fair lasses;
So lovely her aspect,
  I could not suppose her
A simple milk-maiden
  Of rude Finojosa.

I think not primroses
  Have half her smile's sweetness,
Or mild modest beauty;
  (I speak with discreetness).
Oh, had I beforehand
  But known of this Rosa,
The handsome milk-maiden
  Of far Finojosa.

Her very great beauty
  Had not so subdued,
Because it had left me
  To do as I would.
I have said more, oh, fair one!
  By learning 'twas Rosa,
The charming milk-maiden
  Of sweet Finojosa.

The next is by Mr. Lockhart:

DON RODERICK AFTER HIS DEFEAT. (A. D. 711.)

The hosts of Don Rodrigo were scattered in dismay,
When lost was the eighth battle, nor heart nor hope had they;
He, when he saw the field was lost, and all his hope was flown,
He turned him from his flying host, and took his way alone.

His horse was bleeding, blind and lame, he could no farther go;
Dismounted, without path or aim the king stepped to and fro:
It was a sight of pity to look on Roderick,
For sore athirst and hungry, he staggered faint and sick.

All stained and smeared with dust and blood, like to some smoul-
                            dering brand,
Plucked from the flame, Rodrigo showed; his sword was in his hand;
But it was hacked into a saw of dark and purple tint;
His jewelled mail had many a flaw, his helmet many a dint.

He climbed into a hill top, the highest he could see;
Thence all about of that wide route, his last long look took he;
He saw his royal banners where they lay drenched and torn,
He heard the cry of victory, the Arab shout of scorn.

He looked for the brave captains who had led the hosts of Spain,
But all were fled except the dead, and who could count the slain?
Where'er his eye could wander, all bloody was the plain;
And while thus he spoke, the tears he shed ran down his cheeks like rain

"Last night I was the king of Spain — to-day no king am I;
Last night fair castles held my train — to-night, where shall I lie?
Last night a hundred pages did serve me 'on the knee,
To-night not one I call my own — not one pertains to me.

"Oh, luckless, luckless was the hour, and cursed was the day,
When I was born to have the power of this great seignory!
Unhappy one, that I should see the sun go down to-night!
O Death! why now so slow art thou? why fearest thou to smite?"

The third is by Sir John Bowring:

Fount of freshness! fount of freshness!
  Fount of freshness and of love!
Where the little birds of spring-time
  Seek for comfort as they rove:
All except the widowed turtle —
  Widowed, sorrowing turtle-dove.

There the nightingale, the traitor!
  Lingered on his giddy way;
And these words of hidden treachery
  To the dove I heard him say:
"I will be thy servant, lady!
  I will ne'er thy love betray."

"Off! false-hearted! vile deceiver!
  Leave me, nor insult me so;
Dwell I then 'midst gaudy flow'rets?
  Perch I on the verdant bough?
Even the waters of the fountain
  Drink I dark and troubled now.
Never will I think of marriage —
  Never break the widow-vow.

"Had I children, they would grieve me,
  They would wean me, from my woe:
Leave me, false one; — thoughtless traitor
  Base one! — vain one! — sad one! — go!
I can never, never love thee —
  I will never wed thee — no!"

II. Dramatists.

Notwithstanding the reiterated lamentations about the gradual decay of the stage in England, the Victorian Age can still boast of a few dramatic writers, who would have done honour to any period of English literature. Among these the first place, both in seniority and merit, indisputably belongs to

James Sheridan Knowles (1784—1862).

Of this eminent writer the *Edinburgh Review* declared, that he "is, indeed, the most successful dramatist of this day; and, apart from his other efforts, *the Hunchback* and *the Wife* deserve a permanent station in our drama, having combined the greatest literary merit with the most unequivocal success upon the stage." Mr. Knowles, who was related to the Sheridans, was born in Cork, of which city his father, James Knowles, author of an excellent *Dictionary of the English Language*, was likewise a native. So early as 1820, he had began to write for the stage; when his first considerable piece, a tragedy called Caius Gracchus, was produced at Belfast, and subsequently performed at Drury Lane theatre, London. Mr. Knowles wrote altogether sixteen principal plays, tragedies, and comedies, which, however, were not all equally successful. Towards the close of his life, he obtained from Government a pension of £ 200 a-year, and withdrawing from all connexion with the stage, joined the sect of the Baptists, and became a popular preacher. "His works", says an able dramatic critic, "are without a spot; they breathe the noblest sentiments, the purest morality. His characters do honour to human nature. Of filial duty, love of country, independence, liberty, the social virtues, and all the charities that bind man to man, they are bright examples! The female parts are particularly attractive; combining delicacy, firmness, and a high-wrought enthusiasm. . . . Take him for all in all, he is a noble poet, and would have cast a lustre upon any age."

Of Mr. Knowles's tragedies, perhaps the finest is *Virginius*, founded on the well-known old Roman story. It was first produced at Covent Garden, the original Virginius being Mr. Macready. The gloomier features of the tragedy are judiciously relieved by the introduction of the sarcastic old veteran Siccius Dentatus, whose caustic pleasantry never degenerates into buffoonery. One of the most touching scenes is that in which the centurion discovers the concealed, but not unrequited love of his daughter for young Icilius — a discovery, as we learn, neither unexpected by the father, nor unwelcome to him:

> Vir. — Icilius loves my daughter — nay, I know it;
> And such a man would challenge for her husband,
> And only waited, till her forward spring
> Put on, a little more, the genial likeness
> Of colouring into summer, ere I sought
> To nurse a flower, which, blossoming too early,
> Too early often dies; but if it springs
> Spontaneous, and unlook'd for, wooes our hand
> To tend and cherish it, the growth is healthful;
> And 'twere untimely, as unkind, to check it.

Icilius appears; and the father, with faltering voice, commits to him the care of his child's future happiness:

> Icilius. — All that man should be
> To woman, I will be to her!
> Virg. The oath
> Is register'd. Didst thou but know, young man,
> How fondly I have watch'd her since the day
> Her mother died, and left me to a charge
> Of double duty bound — how she hath been
> My ponder'd thought by day, my dream by night,
> My prayer, my vow, my offering, my praise,
> My sweet companion, pupil, tutor, child! —
> Thou would'st not wonder that my drowning eye,
> And choking utterance, upbraid my tongue,
> That tells thee, she is thine!

On the development of the infamous plot of the Decemvir Appius and his creature Claudius, to obtain possession of the person of the young girl, under the false allegation that she was the daughter of Claudius's

slave, and purchased in infancy from the mother by
the childless wife of Virginius, the unhappy father
makes an appeal which must have convinced any less
interested tribunal:

Appius. — Your answer now, Virginius.
Virginius. — Here it is!
   Is this the daughter of a slave? I know
   'Tis not with men as shrubs and trees, that by
   The shoot you know the rank and order of
   The stem. Yet who from such a stem would look
   For such a shoot? My witnesses are these —
   The relatives and friends of Numitoria,
   Who saw her, ere Virginia's birth, sustain
   The burden which a mother bears, nor feels
   The weight, with longing for the sight of it.
   Here are the ears that listened to her sighs
   In nature's hour of labour, which subsides
   In the embrace of joy — the hands, that when
   The day first looked upon the infant's face,
   And never looked so pleased, helped her up to it,
   And blessed her for a blessing. Here, the eyes
   That saw her lying at the generous
   And sympathetic fount, that at her cry
   Sent forth a stream of liquid living pearl
   To cherish her enamelled veins. The lie
   Is most unfruitful then, that takes the flower —
   The very flower our bed connubial grew —
   To prove its barrenness!

Finding this eloquent pleading disregarded, Virginius,
as a last favour, intreats permission to take leave of her
whom at least he had always looked on as his daughter:

Virginius. — Appius, I pray you wait! If she is not
   My child, she hath been like a child to me
   For fifteen years. If I am not her father,
   I have been like a father to her, Appius,
   For even such a time. They that have lived
   So long a time together, in so near
   And dear society, may be allowed
   A little time for parting. Let me take
   The maid aside, I pray you, and confer
   A moment with her nurse; perhaps she'll give me
   Some token will unloose a tie so twined
   And knotted round my heart, that, if you break it,
   My heart breaks with it.
Appius. — Have your wish. Be brief!
   Lictors, look to them.

Virginia. — Do you go from me?
           Do you leave? Father! Father!
Virginius. — No, my child. —
           No, my Virginia — come along with me.
Virginia. — Will you not leave me? Will you take me with you?
           Will you take me home again? Oh, bless you, bless you!
           My father! my dear father! Art thou not
           My father?

It is at this moment that Virginius discovers, in the immediate neighbourhood, a butcher's stall, with a knife upon it.

Vir. — This way, my child — No, no; I am not going
       To leave thee, my Virginia! I'll not leave thee.
App. — Keep back the people, soldiers! Let them not
       Approach Virginius! Keep the people back!
                         [Virginius secures the knife.
       Well, have you done?
Vir. — Short time for converse, Appius,
       But I have.
App. — I hope you are satisfied.
Vir. — I am —
       I am — that she is my daughter!
App. — Take her, lictors!
Vir. — Another moment, pray you. Bear with me
       A little — 'Tis my last embrace. 'Twon't try
       Your patience beyond bearing, if you're a man!
       Lengthen it as I may. I cannot make it
       Long. My dear child! my dear Virginia!
                         [Kissing her.
       There is one only way to save thy honour —
       'Tis this.
                         [Stabs her.
       Lo, Appius, with this innocent blood
       I do devote thee to the infernal gods!
       Make way there!
App. — Stop him! Seize him!
Vir. — If they dare
       To tempt the desperate weapon that is maddened
       With drinking my daughter's blood, why, let them: thus
       It rushes in amongst them. Way there! Way!
                         [Exit through the soldiers.

Mr. Knowles's *William Tell* differs very widely in its treatment from Schiller's tragedy of the same name. The work of the great German poet may be said to be more historically correct; that is. he describes Tell as he would have been, had he really lived; as the honest, simple-minded German-Swiss yeoman, little conversant with abstract notions of liberty, and only stimulated to action by a keen sense of personal wrongs. Knowles, on the contrary, believing himself perfectly justified in idealizing a hero, who never existed save in poetic legend, portrays him as an ardent patriot, continually brooding over the wrongs of his degraded and enslaved country, and who, to quote the words of George Daniels, "feels that to submit to oppression without murmur or resistance, would be to throw away his birthright, and prove himself unworthy of those high immunities that belong to him as the last, the noblest work of the Creator." Mr. Macready, for whom, indeed, Knowles wrote most of his principal characters, was the original William Tell; but it was subsequently performed with no less success by the American tragedian Forrest. The following scene is from Act I.:

  Tell. Ye crags and peaks, I'm with you once again!
I hold to you the hands you first beheld,
To show they still are free. Methinks I hear
A spirit in your echoes answer me,
And bid your tenant welcome to his home.
Again! O sacred forms, how proud you look!
How high you lift your heads into the sky!
How huge you are! how mighty and how free!
How do you look, for all your bared brows.
More gorgeously majestical than kings
Whose loaded coronets exhaust the mine!
Ye are the things that tower, that shine — whose smile
Makes glad — whose frown is terrible — whose forms,
Robed or unrobed, do all the impress wear
Of awe divine — whose subject never kneels
In mockery, because it is your boast
To keep him free! Ye guards of liberty,
I'm with you once again! — I call to you
With all my voice! I hold my hands to you
To show they still are free! I rush to you
As though I could embrace you!

Albert enters, with his back to Tell, not seeing him, and aiming at his mark.
  Albert. I'll hit it now. (*shoots.*)
  Tell. That's scarce a miss, that comes so near the mark!
Well aim'd, young archer! With what ease he bends
The bow! To see those sinews, who'd believe

Such strength did lodge in them? (*Albert shoots.*) Well aim'd
    again!
There plays the skill will thin the chamois' herd,
And bring the lammer-geyer from the cloud
To earth. Perhaps do greater feats — perhaps
Make man its quarry, when he dares to tread
Upon his fellow man. That little arm,
His mother's palm can span, may help, anon,
To pull a sinewy tyrant from his seat,
And from their chains a prostrate people lift
To liberty. I'd be content to die,
Living to see that day. — What, Albert!
    Albert. Ah!
My father!   (*running to Tell, who embraces him.*)
    Emma. (*running from the cottage.*) William! — Welcome!
    welcome, William!
I did not look for you till noon. Joy's double joy,
That comes before the time: it is a debt
Paid ere 'tis due, which fills the owner's heart
With gratitude, and yet 'tis but his own!
And are you well? And has the chase proved good?
How has it fared with you? Come in; I'm sure
You want refreshment.
    Tell.   No; I did partake
A herdsman's meal, upon whose lonely chalet
I chanced to light. I've had bad sport; my track
Lay with the wind, which to the start'lish game
Betray'd me still. Only one prize; and that
I gave mine humble host—true that scaling yonder peak,
I saw an eagle wheeling near its brow:
O'er the abyss his broad expanded wings
Lay calm and motionless upon the air,
As if he floated there without their aid.
By the sole act of his unlorded will,
That buoy'd him proudly up. Instinctively
I bent my bow; yet kept he rounding still
His airy circle, as in the delight
Of measuring the ample range beneath
And round about: absorb'd, he heeded not
The death that threaten'd him. I could not shoot—
'Twas liberty! I turned my bow aside,
And let him soar away.

The incident he has just mentioned recalls to Tell
the happy period of his marriage, and the days when
his country was still the land of freemen.

    Tell. When I wedded thee,
The land was free. Oh! with what pride I used
To walk these hills, and look up to their Maker,

And bless Him that it was so. It was free—
From end to end, from cliff to lake 'twas free!
How happy was I in it then! I lov'd
Its very storms! Yes, Emma, I have sat
In my boat at night, when, midway o'er the lake,
The stars went out, and down the mountain gorge
The wind came roaring—I have sat and eyed
The thunder breaking from his cloud, and smil'd
To see him shake his lightnings o'er my head,
And think I had no master save his own.
You know the jutting cliff, round which a track
Up hither winds, whose base is but the brow
To such another one, with scanty room
For two a-breast to pass? O'ertaken there
By the mountain blast, I've laid me flat along,
And while gust followed gust more furiously,
As if to sweep me o'er the horrid brink;
And I have thought of other lands, whose storms
Are summer flaws to those of mine, and just
Have wished me there—the thought that mine was free,
Has check'd that wish, and I have rais'd my head,
And cried in thraldom to that furious wind,
Blow on! This is the land of liberty!

Old Melctal soon after this appears, blinded as he
is by the cruel orders of Gesler.

Enter Old Melctal, a bandage round his eyes, led by Albert.

Old M. Where art thou, William?

Tell.   Who is't?

Emma. Do you not know him?

Tell.   No!—It cannot be
The voice of Melctal!

Albert.   Father, it is Melctal!

Emma. What ails you, Tell?

Albert. Oh, father, speak to him.

Emma. What passion shakes you thus?

Tell. His eyes—where are they? —
Melctal has eyes.

Old M. Tell! Tell!

Tell.   'Tis Melctal's voice.
Where are his eyes? Have they put out his eyes?
Has Gesler turned the little evening of
The old man's life to-night before its time?
To such black night as sees not with the day
All round it! Father, speak! pronounce the name
Of Gesler!

Old M. Gesler!

Tell.   Gesler has torn out
The old man's eyes! Support thy mother!

(Albert goes to Emma.

Erni? .Where's Erni? Where's thy son! Is he alive?
And are his father's eyes torn out?
    Old M.   He lives, my William,
But knows it not.
    Tell.   When he shall know it!—Heavens!—
When he shall know it!—I am not thy son,
Yet—
    Emma. (*alarmed at his increasing vehemence*) William!
      William!
    Albert.   Father!
    Tell.   Could I find
Something to tear—to rend, were worth it!—something
Most ravenous and bloody—something like
Gesler!—a wolf!—no, no! a wolf's a lamb
To Gesler! 'Tis a natural hunger makes
The wolf a savage: and, savage as he is,
Yet with his kind he gently doth consort.
'Tis but his lawful prey he tears; and that
He finishes—not mangles, and then leaves
To live! He hath no joy in cruelty—but as
It ministers to his most needful want,—
I would let the wolf go free for Gesler!—Water! Water!
My tongue cleaves to its roof! (Emma *goes into cottage.*
    Old M. What ails thee, William?
I pray thee, William, let me hear thy voice!
That's not thy voice!
    Tell. I cannot speak to thee!
    Emma. (*returning, with water*) Here, William!
    Tell.   Emma!
    Emma.   Drink!
    Tell. I cannot drink!
    Emma. Your eyes are fixed.
    Tell.   Melctal!—he has no eyes!
                         (*bursts into tears.*
The poor old man!   (*falls on* Melctal's *neck.*
    Old M.   I feel thee, Tell! I care not
That I have lost my eyes. I feel thy tears—
They're more to me than eyes! When I had eyes,
I never knew thee, William, as I know
Thee now without. I do not want my eyes!

In the plot Mr. Knowles has pretty closely fol-
lowed the French writer Florian, in his *Guillaume Tell.*
As originally composed, the tragedy contained five acts,
but Mr. Macready, thinking it too long for the some-
what meagre incidents, cut it down to three acts, altoge-
ther suppressing an ingenious and amusing underplot.
In this underplot, two young patriotic citizens of Altorf,

Jagheli and Michael, who love respectively the Seneschal's daughter and niece, obtain admission by a stratagem into Gesler's castle, and not only succeed in carrying off the fair ones, "nothing loath". but facilitate the capture of the stronghold by Tell and his Swiss bands. The annexed scene, in which Michael surprises Jagheli rehearsing a serenade to his mistress. will show that Mr. Macready's excision has sacrificed much good and humorous dialogue:

SONG.

> Lady, you're so heavenly fair,
>   Though to love is madness, still
> Who beholds you can't forbear,
>   But adores against his will.
>
> Reason warns the heart in vain
>   Headlong passion won't obey;
> Hope's deceived, and sighs again!
>   Love's abjured, yet holds its sway!

Michael. — I pray you, have the ditty o'er again!
Of all the strains that mewing minstrels sing
The lover's one for me. 1 could expire
To hear a man, with bristles on his chin,
Sing soft, with upturn'd eyes and arched brows.
Which tell of trickling tears that never fell,
And through the gamut whine his tender pain:
While A and B and C such anguish speak
As never lover felt for mistress lost.
Let's have the strain again!
Jagheli. — To make thee mirth?
When I'm thy lackey, honest Michael, I'll
Provide thee music. I'm not in thy pay.
M. No, but I mean
To take thee into it. Wilt thou hire with me?
Nay, hang thy coyness, man! Why, thinkest thou
Thou art the only man in Altorf knows
The Seneschal has a fair daughter?
J. Fair
Or not, she's nought to me.
M. Indeed? Oh, then,
I'll tell her so.
J. You do not know her?
M. No;
For any profit it can bring to thee.
I pray thee, tell me, has she not black teeth?
J. Thou know'st 'twould take the pearl to challenge them.

M. Her nose, 1 think, is somewhat set awry?
J. It sits like dignity on beauty's face.
M. Her hair is a dull black?
J. 'Tis shining gold.
M. Her figure's squat?
J. Between the full and slim —
    A mould where vie the richest charms of both!
M. Well, then, she hobbles in her gait?
J. She moves, the light and flexible chamois, —
    If you could lend the chamois her beauty,
    And add to that her modest stateliness.
M. You are a hopeful painter, sir! How well
    You've drawn the daughter of the Seneschal!
J. Good Michael, thou'rt a jester; but thou'rt kind.
    Thy mirth doth feed at every man's expense:
    Yet with such grace of frankest confidence,
    That none begrudge thee. Wilt thou be my friend?
    I love the daughter of the Seneschal.
    Help me to see her.
M. Come to church with me
    Next Sunday.
J. I was there last Sunday, Michael —
    And Sunday before last — and Sunday, too,
    Preceding that. I ne'er miss church, for there
    I see the daughter of the Seneschal.
M. How wondrously devout thou'rt grown of late!
    They say there is a young man in the church
    That has his prayers by heart — unless, indeed,
    He reads them in a certain angel's face;
    On which he looks, and says them word for word,
    From end to end, nor e'er is seen to turn
    To other page. Can it be thou they mean?
    Thou'lt have a name for most rare sanctity!
J. Good Michael, can'st thou help me?
M. If I knew
    The lady.
J. What! dost thou not know her then?
    With what impediments is love environ'd!
M. Why, that's love's gain! It would not else be love.
    Or wherefore sing it, as your poets do,
    A thing that lives in plots and stratagems?
    They know not love who need but woo to wed,
    But they who fain would wed, but dare not woo!
    That's to be sound in love — to feel it from
    The heart's deep centre to the fingers' ends!
    As sweetest fruit is that which is forbid,
    So fairest maid is she that is withheld.
    Whene'er I fall in love, I'll pick a maid
  · Whose sire has vow'd her to a nunnery;
    And she shall have, moreover, for her wardens,

> Two maiden aunts past wooing, and to these
> I'll add an abigail, who has stood bridesmaid
> To twenty younger cousins, yet has ne'er
> Been ask'd herself; and under her I'll set
> A male retainer of the family,
> For twenty years or more, as surly as
> A mastiff on the chain; and, that my fair
> May lack no sweet provocative of love,
> Her tempting lattice shall be grated, and
> Her bower shall be surrounded with a wall
> Full ten feet high, on which an iron row
> Of forked shrubs shall stand and frown on me;
> And then I'll be a lover!

"The *Hunchback*", says Mr. Daniels, "is a noble play. Massinger might have written it, and lost no reputation by the authorship" Mr. Knowles himself, who was, like Shakespeare, a respectable, though not a great actor, was the original Master Walter, the Hunchback. In the last scene of the play we discover, that Master Walter was the eldest son of the Earl of Rochdale, but disowned from infancy, and disinherited by his father, who

> — would not have a Hunchback for his son;

and though this deformity, adds Master Walter,

> — was no act of mine,
> Yet did it curdle nature's kindly milk
> E'en where 'tis richest in a parent's breast —
> To cast me out to heartless fosterage,
> Not heartless always, as it prov'd — and give
> My portion to another!

The Hunchback finds a wife, notwithstanding, who dies early, leaving him a daughter, and this daughter he resolves to bring up in retirement, as his ward; for, as he subsequently tells her,

> — jealousy of my misshapen back
> Made me mistrustful of a child's affections —
> Who doubted e'en a wife's — so that I dropp'd
> The title of thy father, lest thy duty
> Should pay the debt that love could solve alone.

All this we learn only at the close of the fifth act; and till then must be satisfied with believing Julia to be merely the ward of simple Master Walter, Lord

Rochdale's steward. In the first act we find Julia in
her country-house, with her cousin Helen as a visitor.
Helen loves the town, as Julia loves the country; and
this difference of character gives occasion to a playful
discussion between the two young girls.

Helen.
    The town's the sun, and thou hast dwelt in night
    E'er since thy birth, not to have seen the town!
    Their women there are queens, and kings their men;
    Their houses palaces.
Julia.   And what of that?
    Have your town palaces a hall like this?
    Couches so fragrant? walls so high adorn'd?
    Casements with such festoons, such prospects, Helen,
    As these fair vistas have? Your kings and queens!
    See me a May-day queen, and talk of them!
Helen. Extremes are ever neighbours. 'Tis a step
    From one to the other.
    The odds are ten to one, that this day year
    Will see our May-day queen a city one.
Julia. Never! I'm wedded to a country life.
    O, did you hear what Master Walter says!
    Nine times in ten, the town's a hollow thing,
    Where what things are, is nought to what they shew;
    Where merit's name laughs merit's self to scorn!
    Where friendship and esteem, that ought to be
    The tenants of men's hearts, lodge in their looks
    And tongues alone. Where little virtue, with
    A costly keeper, passes for a heap;
    A heap for none that has a homely one!
    Where Fashion makes the law—your umpire, which
    You bow to, whether it has trains or not.
    Where Folly taketh off his cap and bells,
    To clap on Wisdom, which must bear the jest!
    Where to pass current, you must seem the thing,
    The passive thing, that others think; and not
    Your simple, honest, independent self!

The Hunchback arrives, and introduces Sir Thomas
Clifford, a young gentleman whom Master Walter highly
esteems; nor is it long till Sir Thomas proposes in due
form to Julia; but the young girl hesitates to give
an answer, and inquires:

Julia.   You're from the town;
    How comes it, sir, you seek a country wife?
Cliff. In joining contrasts lieth love's delight.
    Complexion, stature, nature, mateth it,

Not with their kinds, but with their opposites.
Hence hands of snow in palms of russet lie;
The form of Hercules affects the sylph's;
And breasts that case the lion's fear-proof heart
Find their loved lodge in arms where tremors dwell!
So with degrees.
Rank passes by the circlet-graced brow,
Upon the forehead bare of notelessness
To print the nuptial kiss. As with degrees,
So is't with habits; therefore I, indeed
A gallant of the town, the town forsake,
To win a country wife.

Julia accepts Sir Thomas; and in the next act we find the whole party in London, whither they have come to procure the *trousseau* of the bride, and make the other wedding purchases. But Julia, once immersed in the dissipation of polite London life, becomes completely metamorphosed, and can speak and think of nothing but the brilliant and fashionable life she intends to lead as the wife of a wealthy baronet:

Julia. Helen — I shall be
A happy wife! What routs, what balls, what masques.
What gala days! Think not, when I am wed,
I'll keep the house as owlet does her tower,
Alone, — when every other bird's on wing.
I'll use my palfrey, Helen! and my coach;
My barge too, for excursion on the Thames;
What drives to Barnet, Hackney, Islington!
What rides to Epping, Hounslow, and Blackheath!
What sails to Greenwich, Woolwich, Fulham, Kew;
I'll set a pattern to your lady wives!
And what a wardrobe! I'll have change of suits
For every day in the year! and sets for days!
My morning dress, my noon dress, dinner dress,
And evening dress! then will I show you lace
A foot deep, can I purchase it; if not,
I'll specially bespeak it. Diamonds too!
Not buckles, rings, and ear-rings only, — but
Whole necklaces and stomachers of gems!
I'll shine! be sure I will. I will be known
For Lady Clifford all the City through,
And fifty miles the country round about.
Wife of Sir Thomas Clifford, baronet, —
Not perishable knight! who, when he makes
A lady of me, doubtless must expect
To see me play the part of one.

This programme is accidentally overheard by Sir Thomas, who somewhat hastily assumes that Julia accepts him solely on account of his wealth; hence he coldly informs her, that he will keep his word and wed her; that she shall be Lady Clifford, but also that they shall part at the altar. This proposal Julia treats as an insult, and the marriage is broken off. A new suitor for Julia's hand now presents himself — no other, in fact, than Master Wilford, who, on the death of the late Earl of Rochdale without issue, had succeeded to the title and property, in spite of his distant relationship. Julia, in a moment of pique, and ignorant of the just claims of Master Walter to the earldom, signs a marriage contract with the new Lord; but she has scarcely done so when all her tenderness for Clifford revives, and she intreats the Hunchback to save her from the detested union. Master Walter assumes an austere demeanour, and declares that his word has been given, and the marriage contract signed. The wedding-day at length arrives, and only then does the Hunchback reveal himself as Julia's father and the rightful Earl of Rochdale; hence Wilford's signature as Earl was valueless, and the marriage contract null and void. While Julia has thus become an earl's daughter, Clifford has suffered a reverse of fortune, but she proves her affection and disinterestedness by becoming his wife.

One scene in the *Hunchback* is always sure of a good reception from an English audience. The sprightly Helen is loved by her bookworm cousin, Modus, who can never muster courage to woo her, so that she has to meet him more than half way. Julia and Master Walter are both out, and Helen, in wandering through the house meets Cousin Modus, with a book in his hand:

Helen.   What's that you read?
Modus. Latin, sweet cousin.
Helen.   'Tis a naughty tongue
      I fear, and teaches men to lie.
Modus.   To lie!
Helen. You study it. You call your cousin sweet,
      And treat her as you would a crab [1]. As sour

[1] The crab-apple, or wild apple, which is extremely sour.

'Twould seem you think her, so you covet her!
Why how the monster stares, and looks about!
You construe Latin, and can't construe that.
Modus. I never studied women.
Helen.   No: nor men.
  Else would you better know their ways: nor read
  In presence of a lady. *(strikes book from his hand.)*
Modus.   Right you say,
  And well you served me, cousin, so to strike
  The volume from my hand. I own my fault;
  So please you, — may I pick it up again?
  I'll put it in my pocket!
Helen.   Pick it up.
  (aside) He fears me as I were his grandmother!
  What is the book?
Modus.   'Tis Ovid's Art of Love.
Helen. That Ovid was a fool!
Modus.   In what?
Helen.   In that.
  To call that thing an art, which art is none.
Modus. And is not love an art?
Helen.   Are you a fool,
  As well as Ovid? Love an art! No art
  But taketh time and pains to learn. Love comes
  With neither. Is't to hoard such grain as that
  You went to college? Better stay at home,
  And study homely English.
Modus.   Nay, you know not
  The argument.
Helen.   I don't? I know it better
  Than ever Ovid did. The face — the form —
  The heart — the mind we fancy, cousin;
  That's the argument. Why, cousin, you know nothing.
  Suppose a lady were in love with thee,
  Couldst thou by Ovid, cousin, find it out?
  Couldst find it out, wert thou in love thyself?
  Could Ovid, cousin, teach thee to make love?
  I could, that never read him. You begin
  With melancholy; then to sadness; then
  To sickness; then to dying — but not die;
  She would not let thee, were she of my mind;
  She'd take compassion on thee. Then for hope;
  From hope to confidence; from confidence
  To boldness; then you'd speak; at first entreat;
  Then urge; then flout; then argue; then enforce;
  Make prisoner of her hand; besiege her waist;
  Threaten her lips with storming; keep thy word
  And carry her! My sampler 'gainst thy Ovid!
  Why, cousin, are you frighten'd, that you stand
  As you were stricken dumb? The case is clear,

You are no soldier. You'll never win a battle.
You care too much for blows!
Modus.   You wrong me there.
At school I was the champion of my form,
And since I went to college —
Helen.   That for college! (*snapping her fingers.*)
Modus. Nay. hear me!
Helen.   Well? What, since you went to college
You know what men are set down for, who boast
Of their own bravery. Go on, brave cousin,
What, since you went to college? Was there not
One Quentin Halworth there? You know there was,
And that he was your master!
Modus.   He my master!
Thrice was he worsted by me.
Helen.   Still was he
Your master.
Modus.   He allow'd I had the best!
Allow'd it, mark me! nor to me alone,
But twenty I could name.
   Helen.   And master'd you
At last! Confess it, cousin, 'tis the truth.
A proctor's daughter you did both affect —
Look at me and deny it! Of the twain
She more affected you; — I've caught you now,
Bold cousin! Mark you? Opportunity
On opportunity she gave you, sir, —
Deny it if you can! — but though to others,
When you discours'd of her, you were a flame;
To her you were a wick that would not light,
Though held in the very fire! And so he won her —
Won her, because he woo'd her like a man.
For all your cuffings, cuffing you again
With most usurious interest. Now, sir,
Protest that you are valiant!
Modus.   Cousin Helen!
Helen. Well, sir?
Modus.   The tale is all a forgery!
Helen.   A forgery!
Modus. From first to last: ne'er spoke I
To a proctor's daughter while I was at college —
Helen. 'Twas a scrivener's then — or somebody's.
But what concerns it whose? Enough, you lov'd her!
And, shame upon you, let another take her.
Modus. Cousin, I tell you, if you'll only hear me,
I lov'd no woman while I was at college —
Save one, and her I fancied ere I went there.
Helen. Indeed! (*aside*) Now I'll retreat, if he's advancing.
Comes he not on! O what a stock's the man?
Well, cousin?

Modus.   Well! What more would'st have me say,
    I think I've said enough.
Helen.   And so think I.
    I did but jest with you. You are not angry?
    Shake hands! Why, cousin, do you squeeze me so?
Modus. (*letting her go*) I swear I squeezed you not!
Helen. You did not?
Modus.   No! I'll die if I did!
Helen. Why then you did not, cousin.
    So let's shake hands again — (*he takes her hand timidly;
        she looks at him for a minute, then pettishly strikes his
        hand down*) O, go and now
    Read Ovid! (*going off, but returns*) Cousin, will you tell
        me one thing.
    Wore lovers ruffs in Master Ovid's time?
    Behov'd him teach them, then, to put them on; —
    And that you have to learn. Hold up your head!
    Why, cousin, how you blush. Plague on the ruff!
    I cannot give't a set. You're blushing still!
    Why do you blush, dear cousin? So! — 'twill beat me!
    I'll give it up.
Modus.   Nay, prithee don't — try on!
Helen. And if I do, I fear you'll think me bold.
Modus. For what?
Helen.   To trust my face so near to thine.
Modus. I know not what you mean.
Helen.   I'm glad you don't!
    Cousin, I own right well behaved you are,
    Most marvellously well behaved! They've bred
    You well at college. With another man
    My lips would be in danger! Hang the ruff!
Modus. Nay, give it up, nor plague thyself, dear cousin.
Helen. Dear fool! (*throws the ruff on the ground*) I swear
           the ruff is good for just
    As little as its master! There! — 'tis spoiled —
    You'll have to get another. Hie for it,
    And wear it in the fashion of a wisp,
    Ere I adjust it for thee! Farewell, cousin!
    You'd need to study Ovid's Art of Love.
                    Exit Helen.

The Wife, a Tale of Mantua, seems to have been suggested by Massinger's *Duke of Milan*, though the two pieces differ widely in the details. Leonardo Gonzaga, the rightful Duke of Mantua, when wandering through Switzerland, was rescued "from beneath an avalanche, the sole survivor of a company", by Mariana's father, and the young girl, ignorant of his rank, and knowing only that he had come from Mantua, learned to love him while attending his sick-bed:

Mariana. I loved indeed! If I but nursed a flower
   Which to the ground the wind and rain had beaten,
   That flower of all our garden was my pride:
   What then was he to me, for whom I thought
   To make a shroud, when, tending on him still
   With hope, that, baffled still, did still keep up;
   I saw, at last, the ruddy dawn of health
   Begin to mantle o'er his pallid form,
   And glow and glow — till forth at last it burst
   Into confirmed, broad, and glorious day!

The traveller, restored to health, returns home, and leaves for Mariana an aching void behind:

Mar. Cot, garden, vineyard, rivulet, and wood,
   Lake, sky, and mountain, went along with him!
   Could I remain behind? My father found
   My heart was not at home; he loved his child,
   And asked me, one day, whither we should go?
   I said: "To Mantua". I followed him
   To Mantua! to breathe the air he breathed,
   To walk upon the ground he walked upon,
   To look upon the things he looked upon,
   To look, perchance, on him! perchance to hear him,
   To touch him! never to be known to him,
   Till he was told I lived and died his love!

Mariana meets with her princely lover in Mantua, and is made by him the sharer of his ducal throne, to the great chagrin of his cousin, Fernando Gonzaga, the heir to the ducal dignity. Taking advantage of the absence of the Duke on a warlike expedition, the unworthy Fernando attempts to blast, by a vile machination, the fair fame of the young Duchess. For this purpose he throws in Mariana's way a handsome young Swiss adventurer, whom he has made his secretary, and who, though now calling himself Julian St. Pierre, finally turns out to be Mariana's brother Ambrose, a wild youth, who had left his home when Mariana was still a child in the cradle. The young man half suspects who Mariana is, but she has no recollection of him; and attributes the pleasure she finds in her intercourse with him to the reminiscences of her native land which he awakes:

Julian St. Pierre. — It is
> The land of beauty, and of grandeur, lady,
> Where looks the cottage out on a domain
> The palace cannot boast of. Seas of lakes,
> And hills of forests! crystal waves that rise
> 'Midst mountains all of snow, and mock the sun,
> Returning him his flaming beams more thick
> And radiant than he sent them. — Torrents, there.
> Are bounding floods! And there the tempest roams
> At large, in all the terrors of its glory!
> And then our valleys! Ah, they are the homes
> For hearts! Our cottages, our vineyards, orchards! —
> Our pastures, studded with the herd and fold!
> Our native strains, that melt us as we sing them!
> A free — a gentle — simple — honest people!

Julian is plied by Fernando with intoxicating drinks, and then carried, in an unconscious state, into a chamber adjoining that of the Duchess, where he is discovered by the household servants the next morning. But the ruin of Mariana is not yet secured, in spite of this accusatory discovery, and Fernando summons Julian to his presence to give him his further instructions. These Julian desires to have in writing, pleading the weakness of his memory, and at length, partly by address, partly by intimidation, obtains from Fernando what is equivalent to a confession of his guilt, signed by his own hand. Duke Leonardo is still with his army, and Fernando carries off the Duchess as a prisoner to the encampment, where, in the presence of the Duke, he endeavours to substantiate against her the charge of infidelity. Leonardo refuses to admit the truth of the accusation; and a moment afterwards Julian arrives hot and dusty, places in the Duke's hand the papers proving Fernando's treachery, and then falls to the ground mortally wounded by a thrust of the traitor's sword. Before he dies, he has still strength left to make himself known to Mariana as her brother Ambrose.

Of Mr. Knowles's comedies, the most successful is *the Love-Chase*. The scene is London, and the leading characters are Constance and Wildrake, a pair of lovers. who, like Beatrice and Benedick, affect a mutual aversion. but are at last brought to understand themselves and each other by a friendly stratagem on the part of Trueman, who explains in the following terms to Constance's father, how he proposes to proceed:

> Unlike other common flowers,
> The flower of love shows various in the bud;
> 'Twill look a thistle. and 'twill blow a rose!
> And with your leave, I'll put it to the test;
> Affect, myself, for thy fair daughter love —
> Make him my confidant — dilate to him
> Upon the graces of her heart and mind,
> Feature and form — that well may comment bear —
> Till — like the practised connoisseur, who finds
> A gem of art out in a household picture
> The unskill'd owner held so cheap he grudged
> Renewal of the chipp'd and tarnish'd frame,
> But values now as priceless — I arouse him
> Into a quick sense of the worth of that
> Whose merit hitherto, from lack of skill,
> Or dulling habit of acquaintanceship
> He has not been awake to.

The comic effect of the piece is greatly heightened by the scene, in which the elderly Widow Green, imagining that young Waller's attentions to her humble companion, Lydia, are addressed to herself, tries to make him jealous of the antiquated beau, Sir W. Fondlove, who, on his side, is equally certain that the Widow is pining for him.

Of Mr. Knowles's other plays, *Alfred the Great*, and *John of Procida* (based on the Sicilian Vespers), obtained a certain, though an inferior degree of success; and the same may be said of his two comedies, *Love*, and *the Secretary*, in both of which the subject is the love of a humble subordinate for his patroness. *The Beggar of Bethnal Green*, founded on the old popular ballad, was an acknowledged failure; and *the Daughter*, a tale of the wreckers of Cornwall, as the inhuman wretches were called, who made a trade of plundering and sometimes murdering shipwrecked voyagers, though containing some very effective scenes, could not keep its place on the stage. Another piece, *the Rose of Arragon*, resembles rather too closely *the Wife*; and *Woman's Wit; or, Love's Disguises*, the idea of which seems borrowed from Mrs Centlivre's *Bold Stroke for a Wife*, is decidedly too full of masquerading.

Of Mr. Knowles, the *Athenaeum* (Feb. 1847) says, that he is "a writer as full of individuality as of geniality, who has been popular without coarse conception, and received as a poet without making any extraordinary pretensions. The first and last cause of his well-deserved popularity, as a dramatist, is the *heartiness* of his writings. The heart which Mr. Knowles puts into his work lays hold of the hearts of his public; and this is his secret."

Among the dramatists of the period, no mean place must be assigned to

Lord Lytton.

Lord Lytton's most popular play is unquestionably *the Lady of Lyons*, founded on the old French story of *Perourou, or the Bellows-Mender*. Claude Melnotte, the hero, though only a well-to-do gardener's son, loves Pauline Deschapelles, a rich merchant's proud daughter. and in "the ambition to be worthier" of her, makes himself master of several accomplishments usually looked on as the appanage of the wealthier classes. He sends the lady his rarest flowers, and encouraged by observing that she wears them, though ignorant of the quarter whence they come, he ventures to address her in some verses signed with his name. In one of the early scenes, his friend and messenger, Gaspar, returns to report how this tribute of devotion has been received:

(Enter Gaspar).

Melnotte. Welcome, Gaspar, welcome. Where is the letter? Why do you turn away, man? Where is the letter? (*Gaspar gives him one*). This! this is mine, the one I intrusted to thee. Didst thou not leave it?

Gaspar. Yes. I left it.

Mel. My own verses returned to me. Nothing else!

Gas. Thou wilt be proud to hear how thy messenger was honoured. For thy sake, Melnotte, I have borne that which no Frenchman can bear without disgrace.

Mel. Disgrace, Gaspar! Disgrace?

Gas. I gave thy letter to the porter, who passed it from lackey to lackey till it reached the lady it was meant for.

M e l. It reached her, then; — you are sure of that! It reached
her, — well, well!

G a s. It reached her, and was returned to me with blows. Dost
hear, Melnotte? with blows! Death! are we slaves still, that
we are to be thus dealt with, we peasants?

M e l. With blows? No, Gaspar, no; not blows!

G a s. I could show thee the marks if it were not so deep a shame
to bear them. The lackey who tossed thy letter into the mire
swore that his lady and her mother never were so insulted.
What could thy letter contain, Claude?

M e l. Not a line that a serf might not have written to an empress.
No, not one.

G a s. They promise thee the same greeting they gave me, if thou
wilt pass that way. Shall we endure this, Claude?

M e l. Forgive me, the fault was mine, I have brought this on thee;
I will not forget it; thou shalt be avenged! The heartless in-
solence!

G a s. Thou art moved, Melnotte; think not of me; I would go
through fire and water to serve thee; but, — a blow! It is
not the b r u i s e that galls, — it is the b l u s h, Melnotte.

M e l. Say, what message? How insulted? — Wherefore? — What
the offence?

G a s. Did you not write to Pauline Deschapelles, the daughter of
the rich merchant?

M e l. Well? —

G a s. And are you not a peasant — a gardener's son? that was
the offence. Sleep on it, Melnotte. Blows to a French citizen,
blows!

While Melnotte is thirsting for revenge, but still
struggling with love, a letter reaches him from Beau-
seant, a rejected suitor of Pauline's, in which he finds
the mysterious words:

I can secure to thee the realization of thy most sanguine
hopes: and the sole condition I ask in return is, that thou shalt
be steadfast to thine own ends. I shall demand from thee a solemn
oath to marry her whom thou lovest; to bear her to thine home
on thy wedding night. I am serious — if thou wouldst learn more,
lose not a moment, but follow the bearer of this letter.

In the next act, we find Melnotte an honoured guest
in the Deschapelles family, to which he has been in-
troduced by Beauseant as the Prince of Como, having
been previously furnished by him and his friend Glavis,
another luckless lover of Pauline's, with everything
necessary to support the assumed dignity. He now
wooes and soon wins Pauline. On one occasion she desires
to hear from him a description of his palace by the

Lake of Como. Evading her request, while he appears to fulfil it. Melnotte seizes the opportunity, to discover what are her real feelings towards him:

M e l. Nay, dearest, nay, if thou wouldst have me paint
    The home to which, could love fulfil its prayers,
    This hand would lead thee, listen! — A deep vale
    Shut out by Alpine hills from the rude world
    Near a clear lake, margin'd by fruits of gold
    And whispering myrtles; glassing softest skies,
    As cloudless, save with rare and roseate shadows
    As I would have thy fate!
Paul. My own dear love!
M e l. A palace lifting to eternal summer
    Its marble walls, from out a glossy bower
    Of coolest foliage musical with birds,
    Whose songs shall syllable thy name! At noon
    We'd sit beneath the arching vines, and wonder
    Why Earth could be unhappy, while the Heavens
    Still left us youth and love! We'd have no friends
    That were not lovers; no ambition, save
    To excel them all in love; we'd read no books
    That were not tales of love — that we might smile
    To think how poorly eloquence of words
    Translates the poetry of hearts like ours!
    And when night came, amidst the breathless Heavens
    We'd guess what star should be our home when love
    Becomes immortal; while the perfumed light
    Stole through the mists of alabaster lamps,
    And every air was heavy with the sighs
    Of orange-groves and music from sweet lutes,
    And murmurs of low fountains that gush forth
    I' the midst of roses! Dost thou like the picture?
Paul. Oh, as the bee upon the flower, I hang
    Upon the honey of thy eloquent tongue!
    Am I not blest? And if I love too wildly,
    Who would not love thee like Pauline?
M e l. *(bitterly).*   Oh, false one!
    It is the p r i n c e thou lovest, not the m a n:
    If in the stead of luxury, pomp, power,
    I had painted poverty, and toil, and care,
    Thou hadst found no honey on my tongue; — Pauline,
    That is not love!
Paul. Thou wrong'st me, cruel Prince!
    At first, in truth, I might not have been won,
    Save through the weakness of a flatter'd pride;
    But n o w, — oh, trust me, — could'st thou fall from power
    And sink —
M e l.   As low as that poor gardener's son,
    Who dared to lift his eyes to thee?

Paul.   Even then,
     Methinks thou would'st be only made more dear
     By the sweet thought that I could prove how deep
     Is woman's love! We are like the insects, caught
     By the poor glittering of a garish flame;
     But, oh, the wings once scorch'd, the brightest star
     Lures us no more; and by the fatal light
     We cling till death!
Mel.   Angel! *(Aside).* O conscience! conscience!

Though now tortured by remorse, Melnotte fulfils the conditions of his oath, and conducts his young bride, not to the imaginary palace on the Lake of Como, but to the humble cottage of his mother. Of his authority as a husband he makes no other use than to protect her from the triumphant insults of Beauseant, and having announced to the injured Pauline his firm resolution to restore her to her father on the morrow, he confides her for the night to the care of his mother:

Paul.   No, touch me not!
     I know my fate. You are, by law, my tyrant;
     And I — O Heaven! a peasant's wife! I'll work —
     Toil — drudge — do what thou wilt — but touch me not;
     Let my wrongs make me sacred!
Mel.   Do not fear me.
     Thou dost not know me, madam; at the altar
     My vengeance ceased — my guilty oath expired!
     Henceforth, no image of some marble saint,
     Niched in cathedral aisles, is hallow'd more
     From the rude hand of sacrilegious wrong.
     I am thy husband — nay, thou need'st not shudder; —
     Here, at thy feet, I lay a husband's rights.
     A marriage thus unholy — unfulfill'd —
     A bond of fraud — is, by the laws of France,
     Made void and null. To-night sleep — sleep in peace.
     To-morrow, pure and virgin as this morn
     I bore thee, bathed in blushes, from the shrine,
     Thy father's arms shall take thee to thy home.
     The law shall do thee justice, and restore
     Thy right to bless another with thy love.
     And when thou art happy, and hast half forgot
     Him who so loved — so wrong'd thee, think at least
     Heaven left some remnant of the angel still
     In that poor peasant's nature! Ho! my mother!

Melnotte sets out for the army, in company with the eccentric old officer Damas, a connexion of the Deschap-

pelles family, who becomes the friend of the gardener's
son, though he had been the enemy of the Prince; and
for two years and a half nothing is heard of either of
them. In the mean time the merchant Deschappelles
has met with heavy losses. and on the day that Damas
returns as General, and Melnotte as Colonel, they learn
that Pauline, to save her father from bankruptcy, is
about to give her hand to Beauseant, who exacts this
sacrifice as the price of the pecuniary aid he offers.
Damas, being invited to the wedding, takes Melnotte
with him, under the name of Colonel Morier, and apprises
Pauline, in a whisper, that Morier is Melnotte's intimate
friend. While the others are engaged with the marriage
contract, she approaches the stranger, who turns from
her with averted gaze:

Paul. Thrice have I sought to speak; my courage fails me.
    Sir, is it true that you have known — nay, are
    The friend of — Melnotte?
Mel.   Lady, yes! — Myself
    And misery know the man!
Paul.   And you will see him,
    And you will bear to him — ay — word for word,
    All that this heart, which breaks in parting from him,
    Would send, ere still for ever?
Mel.   He hath told me
    You have the right to choose from out the world
    A worthier bridegroom; — he foregoes all claim,
    Even to murmur at his doom. Speak on!
Paul. Tell him for years I never nursed a thought
    That was not his; — that on his wandering way,
    Daily and nightly, pour'd a mourner's prayers.
    Tell him ev'n now that I would rather share
    His lowliest lot, — walk by his side, an outcast, —
    Work for him, beg with him — live upon the light
    Of one kind smile from him — than wear the crown
    The Bourbon lost!

Beauseant, with the bank-notes in his hand, ad-
vances to Deschappelles, and informs him, that they
are his the moment his daughter signs the marriage-
contract. The Notary is about to hand the paper to
Pauline, when Melnotte seizes and tears it:

Beaus.   Are you mad?
Deschap. How, sir! What means this insult?

M e l.   Peace, old man!
    I have a prior claim. Before the face
    Of man and Heaven I urge it; I outbid
    You sordid huckster for your priceless jewel.
                                         (Giving a pocket-book).
    There is the sum twice told! Blush not to take it:
    There's not a coin that is not bought and hallow'd
    In the cause of nations with a soldier's blood!
B e a u s.   Torments and death!
P a u l.   That voice! Thou art —
M e l.   Thy husband!
                                (Pauline rushes into his arms).

The *Duchess de la Vallière*, as the title implies, is
founded on the history of the least unworthy of the
numerous mistresses of Louis XIV., who, overcome by
shame and remorse, withdrew from court, and closed
her life in a Carmelite convent. This piece obtained
only a partial success on the stage, though it can
boast of at least one highly effective scene — that in
which the King encounters Bragelone, the Duchess's
former lover, whom grief and despair have driven to
renounce the world, and to become a monk:

L o u i s.   Save you, father!
B r a g e l o n e.   I thank thee, son.
L o u i s.   He knows me not. Well, monk,
    Are you her grace's almoner?
B r a g e.   Sire, no!
L o u i s.   So short, yet know us?
B r a g e.   Sire, I do. You are
    The man —
L o u i s.   How, priest! — the man!
B r a g e.   The word offends you?
    The k i n g, who raised a maiden to a duchess.
    That maiden's mother was a stainless matron:
    Her heart you broke, though mother to a duchess.
    That maiden was affianced from her youth
    To one who served you well — nay, saved your life:
    His life you robb'd of all that gave life value;
    And yet — you made his fair betroth'd a duchess!
    You are that king. The world proclaims you "Great;"
    A million warriors bled to buy your laurels;
    A million peasants starved to build Versailles:
    Your people famish; but your court is splendid!
    Priests from the pulpit bless your glorious reign;
    Poets have sung you greater than Augustus;
    And painters placed you on immortal canvass,

Limn'd as the Jove whose thunders awe the world:
But to the humble minister of Heaven,
You are the king who has betray'd his trust —
Beggar'd a nation but to bloat a court,
Seen in men's lives the pastime to ambition,
Look'd but on virtue as the toy for vice;
And, for the first time, from a subject's lips,
Now learns the name he leaves to Time and God!

Louis. Add to the bead-roll of that king's offences,
That when a foul-mouthed monk assumed the rebel,
The monster-king forgave him. Hast thou done?

Brage. Your changing hues belie your royal mien;
Ill the high monarch veils the trembling man!

Louis. Well, you are privileged! It ne'er was said
The Fourteenth Louis, in his proudest hour,
Bow'd not his sceptre to the Church's crozier.

Brage. Alas! the Church! 'Tis true, this garb of serge
Dares speech that daunts the ermine, and walks free
Where stout hearts tremble in the triple mail.
But wherefore? — Lies the virtue in the robe,
Which the moth eats? or in these senseless beads?
Or in the name of Priest? The Pharisees
Had priests that gave their Saviour to the cross!
No! we have high immunity and sanction,
That Truth may teach humanity to Power,
Glide through the dungeon, pierce the armed throng,
Awaken Luxury on her Sybarite couch,
And, startling souls that slumber on a throne,
Bow kings before that priest of priests — the Conscience!

Louis (aside). An awful man! — unlike the reverend crew
Who praise my royal virtues in the pulpit,
And — ask for bishoprics when church is over!

Brage. This makes us sacred. The profane are they
Honouring the herald while they scorn the mission.
The king who serves the Church, yet clings to Mammon;
Who fears the pastor, but forgets the flock;
Who bows before the monitor, and yet
Will ne'er forego the sin, may sink, when age
Palsies the lust and deadens the temptation,
To the priest-ridden, not repentant, dotard, —
For pious hopes hail superstitious terrors,
And seek some sleek Iscariot of the Church,
To sell salvation for the thirty pieces!

Louis (aside). He speaks as one inspired!

Brage.   Awake! — awake!
Great though thou art, awake thee from the dream
That earth was made for kings — mankind for slaughter
Woman for lust — the people for the palace!
Dark warnings have gone forth; along the air
Lingers the crash of the first Charles's throne:

Behold the young, the fair, the haughty king!
The kneeling courtiers, and the flattering priests;
Lo! where the palace rose, behold the scaffold —
The crowd — the axe — the headsman — and the victim!
Lord of the silver lilies, canst thou tell
If the same fate await not thy descendant!
If some meek son of thine imperial line   .
May make no brother to yon headless spectre!
And when the sage who saddens o'er the end
Tracks back the causes, tremble, lest he find
The seeds, thy wars, thy pomp, and thy profusion,
Sow'd in a heartless court and breadless people,
Grew to the tree from which men shaped the scaffold, —
And the long glare of thy funereal glories
Light unborn monarchs to a ghastly grave!
Beware, proud King! the Present cries aloud,
A prophet to the future! Wake! — beware!.   (*Exit.*)

Richelieu; or, the Conspiracy, is another historical piece, which closes with the so-called *Day of Dupes*, or the day of Richelieu's triumph over all the enemies who had plotted his ruin. An increased interest is lent to this drama by the introduction of Julie de Mortemar, Richelieu's ward; and its success on the stage was insured by the admirable performance of Mr. and Miss Vandenhoff, in the respective characters of Richelieu and Julie. The mixed character of the great Cardinal, with all its bright and dark traits, is skilfully portrayed in the soliloquy at the beginning of the third act. We quote a few of the most striking passages:

Richelieu. "In silence, and at night, the Conscience feels
    That life should soar to nobler ends than Power."
    So sayest thou, sage and sober moralist!
    But wert thou tried? Sublime Philosophy,
    Thou art the Patriarch's ladder, reaching heaven,
    And bright with beck'ning angels — but, alas!
    We see thee, like the Patriarchs, but in dreams,
    By the first step — dull-slumbering on the earth.
    I am not happy! — with the Titan's lust,
    I woo'd a goddess, and I clasp a cloud.

*   *   *

O ye, whose hour-glass shifts its tranquil sands
In the unvex'd silence of a student's cell;
Ye, whose untempted hearts have never toss'd
Upon the dark and stormy tides where life

Gives battle to the elements, — and man
Wrestles with man for some slight plank, whose weight
Will bear but one — while round the desperate wretch
The hungry billows roar — and the fierce Fate,
Like some huge monster, dim-seen through the surf,
Waits him who drops; — ye safe and formal men,
Who write the deeds, and with unfeverish hand
Weigh in nice scales the motives of the Great,
Ye cannot know what ye have never tried!
History preserves alone the fleshless bones
Of what we are — and by the mocking skull
The would-be wise pretend to guess the features!
Without the roundness and the glow of life
How hideous is the skeleton! Without
The colourings and humanities that clothe
Our errors, the anatomists of schools
Can make our memory hideous!
                    I have wrought
Great uses out of evil tools — and they
In the time to come may bask beneath the light
Which I have stolen from the angry gods,
And warn their sons against the glorious theft,
Forgetful of the darkness which it broke.
I have shed blood — but I have had no foes
Save those the State had — if my wrath was deadly,
'Tis that I felt my country in my veins,
And smote her sons as Brutus smote his own.
And yet I am not happy — blanch'd and sear'd
Before my time — breathing an air of hate,
And seeing daggers in the eyes of men,
And wasting powers that shake the thrones of earth
In contest, with the insects — bearding kings
And braved by lackies — murder at my bed;
And lone amidst the multitudinous web,
With the dread Three — that are the Fates who hold
The woof and shears — the Monk, the Spy, the Headsman.
And this is power? Alas! I am not happy.

Richelieu's chief enemies, the favourite Baradas, and Gaston of Orleans, the King's brother, while bent on removing the Cardinal by any means, assassination not excepted, are at the same time endeavouring, by tampering with the army and confederating secretly with the Spanish enemy, to depose the King, and to proclaim Gaston regent of the kingdom. These manoeuvres are well known to Richelieu, but for the time being, the conspirators have gained the ear of the weak and fickle Louis, and it is only under the pretence of resigning his office, and taking leave of the King, as a "dying servant" that he is allowed to appear in the royal presence. Once here he soon finds an opportunity of exposing the incapacity and treason of Baradas and his accomplices:

Richelieu. You would consign your armies to the baton
    Of your most honoured brother. Sire, so be it!
    Your minister, the Count de Baradas;
    A most sagacious choice! — Your Secretaries
    Of State attend me, Sire, to render up
    The ledgers of a realm. I do beseech you,
    Suffer these noble gentlemen to learn
    The nature of the glorious task that waits them
    Here, in my presence.
Louis. You say well, my lord.

The Secretaries advance to read their reports: while Baradas and Orleans observe the seemingly moribund Richelieu with ill concealed triumph:

First Sec.   The affairs of Portugal,
    Most urgent, Sire: One short month since the Duke
    Braganza was a rebel.
Louis. And is still.
First Sec. No, Sire, he has succeeded! He is now
    Crown'd King of Portugal — craves instant succour
    Against the arms of Spain.
Louis.   We will not grant it
    Against his lawful king. Eh, Count?
Bar.   No, Sire.
First Sec. But Spain's your deadliest foe: whatever
    Can weaken Spain must strengthen France. The Cardinal
    Would send the succours: — balance, Sire, of Europe!
Louis. The Cardinal! — balance! — We'll consider. — Eh, Count?
Bar. Yes, Sir; — fall back!
First Sec.   But —
Bar.   Oh! fall back, Sir.
Second Sec. The affairs of England, Sire, most urgent: Charles
    The First has lost a battle that decides
    One half his realm, — craves moneys, Sire, and succour.
Louis. He shall have both. — Eh, Baradas?
Bar.   Yes, Sire.
Rich. (*feebly, but with great distinctness.*) My liege,
    Forgive me — Charles's cause is lost! A man,
    Named Cromwell, risen — a great man! — your succour
    Would fail — your loans be squander'd! — Pause — reflect!
Louis. Reflect — Eh, Baradas?
Bar. Reflect, Sire.

Louis (*aside*). I half repent! — No successor to Richelieu!
    Round me thrones totter! — dynasties dissolve! —
    The soil he guards alone escapes the earthquake!

While the third Secretary produces the secret correspondence, and alarms Louis with accounts of schemes against himself, Richelieu's faithful page, Francois, is introduced by the Cardinal's confidant, the Capuchin Joseph, and places in Richelieu's hands a document. which he had taken by force from De Beringhen, one of the conspirators. The Secretary continues his report:

Third Sec.   Sire, the Spaniards
    Have reinforced their army on the frontiers.
    The Duc de Bouillon —
Rich.   Hold! — in this department —
    A paper — here, Sire — read yourself — then take
    The Count's advice in't.
Louis (*reading*). To Bouillon — and sign'd Orleans! —
    Baradas, too! — league with our foes of Spain! —
    Lead our Italian armies — what! to Paris! —
    Capture the King — my health requires repose —
    Make me subscribe my proper abdication —
    Orleans, my brother, Regent! Saints of Heaven!
    These are the men I loved!
                (*Baradas attempts to rush out; is arrested.*)
Louis (*rushing to Richelieu*). Richelieu! — Lord Cardinal! — 'tis I resign!
    Reign thou!
Rich. (*feebly*). With absolute power?
Louis.   Most absolute! — Oh! live!
    If not for me — for France!
Rich.   France!
Louis.   Oh! this treason! —
    The army — Orleans — Bouillon — Heavens! — the Spaniard! —
    Where will they be next week?
Rich. (*starting up.*)   There, — at my feet!
               To First and Second Secretaries.)
    Ere the clock strike! — the Envoys have their answer!
              (*To Third Sec., with a ring.*)
    This to De Chavigny — he knows the rest —
    No need of parchment here — he must not halt
    For sleep — for food. — In my name — mine! — he will
    Arrest the Duc de Bouillon at the head
    Of his army! — Ho! there, Count de Baradas,
    Thou hast lost the stake! Away with him!

Of Lord Lytton's comedies, *Not so bad as we seem* is by far the least pleasing and interesting. The scene is London, and the date the reign of George I. There are two peers in the piece, who are engaged in intrigues for the restoration of the Stuarts; but the principal character is Lady Thornside, a married woman, who has left her husband in consequence of his groundless jealousy, and rather strangely taken refuge in an ill-famed street, called Deadman's Lane. At the end of the piece, the lady is reconciled to her husband by the instrumentality of her daughter Lucy. Perhaps the best thing in the comedy is young Lord Wilmot's account of how he had obtained from Sir Robert Walpole, the famous Whig minister and zealous picture-collector, a place in the Treasury for his friend Hardman, by bribing the great man with a Murillo. A vastly superior dramatic work in all respects is *Money;* in which the author illustrates, by the contemptuous neglect shown the eccentric but thoroughly estimable Evelyn when a poor man, and the flattering consideration of which he becomes the object as a rich one, how powerfully most men are influenced, in their estimate of others, by affluence and the social position it confers. In the opening scene we are introduced to Sir John Vesey, a baronet not wealthy, but very desirous of being thought so, and his daughter Georgina, who is supposed, though erroneously, to be the heiress of an uncle recently deceased in India.

(Georgina, and Sir John Vesey.)

Geor. And you really feel sure that poor Mr. Mordaunt has made me his heiress?

Sir J. Ay, the richest heiress in England. Can you doubt it? Are you not his nearest relation? Niece by your poor mother, his own sister. All the time he was making this enormous fortune in India, did we ever miss sending him little reminiscences of our disinterested affection? When he was last in England, and you only so high, was not my house his home? Didn't I get a surfeit out of complaisance to his execrable curries and pillaws? Didn't he smoke his hookah — nasty old — that is, poor dear man — in my best drawing-room? And did you ever speak without calling him your "handsome uncle?" — for the excellent creature was as vain as a peacock, —

Geor. And so ugly, —

Sir J. The dear deceased! Alas he was, indeed. And if, after all these marks of attachment, you are not his heiress, why then the finest feelings of our nature — the ties of blood — the principles of justice — are implanted in us in vain.

Geor. Beautiful, sir. Was not that in your last speech at the Freemasons' Tavern upon the great Chimney-sweep Question?

Sir J. Clever girl! — what a memory she has! Sit down, Georgy. Upon this most happy — I mean melancholy occasion, I feel that I may trust you with a secret. You see this fine house — our fine servants — our fine plate — our fine dinners: every one thinks Sir John Vesey a rich man.

Geor. And are you not, papa?

Sir J. Not a bit of it — all humbug, child — all humbug, upon my soul! As you hazard a minnow to hook in a trout, so one guinea thrown out with address is often the best bait for a hundred. There are two rules in life — First, Men are valued not for what they are, but what they seem to be. Secondly, If you have no merit or money of your own, you must trade on the merits and money of other people. My father got the title by services in the army, and died penniless. On the strength of his services I got a pension of 400 L. a-year — on the strength of 400 L. a-year I took credit for 800 L.: on the strength of 800 L. a-year I married your mother with 10,000 L.: on the strength of 10,000 L., I took credit for 40,000 L., and paid Dicky Gossip three guineas a-week to go about everywhere calling me "Stingy Jack!"

Geor. Ha! Ha! A disagreeable nickname.

Sir J. But a valuable reputation. When a man is called stingy, it is as much as calling him rich; and when a man's called rich, why he's a man universally respected. On the strength of my respectability I wheedled a constituency, changed my politics, resigned my seat to a minister, who, to a man of such stake in the country, could offer nothing less in return than a patent office of 2,000 L. a-year. That's the way to succeed in life. Humbug my dear! — all humbug, upon my soul!

Geor. I must say that you —

Sir J. Know the world, to be sure. Now, for your fortune, — as I spend more than my income, I can have nothing to leave you; yet, even without counting your uncle, you have always passed for an heiress on the credit of your expectations from the savings of "Stingy Jack." The same with your education. I never grudged anything to make a show — never stuffed your head with histories and homilies; but you draw, you sing, you dance, you walk well into a room; and that's the way young ladies are educated now-a-days, in order to become a pride to their parents, and a blessing to their husband — that is, when they have caught him. A propos of a husband: you know we thought of Sir Frederick Blount.

Geor. Ah, papa, he is charming.

Sir J. He was so, my dear, before we knew your poor uncle was dead; but an heiress such as you will be should look out for a duke. — Where the deuce is Evelyn this morning?

Geor. I've not seen him, papa. What a strange character he is — so sarcastic; and yet he can be agreeable.

Sir J. A humorist — a cynic! one never knows how to take him. My private secretary, — a poor cousin, — has not got a shilling, and yet, hang me, if he does not keep us all at a sort of a distance.

Geor. But why do you take him to live with us, papa, since there's no good to be got by it?

Sir J. There you are wrong; he has a great deal of talent: prepares my speeches, writes my pamphlets, looks up my calculations. My report on the last Commission has got me a great deal of fame, and has put me at the head of the new one. Besides, he is our cousin — he has no salary: kindness to a poor relation always tells well in the world; and Benevolence is a useful virtue, — particularly when you can have it for nothing! With our other cousin, Clara, it was different: her father thought fit to leave me her guardian, though she had not a penny — a mere useless incumbrance; so, you see, I got my half-sister, Lady Franklin, to take her off my hands.

Geor. How much longer is Lady Franklin's visit to be?

Sir J. I don't know, my dear; the longer the better, — for her husband left her a good deal of money at her own disposal. Ah, here she comes.

In another scene we find the poor relation Evelyn, his cousin Clara Douglas, and the aristocratic Sir Frederick Blount, a gentleman speaking that lisping dialect, so much affected by fashionable young men, in which the letter *r* is always superseded by a *w*.

Blount. No one in the woom! — Oh, Miss Douglas! — Pway don't let me disturb me. Where is Miss Vesey — Georgina?
                    (*Taking Clara's chair as she rises.*)

Eve. (*looking up, gives Clara a chair and re-seats himself.*) [*Aside.*] Insolent puppy!

Clara. Shall I tell her you are here, Sir Frederick?

Blount. Not for the world. Vewy pwetty girl this companion!

Clara. What did you think of the Panorama the other day, Cousin Evelyn?

Eve. (*reading*). —
    I cannot talk with civet in the room,
        A fine puss gentleman that's all perfume!
    Rather good lines these.

Blount. Sir!

Eve. (*offering the book*). Don't you think so? — Cowper.

Blount. (*declining the book*). Cowper!

Eve. Cowper.

Blount. (*shrugging his shoulders, to Clara*). Stwange person, Mr. Evelyn! — quite a chawacter! — Indeed the Panowama gives you no idea of Naples — a delightful place. I make it a wule

to go there evewy second year. I am vewy fond of twavelling
You'd like Wome (*Rome*) — bad inns, but vewy fine wuins
gives you quite a taste for that sort of thing!

Eve. (*reading*).

How much a dunce that has been sent to roam
Excels a dunce that has been kept at home!

Blount. (*aside*). That fellow Cowper says vewy odd things! —
Humph! — it is beneath me to quawwel. (*Aloud.*) It will not
take long to wead the will, I suppose. Poor old Mordaunt! —
I am his nearest male welation. He was vewy eccentwic. By
the way, Miss Douglas, did you wemark my cuwickle? It is
bwinging cuwickles into fashion. I should be most happy if
you will allow me to dwive you out. Nay — nay — I should
upon my word.   (*Trying to take her hand*).

Eve. (*starting up*). A wasp! — a wasp! — just going to settle.
Take care of the wasp, Miss Douglas!

Blount. A wasp! — where? — don't bwing it this way, some
people don't mind them! I've a particular dislike to wasps;
they sting damnably.

Eve. I beg pardon — it's only a gadfly.

(Enter Servant).

Ser. Sir John will be happy to see you in his study, Sir Frederick.
Blount. Vewy well. Upon my word, there is something vewy
nice about this girl.

To the great disappointment of nearer relations,
it turns out that the deceased nabob has made poor
Evelyn his residuary legatee; and now Sir John forms
all sorts of schemes to bring about a marriage between
Evelyn and his daughter. Though the real object of
Evelyn's attachment is Clara, he seems to meet Sir
John half-way; and this he does all the more readily,
as he has had a misunderstanding with Clara. Suspecting,
however, the disinterestedness of Sir John and Georgina,
he pretends to lose the greater part of his property
at the gaming-table, and the young lady forthwith jilts
him, and accepts the hand of the elegant Blount. Clara,
too, has heard of Evelyn's reverses, but on the contrary
hastens to place her small fortune at his disposal. The
sequel may be guessed. Evelyn assures his future bride,
that she has succeeded where wealth had failed; for
she has reconciled him to the world and to mankind.

In 1869 Lord Lytton surprised the literary world
with a comedy in rhyme, entitled *Walpole; or, Every*

Man has his Price, a well-constructed and amusing piece in the dashing anapaestic metre. The principal personages, besides Walpole himself, are the fashionable Sir Sydney Bellairs, his charming sister Lucy, and Mr. Selden Blount. In the form of a soliloquy he ingeniously makes the Minister describe his own character:

> I wonder what lies the historians will tell
> When they babble of one, Robert Walpole! Well, well;
> Let them sneer at his blunders, declaim on his vices,
> Cite the rogues whom he purchased, and rail at the prices:
> They shall own that all lust for revenge he withstood;
> And, if lavish of gold, he was sparing of blood;
> And when England was threatened by France and by Rome,
> He forced Peace from abroad and encamped her at home;
> And the freedom he left, rooted firm in fair laws,
> May o'ershadow the faults of deeds done in her cause!

Lord Lytton, at his death, left a tragedy in manuscript behind him, founded on the legend of Lucretia and Tarquin, and entitled "Brutus." As two English plays on the same subject already existed (Nathaniel Lee's *Lucius Junius Brutus*, and Payne's *Brutus, or the Fall of Tarquin*), the piece was successively declined by Mr. Phelps of Sadler's Wells Theatre, and by Mr. Irving of the Lyceum, but was at last brought on the stage, with considerable applause, on Feb. 26, 1885, by Mr. Wilson Barrett of the Princess's Theatre, under the name of *Junius, or the Household Gods*. Most of the critical periodicals, however, reserved their judgment till the piece should have appeared in print.

Thomas Noon Talfourd.

Mr. Talfourd has left us four tragedies, *Ion, the Athenian Captive, the Massacre of Glencoe*, and *the Castilian*. Ion, the hero of the first-named piece, is a foundling youth, educated in the temple of Apollo, in Argos, by the High-Priest Medon; and, exemplified in him, the reader of Euripides will soon detect the overruling influence of "Destiny, apart from all moral agencies, combined with the idea of fascination, as an engine by which Fate may work its purposes on the innocent mind." Argos

is devastated by a plague, and it has been announced
by the oracle of Delphi that nothing less than the utter
extirpation of the royal race of Adrastus will appease
the wrath of the Gods; that misrule must terminate
before the pestilence shall be stayed; for

> Argos ne'er shall find release
> Till her monarch's race shall cease.

A conspiracy is formed for the assassination of
Adrastus; lots are drawn, and Ion is fated to strike
the blow. He obtains admission to the presence of the
King, and a number of his friends have been posted
in the precincts of the palace, ready to take advantage
of the consternation caused by the death of the despot.
Ion holds Adrastus at his mercy, and his dagger is
already uplifted, when the High-Priest Medon throws
himself between them, and sternly commands him to
desist. The old man has accidentally discovered, that
Ion is the son of Adrastus, lost in infancy, whose
supposed death, by imbittering the rest of his days,
had changed his character, and plunged him into crime
and debauchery. Father and son are locked in a tender
embrace, when the impatient conspirators invade the
apartment, separate them by force, and murder the
King. This act of violence, however, makes Ion the
sovereign of Argos, and so great is his popularity that
no one dreams of disputing his right to the throne;
but the young King ponders the announcement of the
oracle, and knows well, that as one of the royal race
of Argos, he too is destined to yield up his life, a sacrifice
to the implacable Gods. In tender, but ambiguons words,
he takes leave of his loved Clemanthe, the High-Priest's
daughter:

I o n.   Dark and cold
    Stretches the path which, when I wear the crown,
    I needs must enter: the great gods forbid
    That thou should'st follow in it.
C l e m. O unkind!
    And shall we never see each other?
I o n. (*after a pause*). Yes!
    I have asked that dreadful question of the hills
    That look eternal; of the flowing streams

That lucid flow for ever; of the stars,
Amid whose fields of azure my raised spirit
Hath trod in glory: all were dumb; but now,
While I thus gaze upon thy living face,
I feel the love that kindles through its beauty
Can never wholly perish: we shall meet
Again, Clemanthe!

Ion, of course, refers in this speech to a meeting in a future state of existence; for he is convinced that the salvation of Argos is contingent on his death. The day fixed for his installation in the royal dignity arrives: and he seats himself on the throne.

I o n.   Argives! I have a boon
To crave of you. Whene'er I shall rejoin
In death the father from whose heart in life
Stern fate divided me, think gently of him!
Think that beneath his panoply of pride
Were fair affections crushed by bitter wrongs
Which fretted him to madness; what he did,
Alas! ye know; could you know what he suffered,
Ye would not curse his name. Yet never more
Let the great interests of the state depend
Upon the thousand chances that may sway
A piece of human frailty; swear to me
That ye will seek hereafter in yourselves
The means of sovereignty: our country's space,
So happy in its smallness, so compact,
Needs not the magic of a single name
Which wider regions may require to draw
Their interest into one; but, circled thus,
Like a blest family, by simple laws
May tenderly be governed — all degrees,
Not placed in dexterous balance, not combined
By bonds of parchment, or by iron clasps,
But blended into one — a single form
Of nymph-like loveliness, which finest chords
Of sympathy pervading, shall endow
With vital beauty, tint with roseate bloom
In times of happy peace, and bid to flash
With one brave impulse, if ambitious bands
Of foreign power should threaten. Swear to me
That ye will do this!
M e d o n.   Wherefore ask this now?
Thou shalt live long; the paleness of thy face,
Which late seemed death-like, is grown radiant now,
And thine eyes kindle with the prophecy
Of glorious years.

I o n. The gods approve me then!
    Yet I will use the function of a king,
    And claim obedience. Swear, that if I die,
    And leave no issue, ye will seek the power
    To govern in the free-born people's choice,
    And in the prudence of the wise.
M e d o n a n d o t h e r s. We swear it!
I o n. Hear and record the oath, immortal powers!
    Now give me leave a moment to approach
    That altar unattended.   (*He goes to the altar.*)
                  Gracious gods!
    In whose mild service my glad youth was spent,
    Look on me now, and if there is a power,
    As at this solemn time I feel there is,
    Beyond ye, that hath breathed through all your shapes
    The spirit of the beautiful that lives
    In earth and heaven; to ye I offer up
    This conscious being, full of life and love,
    For my dear country's welfare. Let this blow
    End all her sorrows.   (*Stabs himself.*)

The *Athenian Captive*, likewise a classical drama, nowhere reaches the imposing dignity of *Ion*. Thoas, the Athenian, is brought as a prisoner-of-war to Corinth, where he forms a friendship with King Creon's son, Hyllus. This Hyllus is hated by the King's second wife. the Athenian Ismene. who instigates Thoas to murder the King her husband to recover his liberty, but her main object is to fix the crime on Hyllus. At an assembly of all the principal personages in the temple of Jupiter the Avenger, the spiteful Queen boldly accuses Hyllus of parricide: but Thoas, whom she discovers to be her son, confesses his guilt, and then prays for and receives his death from the hand of Hyllus. In the character of Ismene there are some traits that remind the reader of Gulnare in Byron's *Corsair*.

Glencoe, a drama founded on the terrible massacre of the MacDonalds of Glencoe on 13th Feb. 1689. presents more features of interest to the general reader than the preceding tragedy. The leading characters are: MacIan, chief of the MacDonalds of Glencoe; his sons. John and Alaster; his nephews Halbert and Henry, sons of Lady MacDonald; Helen Campbell, an orphan adopted by Lady MacDonald, and niece to Captain

Robert Campbell of Glenlyon, the officer commanding
the soldiers, on whom the execution of the cruel sen-
tence devolved. At the date of the massacre Helen
Campbell was really the wife of Alaster MacDonald,
but it suited Mr. Talfourd better to make her the
betrothed bride of the fictitious Halbert. As might be
expected, the drama is almost too sombre and distres-
sing for representation on the stage, though the preva-
lent tone of gloom is occasionally relieved by such
exquisite descriptive passages as we find in the follow-
ing scene:

Helen Campbell, Lady MacDonald.

Helen. So early raised to meet the morning's frost?
Lady M. I feel no frost; the ecstasy within me
    Clothes all without with summer; you shall share
    In joy which seldom visits these old walls.
Helen. Oh, say not so; there's not a day but bears
    Its blessing on its light. If nature doles
    Her gifts with sparing hand, their rareness sheds
    Endearments her most bounteous mood withholds
    From greenest valleys. The pure rill which casts
    Its thread of snow-like lustre o'er the rock,
    Which seems to pierce the lowering sky, connects
    The thoughts of earth with heaven, while mightier floods
    Roar of dark passions. The rare sunbeam wins
    For a most light existence human care,
    While it invests some marble heap with gleams
    Of palaced visions. If the tufts of broom
    Whence fancy weaves a chain of gold, appear,
    On nearer visitation, thinly strewn,
    Each looks a separate bower, and offers shade
    To its own group of fairies. The prized harebell
    Wastes not its dawning azure on a bank
    Rough and confused with loveliness, but wears
    The modest story of its gentle life
    On leaves that love has tended; nay, the heath,
    Which, slowly, from a stinted root, unfolds
    Pale lilac blossoms, — image of a maid
    Rear'd tenderly in solitude, is bless'd
    Instead of sharing with a million flowers
    One radiant flush, in offering its faint bloom
    To loving eyes. Say not again, dear lady,
    That joy but seldom visits these old walls.

Mr. Talfourd's posthumous and rather dull tragedy,
the Castilian, has as yet attracted but little notice;

but his prose-works, *Vacation Rambles*, a series of continental tours in 1841—43, and his *Letters* and *Memorials of Charles Lamb*, have added much to his reputation.

Lord Tennyson.

The Laureate, Lord Tennyson, has also competed with some success for the bays of the dramatic poet. In our notice of the dramas he has hitherto produced, we shall begin with *Harold,* which we look on as the first of his dramatic productions in the order of merit.

Harold is a five-act historical tragedy. In the first act we find King Edward the Confessor old and feeble, and vague fears prevail that his dissolution will be the prelude to some national disaster — an apprehension intensified by the sight of Halley's comet flaming over-head. Harold alone seems to enjoy an immunity from the superstition of the age; for when Stigand, the archbishop of Canterbury, apostrophizing the comet, inquires: "Is that the doom of England?" he contemptuously replies: —

> Why not the doom of all the world as well?
> For all the world sees it as well as England.
> These meteors came and went before our day,
> Not harming any: it threatens us no more
> Than French or Norman. War? the worst that follows
> Things that seem jerk'd out of the common rut
> Of Nature is the hot religious fool,
> Who, seeing war in heaven, for heaven's credit
> Makes it on earth.

Harold solicits the permission of the king to go on a hunting expedition to Normandy; and when Edward, in his distrust of the "fox-lion," Duke William, refuses his consent, Harold announces his intention of taking his hounds and hawks to Flanders. In the second act, we find him, notwithstanding, shipwrecked on the coast of Normandy, and a prisoner in the hands of the astute Guy of Ponthieu, who demands a ransom for his liberation. This ransom is paid by Duke William, who brings Harold to his court, with the intention of inducing him, the brother in-law and probable heir of the childless Edward, by force or by fraud, to pledge himself, by a solemn oath, to support William's pretensions to the throne of England, on the death of the king. Overcome by the vehement entreaties of his youngest brother Wulfnoth, then a hostage at the Norman court, who dreads the consequences of his brother's contumacy for them both, persuaded by the friendly Norman noble Malet, and urged by his own longing to return to the fair Edith, King Edward's ward, Harold consents to take an oath, which he does not regard as binding. William begins his manoeuvres by sounding Harold, and inquires: "the heir of England, who is he?" whereupon the dialogue proceeds:

Harold. The Atheling is nearest to the throne.
William. But sickly, slight, half-witted, and a child,
    Will England have him king?
Har.   It may be, no.
Will. And hath King Edward not pronounced his heir?
Har. Not that I know.
Will.   When he was here in Normandy,
    He loved us and we him, because we found him
    A Norman of the Normans.
Har.   So did we.
Will. A gentle, gracious, pure, and saintly man!
    And grateful to the hand that shielded him,
    He promised that if ever he were king
    In England, he would give his kingly voice
    To me as his successor. Knowest thou this?
Har. I learn it now.
Will.   Thou knowest I am his cousin,
    And that my wife descends from Alfred?
Har.   Ay.
Will. Who hath a better claim then to the crown
    So that ye will not crown the Atheling?
Har. None that I know ... if that but hung upon
    King Edward's will.
Will.   Wilt thou uphold my claim?
Malet (*aside to Harold*). Be careful of thine answer, my good friend.
Wulfnoth (*aside to Harold*). Oh! Harold, for my sake and for
    thine own!
Har. Ay ... if the king have not revoked his promise.
Will. But hath he done it then?
Har.   Not that I know.
Will. Good, good, and thou wilt help me to the crown?
Har. Ay ... if the Witan will consent to this.

Will. Thou art the mightiest voice in England, man,
   Thy voice will lead the Witan — shall I have it?
Wulfnoth (*aside to Harold*). Oh! Harold, if thou love thine Edith, ay.
Har. Ay, if —
Malet (*aside to Harold*). Thine "ifs" will sear thine eyes out — ay.
Will. I ask thee, wilt thou help me to the crown?
   And I will make thee my great Earl of Earls,
   Foremost in England and in Normandy;
   Thou shalt be verily king — all but the name —
   For I shall most sojourn in Normandy;
   And thou be my vice-king in England. Speak.
Wulfnoth (*aside to Harold*). Ay, brother — for the sake of Eng-
   land — ay.
Har. My lord —
Malet (*aside to Harold*). Take heed now.
Har.   Ay.
Will.   I am content,
   For thou art truthful, and thy word thy bond.
   To-morrow will we ride with thee to Harfleur.
                             (*Exit* William).
Malet. Harold, I am thy friend, one life with thee,
   And even as I should bless thee saving mine,
   I thank thee now for having saved thyself.
                             (*Exit* Malet).

Har. For having lost myself to save myself,
   Said "ay" when I meant "no," lied like a lad
   That dreads the pendent scourge, said "ay" for "no"!
   Ay! No! — he hath not bound me by an oath —
   Is "ay" an oath? is "ay" strong as an oath?
   Or is it the same sin to break my word
   As break mine oath? He call'd my word my bond!
   He is a liar who knows I am a liar,
   And makes believe that he believes my word —
   The crime be on his head — not bounden — no.

In the third act Harold is again in England, but his beloved Edith is withheld from him by the King, and he reluctantly marries Aldwyth, the widowed Queen of Wales. The terrible comet is still visible:

   It glares in heaven, it flares upon the Thames,
   The people are as thick as bees below,
   They hum like bees — they cannot speak — for awe;
   Look to the skies, then to the river, strike
   Their hearts, and hold their babies up to it;

and other portents announce an impending catastrophe. In the presence of the dying King, Aldred relates how a wayfarer passing by Senlac hill, had heard

> A ghostly horn
> Blowing continually, and faint battle hymns,
> And cries, and clashes, and the groans of men;
> And dreadful shadows strove upon the hill,
> And dreadful lights crept up from out the marsh —
> Corpse-candles gliding over nameless graves.

The name Senlac is caught up by Edward in his troubled sleep, and making a grim play on the word, he murmurs:

> A lake,
> A sea of blood — we are drown'd in blood — for God
> Has filled the quiver, and Death has drawn the bow —
> Sanguelac! Sanguelac! the arrow! the arrow!

And with these words in his mouth he dies.

Harold now becomes king, and the first exercise of his royal power is to crush the rebellion excited by his turbulent brother Tostig, with the aid of the Norwegian King, Harold Hardrada, in the principality of Northumberland. The insurgents are totally routed at Stamford Bridge. Particularly vigorous is the description of the King of Norway's death on the battle-field:

> — when all was lost, he yell'd,
> And bit his shield, and dash'd it on the ground,
> And swaying his two-handed sword about him,
> Two deaths at every swing, ran in upon us,
> And died so.

But in the mean time the Normans under Duke William have landed, and King Harold must gather all his forces without delay, and march southwards to oppose them.

When the fifth act opens, the rival armies stand face to face at Senlac or Hastings. In a dream, the night before the battle, Harold is visited by the ghosts of those whose destiny in life has been in some way or other mixed up with his own, including his brother Tostig and his youngest brother Wulfnoth, though we had supposed the latter to be still a living man. Like Richard III. he suddenly awakes, and springs from his couch, defiantly exclaiming:

Away!

My battle-axe against your voices. Peace!
The king's last word — "the arrow!" I shall die —
I die for England then, who lived for England —
What nobler? men must die.
I cannot fall into a falser world —
I have done no man wrong. Tostig, poor brother,
Art thou so anger'd?
Fain had I kept thine earldom in thy hands
Save for thy wild and violent will that wrench'd
All hearts of freemen from thee.
. . . . Is it possible
That mortal men should bear their earthly heats
Into yon bloodless world, and threaten us thence
Unschool'd of Death? Thus then thou art revenged —
I left our England naked to the South
To meet thee in the North. The Norseman's raid
Hath helpt the Norman, and the race of Godwin
Hath ruin'd Godwin. No — our waking thoughts
Suffer a stormless shipwreck in the pools
Of sullen slumber, and arise again
Disjointed: only dreams — where mine own self
Takes part against myself! Why? for a spark
Of self-disdain born in me when I sware
Falsely to him, the falser Norman, over
His gilded ark of mummy-saints, by whom
I knew not that I sware, — not for myself —
For England.

During the battle the stage is occupied by Stigand and Edith, and it is only from the disjointed description of the archbishop that we can glean the incidents of the fight, and the fall of Harold. William at length enters victorious; and Edith, after acknowledging herself to be Harold's wife — which is rather puzzling after the marriage with Aldwyth — dies, as it appears, of a broken heart.

Though we may find, scattered through this tragedy, many happy ideas elegantly expressed, yet something more is necessary to meet the requirements of dramatic art; and perhaps a reviewer did not say too much when he averred, that the failure of *Harold* to satisfy these exigencies does more than prove that Lord Tennyson has no great aptitude for dramatic composition.

Queen Mary (originally named *Mary Tudor),* met with a very cold reception on the stage. Though the future Queen Elizabeth is one of the dramatis personae, and the most is made of Wyatt's rash rebellion, the piece from beginning to end is dull. We feel but small sympathy with a fanatical, unlovable woman wedded to an atrabilious, unloving Spanish husband, and vainly sighing for the joys of maternity. The finest thing in the drama, in our opinion, is the fifth scene of the fifth act, where Mary complains with indignant bitterness of Philip's indifference, and bewails the loss of the old English stronghold Calais, which had been sacrificed to the crooked and selfish policy of Spain:

Alice. Madam, who goes? King Philip?
Mary. No, Philip comes and goes, but never goes.
    Women, when I am dead,
    Open my heart, and there you will find written
    Two names, Philip and Calais; open his, —
    So that he have one, —
    You will find Philip only, policy, policy, —
    Ay, worse than that, not one hour true to me!
    Foul maggots crawling in a fester'd vice!
    Adulterous to the very heart of Hell.
    Hast thou a knife?
A. Ay, Madam, but o' God's mercy —
M. Fool, think'st thou I would peril mine own soul
    By slaughter of the body? I could not, girl,
    Not this way — callous with constant stripe.
    Unwoundable. Thy knife!
A. Take heed, take heed!
    The blade is keen as death.
M. This Philip shall not
    Stare in upon me in my haggardness;
    Old, miserable, diseased,
    Incapable of children. Come thou down.
             (Cuts out the picture, and throws it down.)
    Lie there. (*Wails*). O God, I have kill'd my Philip.
A.   No,
    Madam, you have but cut the canvas out,
    We can replace it.
M. All is well, then; rest —
    I will to rest; he said, I must have rest.

The Falcon is a trifling one-act piece, founded on the ninth tale of the fifth day in Boccaccio's *Decamerone*. A young Florentine, called Federigo degli Alberighi, the Italian story-teller relates, loved a certain Madam Giovanna, and spent his whole moderate fortune

in procuring her such diversions as balls, tilts. and
pleasure-parties, and in making her elegant and costly
presents. Reduced to poverty, he withdraws to the
country, where he finds himself entirely dependent for
sustenance on the booty made by his well-trained hawk.
After some time. the lady, now a widow, goes into
retirement with her son; and as she has settled in the
same neighbourhood. the young lad often meets Fe-
derigo, and cannot enough admire his wonderful bird.
The child falls dangerously ill, and all the remedies
of the doctor avail nothing, for the little patient pines
for the much-prized hawk. Alarmed at the critical
condition of her darling, Madam Giovanna pays a visit
to Federigo, with the intention of begging him to give
her the falcon. She is received with due respect by
the young gentleman, who desires to offer her a col-
lation, but having nothing else at hand, the poor fellow,
at his wits' end, makes up his mind to sacrifice his
priceless feathered friend. When the lady has finished
her meal, she brings forward her request; which Federigo
of course is unable to grant, but the lady, on learning
the truth, is so touched that when her son soon after-
wards dies, she marries Federigo, who, we are told,
lived very happily with her, and became a good manager
of the considerable property brought him by his wife.
Such is Boccaccio's story, but is has been a good deal
modified by Lord Tennyson, who still leaves Count
Federigo two domestics in all his indigence — his old
nurse Elisabetta, and his serving-man and foster-brother,
Filippo. This Filippo is a half-comic character, con-
tinually indulging in jokes about the poverty of the
household; as he does in the following dialogue:

Count. Come, come, Filippo, what is there in the larder?
Filippo. Shelves and hooks, shelves and hooks, and when I see
    the shelves, I am like to hang myself on the hooks.
Count. No bread?
Filippo. Half a breakfast for a rat!
Count. Milk?
Filippo. Three laps for a cat!
Count. Cheese?
Filippo. A supper for twelve mites.

Count. Eggs?
Filippo. One, but addled.
Count. No bird?
Filippo. Half a tit and a hern's bill.

The Lady Giovanna arrives, and the Count wel-
comes her with the words:

> Lady, you bring your light into my cottage
> Who never deign'd to shine into my palace.
> My palace wanting you was but a cottage;
> My cottage, while you grace it, is a palace.

In the course of the ensuing conversation we find
some lines that merit quotation. Thus, he assures the
lady:

> You can touch
> No chord in me that would not answer you
> In music;

and referring to a warlike exploit in which he wore
her wreath, he declares:

> I wore the lady's chaplet round my neck;
> It served me for a blessed rosary.

On her side, the Lady, returning some diamonds
he had presented her with, in more prosperous days,
exclaims:

> No other heart
> Of such magnificence in courtesy
> Beats — out of heaven.

At the end of the piece the child still lives, and
Federigo addresses the Lady, now his betrothed bride,
in these words:

> We two together
> Will help to heal your son — your son and mine —
> We shall do it — we shall do it.
> The purpose of my being is accomplish'd,
> And I am happy!

Another version of this same story, *the Falcon*, may
be found in Longfellow's *Tales of a Wayside Inn*, as
the *Student's Tale;* and it likewise forms the subject
of Gounod's opera, *La Colombe.*

Of the two-act tragedy, *the Cup*, it will suffice to
say, that the heroine, Camma, wife of Sinnatus, Tetrarch

of Galatia, after the murder of her husband by the
ex-Tetrach Synorix, at once revenges herself on the
assassin, and puts an end to her own existence, by
inducing Synorix, under pretence of a marriage between
them, to partake with her of a cup of poisoned wine.

More interesting, in all respects, is the five-act
tragedy, *Becket*. The list of *dramatis personae* includes
King Henry II., Queen Eleanor, Becket, Rosamund
Clifford, and most of the other historical personages
who at that time played a part of any importance on
the political stage. In a Prologue, which is itself as
long as an ordinary act, Becket and the King are in-
troduced to us, seated at chess, and the impatient and
choleric temper of Henry, manifested by the rashness
of his moves, is skilfully contrasted with the calculating
coolness of his antagonist, who wins the game. On
the whole, Lord Tennyson in his tragedy respects the
facts of history, if we except the scene in the fourth
act, where Becket rescues Rosamund Clifford out of
the murderous hands of the vindictive Queen Eleanor,
and the last scene of the fifth act, when Rosamund.
in her turn, endeavours though unsuccessfully to repay
the obligation by shielding the life of her benefactor.
The last-mentioned scene is the most stirring and ex-
citing in the tragedy. Becket, who had been the friend
and servant of the King as Chancellor, becomes as
Archbishop a dangerous competitor for popularity and
power. Out of favour at Court, he sullenly retires to
his see of Canterbury, whither he is pursued by four
knights, devoted partisans of Henry, who have vowed
the death of the audacious priest. How they discharged
this rash vow we shall leave the poet himself to tell.
The scene is the North Transept of Canterbury Cathedral:

Monks.   Oh, my lord Archbishop,
    A score of knights all arm'd with swords and axes —
    To the choir, to the choir!
        (*Monks divide, part flying by the stairs on the right, part by
        those on the left*).
Becket. Shall I too pass to the choir,
    And die upon the Patriarchal throne
    Of all my predecessors?

John of Salisbury.   No, to the crypt!
    Twenty steps down. Stumble not in the darkness,
    Lest they should seize thee.
Grim.   To the crypt? no — no,
    To the chapel of St. Blaise beneath the roof!
John of S. (*pointing upward and downward.*)
    That way, or this! Save thyself either way.
Becket. Oh, no, not either way, nor any way
    Save by that way which leads thro' night to light.
    Not twenty steps, but one.
    And fear not I should stumble in the darkness,
    Not tho' it be their hour, the powers of darkness,
    But my hour too, the power of light in darkness!
    I am not in the darkness but the light,
    Seen by the Church in Heaven; the Church on earth —
    The power of life in death to make her free!
            (*Enter the four Knights. John of Salisbury flies to the altar
        of St. Benedict.*)
Fitzurse. Here, here, King's men!
                    (*Catches hold of the last flying Monk.*)
    Where is the traitor Becket?
Monk. I am not he! I am not he, my lord.
    I am not he, indeed!
Fitzurse.   Hence to the fiend!
                    (*Pushes him away.*)
    Where is this treble traitor to the King?
De Tracy. Where is the Archbishop, Thomas Becket?
Becket.   Here.
    No traitor to the King, but Priest of God,
    Primate of England.
                    I am he ye seek.
    What would ye have of me?
Fitzurse.   Your life.
De Morville. Save that you will absolve the bishops.
Becket.   Never, —
    Except they make submission to the Church.
    You had my answer to that cry before.
De Morville. Why, then you are a dead man; flee!
Becket.   I will not.
    I am readier to be slain, than thou to slay.
    Hugh, I know well thou hast but half a heart
    To bathe this sacred pavement with my blood.
    God pardon thee and these, but God's full curse
    Shatter you all to pieces, if ye harm
    One of my flock!
Fitzurse. Was not the great gate shut?
    , They are thronging in to vespers — half the town.
    We shall be overwhelm'd. Seize him and carry him!
    Come with us — nay — thou art our prisoner — come!
De Morville. Ay, make him prisoner, do not harm the man.

Becket. Touch me not!
De Brito.   How the good priests gods himself!
        He is not yet ascended to the Father.
Fitzurse. I will not only touch, but drag thee hence.
Becket. Thou art my man, thou art my vassal. Away!
                                        (*Flings him off.*)
De Tracy. Come; as he said, thou art our prisoner.
Becket.   Down!
                                  (*Throws him headlong.*)
Fitzurse (*advances with drawn sword.*)
        I told thee that I should remember thee!
Becket. Profligate pander!
Fitzurse.   Do you hear that? strike, strike.
        (*Strikes off the Archbishop's mitre, and wounds him in the forehead.*)
Becket. I do commend my cause to God, the Virgin,
        St. Denis of France and St. Alphege of England,
        And all the tutelar Saints of Canterbury.
                  (*Grim wraps his arms about the Archbishop.*)
        Spare this defence, dear brother.
                          (*Tracy approaches hesitatingly*).
Fitzurse.   Strike him, Tracy!
Rosamund (*rushing down from the choir*).
        No, no, no, no!
Fitzurse.   This wanton here! De Morville,
        Hold her away.
De Morville.   I hold her.
Rosamund.   Mercy, mercy,
        As you would hope for mercy.
Fitzurse.   Strike, I say.
Grim. O God, O noble knights, O sacrilege!
        Strike our Archbishop in his own cathedral!
        The Pope, the King, will curse you — the whole world
        Abhor you; ye will die the death of dogs!
        Nay, nay, good Tracy.   (*Lifts his arm.*)
Fitzurse.   Answer not, but strike.
De Tracy. There is my answer then.
                          (*Sword falls on Grim's arm.*)
Grim.   Mine arm is sever'd.
        I can no more -- fight out the good fight — die
        Conqueror.   (*Staggers into the chapel of St. Benedict.*)
Becket (*falling on his knees*).
                  At the right hand of Power —
        Power and great glory — for thy Church, O Lord —
        Into Thy hands, O Lord — into Thy hands! —
                                  (*Sinks prone*).
De Brito. This last to rid thee of a world of brawls! (*Kills him*).
        The traitor's dead, and will arise no more.

If we carefully compare the dramas of Lord
Tennyson with those of Lord Lytton, candour we be-

lieve will compel us to acknowledge, that whatever superiority the former may justly claim over his old rival, as a poet, is strictly limited by the line which divides the realm of lyrical from that of dramatic poetry. Beyond that boundary Lord Lytton's pre-eminence is unquestionable.

Robert Browning.

We have already mentioned Mr. Browning's two early tragedies, *Strafford* and *the Blot on the Scutcheon*. The subject of the first is of course historical. In the second, a proud and punctilious nobleman, Lord Thorold Tresham, accidentally discovers that his sister Mildred accords secret nocturnal interviews to his friend, Earl Mertoun, and the consequences are fatal to all parties. The frigid reception both these tragedies found on representation would have deterred almost any other man from making fresh attempts of the same kind, but Browning, nowise dismayed, subsequently produced: *King Victor and King Charles, a tragedy; Colombe's Birthday, a play; a Soul's Tragedy; the Return of the Druses, a tragedy; and Luria, a tragedy*. No attempt has been made to bring any of these on the stage. In the first-named piece, the principal personages are the first King of Sardinia, Victor Amadeus, and his son Charles Emmanuel; and the main incident is a pretended abdication on the part of the father in favour of his son. Victor afterwards resumes his royal dignity, but only to die as king. There is much in the drama that is anything but clear. *Colombe* is a German princess, Duchess of Juliers and Cleves, and here we have to do with a real abdication, prompted by the Duchess's love for the humble Valence, in favour of the claimant, Prince Berthold. The plot of *a Soul's Tragedy* is rather ingenious. Luitolfo commits a political murder, and is forced to fly. His friend Chiappino, desirous of favouring his escape, and moved by the despair of Luitolfo's betrothed, Eulalia, takes the crime on himself, and is ready to mount the scaffold; but to his great surprise he is not only publicly thanked for the deed by his fellow-citizens, but elected provost in the murdered man's place. He soon becomes corrupted by prosperity, and thinks no more of the fugitive Luitolfo, who after a time returns to find his faithless friend a suitor for Eulalia's hand. As may be supposed, the catastrophe is highly tragic. The scene of *the Return of the Druses* is an islet of the southern Sporades colonised by Druses of Lebanon, and garrisoned by the Knights-Hospitallers of Rhodes. An unpopular Prefect is assassinated, and the colonists are only saved from the vengeance of the Knights by the intervention of the Venetians, who transport them back to their own country. The romantic part of the intrigue is represented by the maiden Anael and her two rival lovers, the Druse Djabal and the French Loys. *Luria,* who gives his name to the next tragedy, is a Moorish general in the service of the Florentine Republic, then at war with Pisa. Being wrongfully accused of treason, he is urged by his fair friend Domizia to revenge himself by marching with his mercenaries against the ungrateful Florence, but he prefers death to dishonour, and stabs himself. These later dramas of Browning's are even less suitable as acting plays than the two earlier ones; but amid their prevalent obscurity, their strange phraseology and their bewildering inversions, the patient reader may find many beauties. In fact, they are rather dramatic poems than dramas. The dialogue produces the effect of a series of monologues pronounced by each of the characters in turn, and we miss that rapid interchange of thought which is so indispensable to excite the interest and secure the attention of the reader or the listener.

Douglas Jerrold.

Besides two or three novels, and his famous contributions to the London *Punch,* Mr. Jerrold (1803—1857) has written some excellent comedies and farces. Of

these, one of the best, *Black-Eyed Susan*, is founded
on John Gay's well-known ballad:

All in the Downs the fleet was moored;

and such was the popularity it attained that Mr. T.
P. Cooke, the original William, appeared no less than
four hundred times successively in the same character,
partly at the Surrey Theatre in London and partly in
the provinces. William, a sailor aboard a man-of-war,
is Susan's husband; and his captain, whose name is
Crosstree, having one day when intoxicated insulted
Susan in the public street, William sees himself com-
pelled to strike him in defence of his wife. For a
sailor, however, to strike his captain, even under the
greatest provocation, is a most serious offence, and it
results in the arrest of William, and his trial before a
court-martial presided over by the admiral. Witnesses
are called, who make their depositions, and the case
is submitted to a jury of captains for their decision:

Admiral. Gentlemen, nothing more remains for us than to con-
sider the justice of our verdict. Although the case of the
unfortunate man admits of many palliatives, still, for the up-
holding of a necessary discipline, any commiseration would
afford a dangerous precedent, and I fear cannot be indulged.
Gentlemen, are you all determined in your verdict? Guilty or
not guilty? — Guilty? (*after a pause, the Captains bow assent.*)
It remains then for me to pass the sentence of the law? (*Cap-
tains bow.*) Bring back the prisoner.

Re-enter William and Master-at-arms.

Adm. Prisoner — after a patient and impartial investigation of
your case, this Court has unanimously pronounced you — Guilty!
(*pause.*) If you have anything to say in arrest of judgment …
now is your time to speak.

William. In a moment, your honours. — My top-lights[1]) are rather
misty. Your honours, I had been three years at sea, and had
never looked upon or heard from my wife — as sweet a little
craft as was ever launched — I had come ashore, and I was
as lively as a petrel in a storm; I found Susan — that's my
wife, your honours — all her gilt[2]) taken by the land-sharks,[3])
but yet all taut,[4]) with a face as red and rosy as the King's
head on the side of a fire-bucket. Well, your honours, when

---

[1]) My eyes (Mastlichter). [2]) Money. [3]) Knavish creditors, swindlers.
[4]) In good order, neat.

we were as merry as a ship's crew on a pay-day, there comes
an order to go aboard; I left Susan, and went with the rest
of the liberty men to ax leave of the first lieutenant. I hadn't
been gone the turning of an hour-glass, when I heard Susan
giving signals of distress, I out with my cutlass, made all
sail, and came up to my craft — I found her battling with a
pirate — I never looked at his figure-head, never stopped —
would any of your honours? long live you and your wives say
I! — would any of your honours have rowed alongside as if
you'd been going aboard a royal yacht? — no, you wouldn't;
for the gilt swabs[1]) on the shoulders can't alter the heart
that swells beneath; you would have done as I did; — and
what did I? why, I cut him down like a piece of old junk;[2])
had he been the first lord of the Admiralty, I had done it!
(*overcome with emotion.*)

A d m. Prisoner, we keenly feel for your situation; yet you, as a
good sailor, must know that the course of justice cannot be
evaded.

W i l. Your honours, let me be no bar to it; I do not talk for my
life. Death! why if I 'scaped it here — the next capful of
wind might blow me from the yard-arm. All I would strive
for, is to show I had no malice; all I wish whilst you pass
sentence, is your pity. That, your honours, whilst it is your
duty to condemn the sailor, may, as having wives you honour
and children you love, respect the husband.

A d m. Have you anything further to advance?

W i l. All my cable is run out[3]) — I'm brought to.

A d m. (*and all the Captains rise.*) Prisoner! it is now my most pain-
ful duty to pass the sentence of the Court upon you. The Court
commiserates your situation, and, in consideration of your services,
wil see that every care is taken of your wife when deprived of
your protection.

W i l. Poor Susan!

A d m. Prisoner! your case falls under the twenty-second Article
of War. (*reads.*) "If any man in, or belonging to the Fleet,
shall draw, or offer to draw, or lift up his hand against his
superior officer, he shall suffer death." (*putting on his hat.*) The
sentence of the Court is, that you be hanged at the fore-yard-
arm of this his Majesty's ship, at the hour of ten o'clock.
Heaven pardon your sins, and have mercy on your soul! This
Court is now dissolved.

William, condemned to death, bids a tender farewell
to his unhappy wife; but he ultimately escapes, being
at the last moment saved by the timely intervention
of the now penitent Captain Crosstree:

---

[1]) Officer's epaulets.   [2]) Old cable or cordage.   [3]) I have told
my story.

William and Susan.

Wil. Oh Susan! Well, my poor wench, how fares it?

Susan. Oh, William! and I have watched, prayed for your return — smiled in the face of poverty, stopped my ears to the reproaches of the selfish, the worst pity of the thoughtless — and all, all for this!

Wil. Ay, Sue, it's hard; but that's all over — to grieve is useless. Susan, I might have died disgraced — have left you the widow of a bad, black-hearted man; I know 'twill not be so — and in this, whilst you remain behind me, there is at least some comfort. I died in a good cause; I died in defence of the virtue of a wife — her tears will fall like spring rain on the grass that covers me.

Susan. Talk not so — your grave! I feel it is a place where my heart must throw down its heavy load of life.

Will. Come, Susan, shake off your tears. There, now, smile a bit — we'll not talk again of graves. Think, Susan, that I am a going on a long foreign station — think so. Now, what would you ask — have you nothing, nothing to say?

Susan. Nothing! oh, when at home, hoping, yet trembling for this meeting, thoughts crowded on me, I felt as if I could have talked to you for days. Stopping for want of power, not words. Now the terrible time is come — now I am almost tongue-tied — my heart swells to my throat, I can but look and weep. (*gun fires.*) That gun! oh, William! husband! is it so near! — You speak not — tremble.

Wil. Susan, be calm. If you love your husband, do not send him on the deck a white-faced coward. Be still, my poor girl, I have something to say — until you are calm, I will not utter it; now Susan — —

Susan. I am cold, motionless as ice.

Wil. Susan! you know the old aspen that grows near to the church porch; you and I, when children, almost before we could speak plainly, have sat and watched, and wondered at its shaking leaves — I grew up, and that tree seemed to me a friend that loved me, yet had not the tongue to tell me so. Beneath its boughs our little arms have been locked together — beneath its boughs I took the last kiss of your white lips when hard fortune made me turn sailor. I cut from that tree this branch (*produces it*). Many a summer's day aboard, I've lain in the top and looked at these few leaves, until I saw green meadows in the salt sea, and heard the bleating of the sheep. When I am dead, Susan, let me be laid under that tree.

 Gun fires. — Slow Music. — William gives Susan in charge of Seaweed, kisses her, and she is carried off.

Last Scene.

The Forecastle of the Ship. — Procession along the starboard gangway.

Master-at-Arms. Prisoner, are you prepared?

Wil. Bless you! Bless you all — (*mounts the platform*).

Captain Crosstree (*rushes on from gangway*). Hold! Hold!
Adm. Captain Crosstree — retire, sir, retire.
Cross. Never! if the prisoner be executed, he is a murdered man.
  I alone am the culprit — 'twas I who would have dishonoured him.
Adm. This cannot plead here — he struck a superior officer.
Cross. No!
All. No?
Cross. He saved my life; I had written for his discharge — vil-
  lainy has kept back the document — 'tis here dated back; when
  William struck me he was not the king's sailor   I was not
  his officer.
Adm. (*taking the paper -   Music*). He is free!

Bubbles of the Day, said Charles Kemble the actor,
has wit enough for three pieces. A few extracts will
suffice to prove that this is a well-earned eulogium.

Sir Phenix Clearcake and Lord Skindeep.

Sir Phenix. My lord, I come with a petition to you — a petition
  not parliamentary, but charitable. We propose, my lord, a
  fancy fair[1]) in Guildhall: its object so benevolent, and more than
  that, so respectable!
Skindeep. Benevolence and respectability! of course, I'm with
  you. Well, — the precise object?
Sir Ph. It is to remove a stain — a very great stain from the
  city; to exercise a renovating taste at a most inconsiderable
  outlay; to call up as it were the snowy purity of Greece in
  the coal-smoke atmosphere of London; in a word, my lord —
  but as yet 'tis a profound secret — it is to paint St. Paul's!
Skind. A gigantic effort!
Sir Ph. The fancy fair will be on a most comprehensive and
  philanthropic scale. Every alderman takes a stall; — and, to
  give you an idea of the enthusiasm in the city — but this is
  also a secret — the Lady Mayoress has been up three nights
  making pincushions.
Skind. But you don't want me to take a stall — to sell pincushions?
Sir Ph. Certainly not, my lord. And yet your philanthropic speeches
  in the house, my lord, convince me that to obtain a certain
  good you would sell anything.
Skind. Well, well; command me in any way; benevolence is my
  foible. I tell you what; I've some splendid Chinese paintings
  on rice-paper. They're not of the least use to me, so you may
  have them for the charity.

Another projector, Captain Smoke, who has served,
as he says, in the "Madras Fusileers," now enters, and

---

[1]) A temporary bazaar, conducted by ladies, for some charitable
object.

introduces another ingenious scheme, for which he
solicits the co-operation of his Lordship's friends, Mr.
Brown and Mr. Chatham Brown:

Smoke. Our family was always military — always distinguished.
But now I 've cut up my sword into steel pens and flourish
the weapons in the cause of commerce. We are about to start
a company to take on lease Mount Vesuvius for the manufactory
of lucifer-matches.

Sir Ph. A stupendous speculation! I should say, that when its
countless advantages are duly numbered, it will be found a
certain wheel of fortune to the enlightened capitalist.

Smoke. Now, sir, if you would but take the chair at the first
meeting (*Aside to Chatham*) we shall make it all right about the
shares, — if you would but speak for two or three hours on
the social improvement conferred by the lucifer-match, with the
monopoly of sulphur secured to the company — a monopoly
which will suffer no man, woman, or child to strike a light
without our permission — —

Brown. He 'll do it, of course he 'll do it.

Chat. Truly, sir, in such a cause, to such an auditory —

Smoke. Sir, if you would speak well anywhere, there 's nothing
like first grinding your eloquence on a mixed meeting. Depend
on 't, if you can only manage a little humbug with a mob, it
gives you great confidence for another place.

Skind. Smoke, never say humbug; it 's coarse.

Sir Ph. And not respectable.

Smoke. Pardon me, my lord: it was coarse. But the fact is, humbug
has received such high patronage, that now it 's quite classic.

Chat. But why not embark his lordship in the lucifer question?

Smoke. I can't: I have his lordship in three companies already.
Three. First, there's a company — half a million capital —
for extracting civet from assafoetida. The second is a company
for a trip all round the world. We propose to hire a three-
decker of the Lords of the Admiralty, and fit her up with
every accommodation for families. We 've already advertised
for wet-nurses and maids-of-all-work.

Sir Ph. A magnificent project! And then the fittings-up will be
so respectable. A delightful billiard-table in the ward-room; [1])
with, for the humbler classes, skittels on the orlop-deck.[2]) Swings
and archery for the ladies, trap-ball and cricket for the children,
whilst the marine sportsman will find the stock of gulls un-
limited. Weippert's quadrille band is engaged, and — —

Smoke. For the convenience of lovers, the ship will carry a parson.

Chat. And the object?

Smoke. Pleasure and education. At every new country we shall
drop anchor for at least a week, that the children may go to

----

[1]) Officers' mess-room. [2]) Upper deck in trading vessels.

school and learn the language. The trip must answer: 'twill
occupy only three years, and we 've forgotten nothing to make
it delightful — nothing, from hot rolls to cork jackets.
Brown. And now, sir, the third venture?
Smoke. That, sir, is a company to buy the Serpentine River for
a Grand Junction Temperance Cemetery.
Brown. What! so many watery graves?
Smoke. Yes, sir, with floating tombstones. Here 's the prospectus.
Look here; surmounted by a hyacinth — the very emblem of
temperance — a hyacinth flowering in the limpid flood. Now,
if you don't feel equal to the lucifers — I know his lordship's
goodness, — he 'll give you up the cemetery. (*Aside to Chatham*)
A family vault as a bonus to the chairman.
Sir Ph. What a beautiful subject for a speech! Water-lilies and
aquatic plants gemming the translucent crystal, shells of rainbow
brightness, a constant supply of gold and silver fish, with the
right of angling secured to shareholders. The extent of the
river being necessarily limited, will render lying there so select,
so very respectable.

In *Retired from Business*, we have an amusing
picture of a shopkeeper colony in the village of Pump-
kinfield. Mr. Pennyweight, a retired green-grocer in
comfortable circumstances, on settling down in the
village with his family, is informed, by Mr. Puffins,
"the great Russia merchant," that society in Pumpkin-
field consists of two classes, the billocracy and the
tillocracy, the former comprising the aristocratic traders
who had enjoyed a bank-credit and drawn bills of ex-
change, the latter including the plebeian retailers who
had no other bank than the till, or money-drawer in
the shop-counter. "The counting-house," says Mr. Puf-
fins, "knows not the shop. The wholesale merchant
never crosses the till." In spite of this strict line of
demarcation, however, there are presumptuous persons.
like the retired pawnbroker Jubilee, who are always
pushing themselves in the circle of the billocrats, and
are too cool and self-possessed to be easily snubbed.
Mr. Jubilee one day takes occasion to tell his acquain-
tances, how hard he finds it to forget the palmy days
when he dwelt beneath the shadow of the golden balls:

Jubilee. Beg pardon, but the shop will rise. Though we are
retired from business, business will come back to us. I dare
say now, on winter nights, when you 're looking at the candles,

your thoughts will smell the dear old Russia tallow, eh? And you, Mr. Creepmouse; when in your walks you see the bright poppies among the corn, doesn 't your heart melt again towards the soldiers' coats — the scarlet cloth you 've made your money on? To be sure; nature, even in an army tailor, will work. I know by myself. — For, last week there was a party at the Sycamores. — Very fine folks. Breaking up — night air cold: a lady — sweet woman — gave me her shawl to wrap about her: such a lovely cachemere! Took my thoughts back in a minute behind the counter. Well, still looking at the shawl, the lady still waiting, and never dreaming where I was, would you think it, I asked — 'What on this?''

Poor Mr. Jubilee is persecuted by the attentions of Miss Chipp, an elderly milliner, who aspires to be the second Mrs. Jubilee. Having caught a glimpse of the recalcitrant lover at the Pennyweights' door, Miss Chipp resolves on a visit to the new-comers. Mrs. Pennyweight, or as she now aspires to be called, Mrs. Fitzpennyweight, receives the milliner very coldly, but all the ice soon thaws, when Miss Chipp proceeds to speak of the distinguished families, with whom she represents herself as on terms of intimacy:

Miss Chipp. Happy, me'm, to meet you. (*Aside.*) He 's in the garden.
Mrs. Penny. You 're very good, ma'am. (*Aside.*) She talks retail; her mouth looks like a till. But no — trust me! — she doesn't sit down in my house.
Miss Chipp. Nice place, Pumpkinfield; the name odd. Might be prettier with another name.
Mrs. Penny. Yes, Miss Chipp; perhaps some places, like some people, would be very glad to change their names.
Miss Chipp. He! he! Change? No doubt; and some people do change — do — do — Mrs. Fitzpennyweight.
Mrs. Penny. (*Aside.*) Oh! if she 's coming to insinuations, I should think I could match her there. (*Aloud.*) The fact is, ma'am —
Miss Chipp. I ought to apologize. But I thought, as there was a slight tie between us — I may say, a little cobweb tie, that — —
Mrs. Penny. I for myself, ma'am, don't encourage cobwebs.
Miss Chipp. You see, my dear friend, Lady Buckle —
Mrs. Penny. Who?
Miss Chipp. Lady Buckle, the cousin of the charming Countess de Crochet, whose niece, the Marchioness of Odonto — the sister-in-law of that sparkling creature, the Duchess of Macassar —

Mrs. Penny. (*Who has drawn down a chair.*) And I vow, you 're standing! Pray take a chair, Miss Chipp.

Miss Chipp. You 're very good. (*They sit.*) I was about to say — lud! where did I begin?

Mrs. Penny. At the tie between us, at that dear little cobweb.

Miss Chipp. True. Well, Lady Buckle has a little girl at Calais, at the same school with your Kitty; and hearing that your daughter was come home, I wished to enquire about the child, because I promised to write to poor Lady Buckle, who is anxious that the countess should communicate with the marchioness, in order that her grace the duchess may have the first intelligence. And I thought that — pray pardon me, the tie — the — he! he! — the — excuse me — the cobweb —

Mrs. Penny. A cobweb, ma'am, I 'm proud to be in.

Miss Chipp. Already my friends have heard of your sweet child, Miss Pennyweight — pardon me — Miss Fitzpennyweight: — by the way, you 've lately had an increase in your family name?

Mrs. Penny. Ye — es.

Miss Chipp. Have you not yet been in the Gazette?

Mrs. Penny. Ma'am!

Miss Chipp. Always done. To pass a new name without the crown stamp, isn't a bit more reputable than to pass counterfeit money.

Mrs. Penny. (*Aside.*) La! I shall never hear the name without thinking myself a pocket-piece. I 'll stop this. (*Aloud.*) Pray, ma'am, do you know a person called Jubilee — a pawnbroker?

Miss Chipp. I knew his wife. And though she did marry a tradesman, I must say it, I stood by her to the last.

Mrs. Penny. Really?

Miss Chipp. For Emma was such a fairy: but, dear Mrs. Fitzpennyweight, can you imagine a fairy at a pawnbroker's?

Mrs. Penny. I shudder at the recollec — at the idea of it.

One of the best characters is Lieutenant Tackle, an old sailor who has taken to gardening. Though not very successful in his new pursuit, he gives young Woodburn his notion of what an average crop of fruit should be:

Tackle. Do you know what I 'm on the look-out for?

Woodburn. Snails?

Tackle. Snails! No — though they 're the plague of my heart. Snails! I don't grudge 'em what they eat, for we all must live — but, damn 'em, it 's what they spoil.

Wood. And how thrives your garden, Lieutenant?

Tackle. Capital! In another year or two I shall eat my own radishes. And what a season we shall have for cherries, to be sure!

Wood. Enough, eh?

Tackle. Why, in the matter of cherries, plums, apples, and such
   like, enough isn't enough — if it isn't enough three times over.
Wood.   Three times?
Tackle. Yes. Enough for the birds, enough for the boys, and
   enough for the master. That 's what I call an average crop.

In his youth, Mr. Jerrold was for some time a
midshipman aboard the *Ernest* gun-brig, which will
partly explain the happy knack he possessed in drawing
sailors' characters. Among his other successful pieces
we shall mention, *Nell Gwynne*, *the Rent Day* (founded
on Sir David Wilkie's two celebrated pictures), *the
Prisoner of War*, *Time works Wonders*, and *Heart of
Gold*. All these are rich in shrewd drollery and pungent
wit, dashed here and there with a flash of poetry.
Thus, in the *Prisoner of War*, Captain Channel, reproving
his daughter for wasting her time in reading trashy,
sensational novels, says:

When I was young, girls used to read Pilgrim's Progress,
Jeremy Taylor, and such books of innocence; now young ladies
know the ways of Newgate as well as the turnkeys. These books
gave girls hearty, healthy food; now, silly things, like larks in
cages, they live upon hemp-seed;

and in *Time works Wonders* we find:

Florentine. Oh, sir, the magic of five long years! We paint
   Time with glass and scythe — should he not carry harlequin's
   own wand? for, oh, indeed, Time's changes!
Clarence. Are they, in truth, so very great?
Flor. Greater than harlequin's; but then Time works them with
   so grave a face, that even the hearts he alters doubt the change,
   though often turned from very flesh to stone.
Clar. Time has its bounteous changes too; and sometimes to the
   sweetest bud will give an unimagined beauty in the flower.

John Poole.

Mr. Poole, the popular dramatist, was born in 1792,
and his first piece, entitled *Who's who?* was performed
at Drury Lane Theatre so early as 1815. From that
year till the time of his death (about 1871) he produced,
besides numerous contributions to the Magazines, a large
number of dramatic pieces, including *Deaf as a Post,*

Paul Pry, Simpson and Co., Turning the Tables, Patrician and Parvenu, Matchmaking, and *'Twixt the Cup and the Lip*. The two first-named pieces belong to the greatest theatrical hits of the day, and their success was confirmed by the admirable acting of Mr. Liston in the respective characters of Tristram Sappy and Paul Pry. From the *New Monthly Magazine* we learn that the idea of the caracter of Paul Pry was suggested to Mr. Poole by an intimate friend, the original being an idle and inquisitive old lady living in his neighbourhood, but the dramatist, wishing to avoid personalities, decided on taking a man as the representative of a class. The plot to a certain point is the same as that of the *Vieux Célibataire* of Collin Harleville; and, like the hero of the French piece, Witherton the old bachelor is governed and bamboozled by two tyrannical and artful domestics, who intercept his nephew's letters. So far only does Mr. Poole follow the French writer; for he brings about a satisfactory denonement at last exclusively by means of the continual intrusions and indiscretions of Paul Pry. Mr. Poole says of the piece: "it is original in structure, plot, character and dialogue, such as they are. The only imitation I am aware of, is to be found in part of the business in which Mrs. Subtle (the house-keeper) is engaged."

Simpson and Co. is a highly amusing piece. The senior partner, a steady-going elderly business man, has a wife who is jealous without a shadow of reason, while the junior partner, a gay, flirting young husband, is blessed with a most confiding and unsuspicious con-sort. An accidental exchange of pocket-books between the partners, and the discovery of a woman's portrait by the jealous elder lady in the one which is moment-arily in possession of her husband, gives rise to the most comic situations and the drollest *quiproquos*.

In *Patrician and Parvenu*, two characters are pre-sented to us in strong contrast with each other, the real man of quality, Sir Osbaldiston de Mowbray, Bart., and the former cheesemonger, Sir Timothy Stilton, Knight. The plot is made up of a series of amusing misunderstandings, which for a time create inextricable confusion, and cause a constant and lively though accidental, and on the part of the baronet displeasing intercourse, between the refined Patrician and the ignorant and presumptuous Parvenu.

Of *Paul Pry* there is another version, which has appeared under the name of *Douglas Jerrold*, but it differs considerably from the original piece by Mr. Poole.

Charles Reade. — Tom Taylor.

Charles Reade, the novelist, has dramatised two of his own novels, *It's never too late to mend*, and *Put yourself in his Place*. Mr. Reade was born at Ipsden House, Oxfordshire, in 1814, and after studying at Cambridge, was called to the bar in 1843, but soon abandoned the law to devote himself to literature. When the first of these pieces, in which the author exposes the cruelties inflicted on prisoners by tyrannical governors of gaols, was produced at the Princess's Theatre, a dramatic critic, called Tomlins, rose and protested against the exaggeration of the play, a step which led to a violent discussion between him and Mr. Reade in the newspapers. The other piece, *Put yourself in his Place*, depicts the struggles of a skilled workman to rise in the world. and the persecution he suffers from certain Trades' Unions, to which he has become obnoxious. Both these dramas were successful on the stage. Mr. Reade likewise wrote several dramatic pieces in conjunction with Mr. Tom Taylor, the best of which was entitled *Masks and Faces*. He died in 1884.

Mr. *Tom Taylor*, born in Sunderland in the year 1817, is the author of the dramas: *Joan of Arc, 'Twixt Axe and Crown*, and *the Fool's Revenge;* besides the amusing comedies, *the contested Election, an unequal Match, Still Waters are deep, the Overland Route*, and some other pieces. A parlamentary election in the little town of Flamborough forms the subject of the first-named of these comedies. Mr. Honeybun, a retired grocer, fond of his ease, is pushed forward as a candidate, very much against his will, by his ambitious wife and the intriguing attorney Dodgson. Perhaps the best scene is where two deputations — one from each of the two political parties that divide the borough — arrive at the same moment to worry the perplexed Honeybun with teasing and embarrassing questions; but Dodgson with great dexterity always intervenes to spare him the necessity of attempting explanations:

(Enter the two deputations. Spitchcock heads the one, Gathercole the other, followed by Crawley, Copperthwaite, Oldwinkle, and Electors, shown in by James and another Servant, who place chairs on each side of stage.)

Dodgson. Pray be seated, gentlemen. Chairs for the deputation. James. *(introducing)* Mr. Honeybun, Mr. Gathercole — the enlightened editor of the Flamborough Beacon; Mr. Spitchcock, editor and proprietor of the Flamborough Patriot; Mr. Copperthwaite, Mr. Crawley. Mr. Oldwinkle. and other influential members of the constituency *(they all sit)*. Mr. Honeybun is most anxious to give the fullest explanation in answer to any questions you may put to him; at the same time. he claims the right to maintain that reserve which befits one about to enter on the arduous and responsible duty of legislation. Now, gentlemen.

Gathercole *(rises, and speaks over back of his chair)*. As one of those who signed the requisition to you, sir, on this occasion, and as the mouth-piece of advanced Liberalism in this borough. I have been requested to obtain from you, sir, a categorical expression of your views on the subject of the ballot, — whether you consider that measure is not necessary to secure the humbler class of voters from oppression. *(sits.)*

Spitchcock *(breaking in and rising)*. Or if its effect will not be rather to give a premium to deception; to encourage cowardice, and to destroy that manly and open avowal of political opinion which has hitherto been the proud characteristic of the Englishman. *(sits.)*

(While these contradictions are being exchanged, Mr. Honeybun keeps looking from one speaker to the other.)

Gather. *(interrupting and rising.)* I can readily understand, with Mr. Spitchcock's well known and hebdomadally reiterated opinions, that he should be averse to any change which will limit the oppressive influence of territorial interests. *(sits.)*

Spitch. *(rises.)* And it is no secret, at least within the limited circulation of the Beacon, that the ballot must be acceptable to any party whose aim is to strengthen the hands of the demagogue, and to deprive the humble voter of the parental guidance of his natural protectors. I should be glad to know which of these two views best embodies the political sentiments of Mr. Honeybun. (*sits.*)

Honeybun. (*rises.*) Well, really, gentlemen, I must observe that there seems to be a great deal to say on both sides. (*sits, and wipes perspiration from his face.*)

Dodgson. (*rises.*) That must be evident to all who have the advantage of perusing our own admirable local prints; and such has been the effect of the consummate power with which these organs have wielded the opposing arguments on the subject of the ballot, that Mr. Honeybun's opinion remains suspended, and he demands a further opportunity for mature consideration before he commits himself unreservedly upon this most interesting question. (*sits.*)

Spitch. (*rises.*) If Mr. Honeybun is satisfied that the ballot is cowardly and un-English — (*sits.*)

Dod. (*rises.*) He authorized me to say that he will oppose it to the uttermost. (*sits.*)

Hon. To the uttermost!

Gather. (*rises.*) But if he be convinced that without it the real opinions of the voters cannot be freely expressed — (*sits.*)

Dod. It will find in him a strenuous and consistent supporter.

Hon. That it will.

Spitch. The destruction of territorial and intellectual influence —

Dod. He holds, with you, would be most mischievous to the country.

Hon. Most mischievous.

Gather. To impose a check on every oppressive and injurious exercise of the power of capital —

Dod. He is as firmly convinced as you or any man, is the imperative duty of an enlightened legislature.

Hon. Imperative. (*pause.*)

Dod. Mr. Honeybun having now stated his views on the subject of the ballot, he will be glad to give an equally explicit answer on any other subject to which the deputation may wish to direct his attention.

Copperthwaite. I should like to know how you would vote on a reform bill disfranchising this here borough.

Hon. Well, if you ask me, I should decidedly support —

Dod. Any measure which might tend to secure the full representation of every class of the community; but as the disfranchisement of Flamborough would be a step in quite the opposite direction —

Omnes. Hear, hear.

Dod. Mr. Honeybun would be found, at whatever risk of forfeiting your favour, most decidedly opposed to such a proceeding.

Omnes. Hear, Hear.

Cop. I'm glad to hear that, sir. We're all reformers in a general way; but reform ain't like charity, sir, — it don't begin at home. We don't see why we should be reformed out of our votes. (*sits.*)

Crawley (*rises.*) Which, 'owever 'umble, we have always done the best with 'em for ourselves and our families. (*sits.*)

Dod. Really this is a very original way of putting it, Mr. Crawley; don't you think so, Mr. Honeybun?

Hon. Oh, very!

Dod. The general good being the sum of individual goods, every man is only to do what is best for himself in order that the country may obtain what is best for all.

Oldwinkle (*rises.*) I should like to hear Mr. Honeybun's opinion about game laws.

Hon. (*rises.*) Well, I'm not a sportsman, myself, and — (*sits.*)

Gather. (*rises.*) Therefore, sir, I trust cannot advocate any system of laws which encourages poaching, leads to numerous breaches of the peace, and fills the county gaols. (*sits.*)

Dod. Certainly not!

Hon. Certainly not!

Spitch. At the same time, Mr. Honeybun can scarcely deny that to put an end to the sports of the field would be to discourage manly activity; to remove a great inducement to resident owner-ship; and to largely diminish a wholesome, a favourite, and a succulent article of culinary consumption.

Dod. Mr. Honeybun would be the last man to deny conclusions which, thus stated, must commend themselves to the meanest capacity.

Hon. To the meanest capacity.

Cop. How about Church-rates?

Craw. Ought refreshments to be allowed to voters?

Dod. Really, gentlemen, Mr. Honeybun cannot be expected to answer you all at once; but one of your questions he did catch distinctly: whether refreshments ought to be allowed to voters? a question he is prepared to answer with equal distinctness, by requesting that you will do him the honour of partaking of lunch, which you will find ready in the dining-room.

Omnes. Hear, hear.

Gather. He's very kind, I'm sure. What do you say, Spitchcock?

Spitch. With all my heart. Political differences should never narrow the field of social intercourse.

Craw. Well, I must say, Mr. Honeybun, you've met us as fair and pleasant as any gentleman could, and we shall be proud and happy to drink your very good health, sir; and success to your election, sir. (*They all rise.*)

Cop. And I only wish I could be a deputation every day of the week to hear such a werry satisfactory statement of opinions as you've guv' us this morning.

Dod. (*showing them out.*) This way, gentlemen — (*Exit deputation, Dodgson rushing back to Honeybun.*) My dear sir, you managed them beautifully.

The subject of "An unequal Match" is the marriage of a man of rank, Sir Harry Arncliffe, with Hester

Grazebrook, a blacksmith's handsome daughter, and the intrigues of Mrs. Montressor, an envious coquettish widow, to mar their domestic happiness. Sir Harry is for a time deceived by the artifices of the widow, whom he takes for his sincere friend, but Hester is more clear-sighted. The following encounter between the two ladies will remind the reader of that "thrust-and-parry" wit, of which Sheridan was such a master:

Mrs. Montressor. Oh, my dear Lady Arncliffe, I should apologise for playing truant so long this morning; but I find that you have been very naughty, too.

Hester. Did Sir Harry complain of me to you?

Mrs. M. Oh, no; he knows I always take your part.

Hester. You take my part!

Mrs. M. Yes; men are so unreasonable, they never will make allowances.

Hester. Few women like to admit that they require them.

Mrs. M. As I tell him; when he has picked a cowslip, it is most unfair to be angry that it is not an exotic. You wild flowers have quite advantages enough over us poor sickly products of the conservatory without insisting on adding our cultivated graces to your native freshness. For my part, I adore wild flowers. I dare say now, my dear Lady Arncliffe, you wouldn't believe me if I confessed to you that I envy you terribly.

Hester. You could tell me few things, Mrs. Montressor, that would less surprise me.

Mrs. M. Satirical, eh? Oh fie! Pray, my dear, don't try to teach that innocent little tongue of yours the art of stabbing; leave that to women of the world.

Hester. I know I am no match for you in the power of inflicting pain.

Mrs. M. Take care! That's an admission of inferiority. The power of inflicting pain is generally proportionate to the capacity for giving pleasure.

Hester. Then you must have a good deal of that capacity, Mrs. Montressor.

Mrs. M. Well, I think, without flattering myself, I have a fair share; that is, if the lords of the creation may be believed.

Hester. Even I have heard of the numbers you have enslaved.

Mrs. M. You are complimentary. I suppose Sir Harry has given you a sad idea of me. But a rejected admirer, you know, dear, is not always to be relied on. Of course, you are aware I refused him?

Hester. I have heard so.

Mrs. M. By-the-by, it was just before we met him at your father's.

Hester. And when my father saved your life.

Mrs. M. Precisely; your family is so muscular. By-the-way, I hear the worthy old man has paid you a visit. How delighted Sir Harry must be to see him. What a refreshing contrast to everything round about him; and how amusingly embarrassed he'll be in the midst of your new splendour!

Hester (*rising.*) My father, Mrs. Montressor, is a homely, but an honest man; if he is embarrassed, it must be from contact with hypocrisy, heartlessness, and affectation.

Mrs. M. (*rising.*) Our friends in the breakfast-room may share that amongst them. But I admire you firing up for your father, and I'll take care to remember that pretty sentence of yours in case Sir Harry should appeal to me on the subject.

Hester. My husband appeal to you!

Mrs. M. Poor fellow! old associations are so strong. He will not forget that I've no longer any right to be his confidante.

Hester. Have you done your best to make him forget it? Have you not rather tried to bring him once more to your feet? to rivet afresh the broken chain?

Mrs. M. That metaphor is too strong of the forge for you to venture upon, my dear Lady Arncliffe. As for my influence with Sir Harry, it's perhaps lucky for you that I'm not quite so eager for conquest as you fancy. Did I rate my own fascinations so highly I might be tempted to hold up my finger and see if he would follow. A man must have some woman who understands him and the way of his world. There are social as well as personal sympathies; you know he cannot find both in you.

Hester (*with a strong effort.*) All that woman can contribute to man's happiness I claim to give my husband, and I alone. I was happy till you came here; my husband never blushed for me till you taught him, but now there is a cloud between us that darkens our happy home — it is you who have raised it. Mrs. Montressor, there must be no disguise between us now — this house is no place for you and me together. I am its mistress!

Mrs. M. Unluckily it was Sir Harry who invited me. You had better ask him to give me my congé, and tell him the reason.

Hester. Take care! Shall I tell him that the woman he had invited here to be his wife's friend and example had used her time to poison the wife's faith, to undermine the husband's love? He might blame me for being jealous; he must despise you, because you are treacherous and base.

Mrs. M. And yet you fear me.

Hester. Only while you wear your mask. If I tear it off you are harmless.

Mrs. M. Lady Arncliffe, is this defiance?

Hester. No, Mrs. Montressor; it is detection! (*Exit Hester.*)

Thomas William Robertson.

Mr. Robertson, born in 1839 at Newark-on-Trent, Nottinghamshire, the son of an actor and an actor himself, is the author of *Ours, Society, School, Play, Caste*, and some other pieces, which are all neatly and ingeniously constructed, but not remarkable for strength, pathos or humour. Mr. Robertson, who is married to a German lady, spent some time in Germany, and it was from a play then popular on the German stage, called *Aschenbrödel*, that he got the first idea of *School*. When the last-named piece was produced in London, the author was assailed in an angry letter in the *Times* as a plagiarist; but his defence was undertaken by Mr. John Oxenford, who showed that the piece had been so much altered and made so thoroughly English, by Mr. Robertson, that it had just claims to be considered a new play. *Ours* (that is, *Our Regiment)* has a plot based on the Crimean War, and was made popular by the three leading characters: Mary Nesley, a light-hearted young girl, strong in her own innocence; Hugh M'Alister, an amiable male flirt, given to verse-making; and Sergeant Jones, the honest and affectionate soldier. But Mr. Robertson's most popular production is his three-act comedy, *Society*. We subjoin the capital scene, in which the vulgar but wealthy upstart, Mr. John Chodd, does his utmost to entice the impecunious young barrister, Sidney Daryl, to introduce him into the circles to which his riches have hitherto proved no passport:

Chodd, jun. Business is business — so I'd best begin at once. The present age is, as you are aware — a practical age. I come to the point — it's my way. Capital commands the world. The capitalist commands capital, therefore the capitalist commands the world.

Sidney. But you don't quite command the world, do you?

Chodd, jun. Practically, I do. I wish for the highest honours — I bring out my cheque-book.[1] I want to get into the House of Commons — cheque-book. I want the best legal opinion in the House of Lords — cheque-book. The best house —

---

[1] A book containing blank money-orders on a bank.

cheque-book. The best turn-out — cheque-book. The best
friends, the best wife, the best-trained children — cheque-book,
cheque-book, and cheque-book.

Sidney. You mean to say with money you can purchase any-
thing?

Chodd, jun. Exactly. This life is a matter of bargain.

Sidney. But "honour, love, obedience, troops of friends."

Chodd, jun. Can buy 'em all, sir, in lots as at an auction.

Sidney. Love, too?

Chodd, jun. Marriage means a union mutually advantageous. It
is a civil contract like a partnership.

Sidney. And the old-fashioned virtues of honour and chivalry?

Chodd, jun. Honour means not being a bankrupt. I know nothing
at all about chivalry, and I don't want to.

Sidney. Well, yours is quite a new creed to me, and I confess
I don't like it.

Chodd, jun. The currency, sir, converts the most hardened sceptic.
I see by the cards on your glass that you go out a good deal.

Sidney. Go out?

Chodd, jun. Yes, to parties (*looking at cards on table.*) There's
my Lady this, and the Countess t'other, and Mrs. somebody
else. Now that's what I want to do.

Sidney. Go into society?

Chodd, jun. Just so. You had money once, hadn't you?

Sidney. Yes.

Chodd, jun. What did you do with it?

Sidney. Spent it.

Chodd, jun. And you've been in the army?

Sidney. Yes.

Chodd, jun. Infantry?

Sidney. Cavalry.

Chodd, jun. Dragoons?

Sidney. Lancers.

Chodd, jun. How did you get out of it?

Sidney. Sold out. [1])

Chodd, jun. Then you were a first-rate fellow, till you tumbled
down?

Sidney. Tumbled down!

Chodd, jun. Yes, to what you are.

*　*　*

Chodd, jun. As I was saying, you know lots [2]) of people at clubs,
and in society.

Sidney. Yes.

Chodd, jun. Titles and Honourables, and Captains, and that.

Sidney. Yes.

---

[1]) English officers were formerly permitted to sell their com-
missions on retiring from the service. [2]) A familiar word, meaning
"a great number."

Chodd, jun. Tiptoppers[1]) (*after a pause.*) You're not well off?
Sidney (*getting serious.*) No.
Chodd, jun. I am. I've heaps of brass.[2]) Now I have what you
    haven't, and I haven't what you have. You've got what I
    want, and I've got what you want. That's logic, isn't it?
Sidney (*gravely.*) What of it?
Chodd, jun. This: suppose we exchange or barter. You help me
    to get into the company of men with titles, and women with
    titles; swells,[3]) you know, real uns, and all that.
Sidney. Yes.
Chodd, jun. And I'll write you a cheque for any reasonable sum
    you like to name.

*   *   *

Sidney. Mr. Chodd, I cannot entertain your very commercial pro-
    position. My friends are my friends; they are not marketable
    commodities. I regret that I can be of no assistance to you.
    With your appearance, manners, and cheque-book, you are sure
    to make a circle of your own.
Chodd, jun. You refuse, then —
Sidney. Absolutely. Good morning.

Other dramatic Writers.

Mr. *Leigh Hunt* produced, in 1840, a play called
a Legend of Florence, in which the part of the heroine
— a wife buried while in a trance, who, on escaping
from the tomb, is disowned by her husband — was
performed with great applause by Miss Ellen Tree
(afterwards Mrs. Charles Kean); and in 1858, a year
before the author's death, another piece of his, called
Lovers' Amazements, was brought successfully on the
stage. Several dramas have been also written by Dr.
Westland Marston. One of these, *the Patrician's Daughter,*
a love-tale, in which the hero is a poor but rising young
politician, and the heroine the daughter of a nobleman
and minister of state, was brought into high favour
with the public by the admirable acting of Miss Helen
Faucit. *The Heart of the World,* and a tragedy called
Strathmore, obtained, on the other hand, a very moderate
success. In his latest dramatic work, *Under Fire,* Dr.

---

[1]) Slang for "people of rank." [2]) Slang term for "money."
[3]) Dandies, or people in good society.

Marston introduces us to a lady in high life, who having begun her career as a public concert-singer, is morbidly sensitive to the faintest allusion to professional musicians, and this is the pivot on which a rather meagre plot turns. Mr. *Mark Lemon,* Mr. *Gilbert Abbot à Beckett,* and Mr. *Shirley Brooks,* all wrote farces and little comedies, but they gained their literary laurels chiefly as contributors to the London *Punch.* Mr. *Wilkie Collins* produced two sensational dramas, *the Light-house* and *the Frozen Deep.* The last-named piece, in which a young naval officer, who has joined a polar expedition, discovers in a sick and helpless comrade his detested, though till then unknown rival, but overcome by pity and a sense of duty, rescues him from certain death at the cost of his own life, met with an enthusiastic reception from the public; to which, it must be confessed, such accessories as the grand and wonderful Arctic scenery, with its glaciers, icebergs, and snowpeaks, not a little contributed. Mr. *Planché* has written some good pieces, particularly an historical comedy, called *Charles XII.* The scene is the island of Rügen, and the date is the time of Charles's hasty return, under a borrowed name, from Bender in Turkey. Mr. *Pinero's* principal work is the *Money-Spinner,* a piece with two interesting and amusing characters, a French detective officer and the eccentric Baron Croodle. Mr. *Buckstone,* Mr. *Charles Matthews* the younger, Mr. *Howard Paul,* Mr. *Dion Bourcicault,* and Mr. *J. Oxenford,* have successfully imitated or adapted several pieces by French dramatists. The two last-mentioned writers have also produced in collaboration the text of a highly successful opera, entitled the *Lily of Killarney,* founded on Gerald Griffin's fine novel, *the Collegians,* and set to music by the late Sir Julius Benedict. Mr. *Brough,* Mr. *Leman Rede,* Mr. *Fitzball,* Mr. *Coyne,* and Mr. *Sullivan* have likewise written several dramas, comedies or farces greeted with an ephemeral success, but of which very few seem likely to secure a permanent place on the stage or in the annals of English literature.

AMERICAN POETS AND DRAMATISTS.

In every work on English literature in the Victorian Age, an honourable place must be assigned to those American writers who during the same period have so well sustained the poetical reputation of their country. Not only are their productions English, in the sense of being composed in the English language, but some of them were originally published by their authors in London, while many others appeared simultaneously in England and America; hence no mean portion of modern American literature has been, so to speak, naturalized on English soil.

The most esteemed American poets belong to the lyrical school. Didactic poetry is less cultivated in America; and though a few poems — especially Longfellow's longer ones — have been called epics, nothing as yet has been produced in America which European critics would regard as a true epic poem. In dramatic composition, too, America has achieved but little. Hillhouse, Longfellow, Bayard Taylor, and some other poets, have no doubt written dramas, but still America cannot yet boast of a great dramatist, and the *repertoire* of the American theatres is on the whole identical with that of the English stage.

In the space at our disposal, we cannot pretend to do more than offer the reader a summary of the most noted American writers, in this department of literature, who were still writing in 1837, or have since then appeared, giving at the same time a few selected specimens from their works. We shall begin with

E. A. Poe.

The unfortunate genius, *Edgar Allan Poe*, was born in Baltimore, in January 1811. His father, David Poe, was for some years a law-student, but having made the acquaintance of a young English actress, called Elizabeth Arnold, he married her, and became an actor himself. About seven years later, they both died, within a few weeks of each other, leaving three children quite unprovided for. Edgar, the second of the family, was adopted by a wealthy and benevolent merchant, Mr. John Allan, who was married but childless. In 1816, this gentleman took young Poe with him to England, and put him to school at Stoke Newington, near London. When the lad returned to America in 1822, he for some time attended an academy in Richmond, and then went to the University at Charlottesville, where he fell into that dissipated course of life, from which he never afterwards could be reclaimed. Manners at Charlottesville were generally dissolute, but of all the students Poe was the wildest and the most reckless. Being desirous of embracing the military profession, he was sent by his kind patron, Mr. Allan, to West Point Academy, but though at first a favourite with the professors and the other cadets, he soon renewed his irregularities, and ten months after his matriculation was expelled from the institution. In the mean time Mr. Allan had re-married, and when he died in 1834, he left three children to inherit his property, and bequeathed nothing to his former *protégé*. From 1834 to 1837 Poe wrote for the *Southern Literary Messenger* in Richmond, and during this time he married his cousin, Virginia Klemm. She was as poor as himself, but he was warmly attached to her, and by her patience and tenderness she exercised a salutary influence on her unfortunate husband till her death in 1846. The poet has immortalized her in his beautiful poem, *Annabel Lee*. Three years later — on the 7th Oct. 1849, Poe died of *delirium tremens* in a Baltimore hospital, at the age of thirty-eight.

The most characteristic of Poe's poems is probably the gloomy and fantastic *Raven*, though we confess we have never read it with pleasure. Sitting alone in his chamber in "bleak December," the poet hears a tapping at his window lattice, and on opening the shutter there steps in "a stately Raven of *the saintly days of yore.*" This "ebony bird" perches on a bust of Pallas, and in reply to the questions or thoughts of his host, croaks forth the same ill-omened reply, "Nevermore!" Passing over these sombre verses, we select as our specimens one of Poe's most varied and powerful poems, and the sweet and tender lines to which we have already alluded; both of which have been set to music by Balfe, the composer of *the Bohemian Girl*.

THE BELLS.

I.

Hear the sledges with the bells —
Silver bells!
What a world of merriment their melody foretells!
How they tinkle, tinkle, tinkle,
In the icy air of night!
While the stars that oversprinkle
All the heavens, seem to twinkle
With a crystalline delight;
Keeping time, time, time,
In a sort of Runic rhyme,
To the tintinnabulation that so musically wells
From the bells, bells, bells, bells,
Bells, bells, bells —
From the jingling and the tinkling of the bells.

II.

Hear the mellow wedding bells,
Golden bells!
What a world of happiness their harmony foretells!
Through the balmy air of night
How they ring out their delight!
From the molten-golden notes
And all in tune,
What a liquid ditty floats
To the turtle-dove that listens while she gloats
On the moon!

Oh, from out the sounding cells,
What a gush of euphony voluptuously wells!
How it swells
How it dwells
On the Future! how it tells
Of the rapture that impels
To the swinging and the ringing
Of the bells, bells, bells,
Of the bells, bells, bells, bells,
Bells, bells, bells —
To the rhyming and the chiming of the bells!

III.

Hear the loud alarum bells —
Brazen bells!
What a tale of terror now their turbulency tells!
In the startled ear of night
How they scream out their affright!
Too much horrified to speak,
They can only shriek, shriek,
Out of tune,
In a clamorous appealing to the mercy of the fire,
In a mad expostulation with the mad and frantic fire
Leaping higher, higher, higher,
With a desperate desire,
And a resolute endeavour
Now — now to sit or never,
By the side of the pale-faced moon.
Oh, the bells, bells, bells!
What a tale their terror tells
Of Despair!
How they clang, and clash, and roar,
What a horror they outpour
On the bosom of the palpitating air!
Yet the ear it fully knows
By the twanging,
And the clanging,
How the danger ebbs and flows;
Yet the ear distinctly tells
In the jangling,
And the wrangling,
How the danger sinks and swells,
By the sinking or the swelling in the anger of the bells —
Of the bells —
Of the bells, bells, bells, bells,
Bells, bells, bells —
In the clamour and the clangour of the bells!

IV.

Hear the tolling of the bells —
Iron bells!
What a world of solemn thought their monody compels!
In the silence of the night,
How we shiver with affright
At the melancholy menace of their tone!
For every sound that floats
From the rust within their throats
Is a groan.
And the people — ah, the people —
They that dwell up in the steeple
All alone,
And who tolling, tolling, tolling,
In that muffled monotone,
Feel a glory in so rolling
On the human heart a stone —
They are neither man nor woman —
They are neither brute nor human —
They are Ghouls:
And their king it is who tolls;
And he rolls, rolls, rolls,
Rolls
A paean from the bells!
And his merry bosom swells
With the paean of the bells!
And he dances, and he yells;
Keeping time, time, time,
In a sort of Runic rhyme
To the paean of the bells —
Of the bells:
Keeping time, time, time,
In a sort of Runic rhyme,
To the throbbing of the bells —
Of the bells, bells, bells,
To the sobbing of the bells;
Keeping time, time, time,
As he knells, knells, knells,
In a happy Runic rhyme
To the rolling of the bells —
Of the bells, bells, bells —
To the tolling of the bells,
Of the bells, bells, bells, bells,
Bells, bells, bells —
To the moaning and the groaning of the bells.

ANNABEL LEE.

It was many and many a year ago,
    In a kingdom by the sea, [1])
That a maiden there lived whom you may know
    By the name of Annabel Lee;
And this maiden she lived with no other thought
    Than to love and be loved by me.

I was a child and she was a child,
    In this kingdom by the sea:
But we loved with a love that was more than love —
    I and my Annabel Lee;
With a love that the winged seraphs of heaven
    Coveted her and me.

And this was the reason that, long ago,
    In this kingdom by the sea,
A wind blew out of a cloud, chilling
    My beautiful Annabel Lee;
So that her high-born kinsmen came
    And bore her away from me,
To shut her up in a sepulchre
    In this kingdom by the sea.

The angels, not half so happy in heaven,
    Went envying her and me —
Yes! — that was the reason (as all men know,
    In this kingdom by the sea)
That the wind came out of the cloud by night,
    Chilling and killing my Annabel Lee.

But our love it was stronger by far than the love
    Of those who were older than we —
    Of many far wiser than we —
And neither the angels in heaven above,
    Nor the demons down under the sea,
Can ever dissever my soul from the soul
    Of the beautiful Annabel Lee.

For the moon never beams, without bringing me dreams
    Of the beautiful Annabel Lee;
And the stars never rise, but I feel the bright eyes
    Of the beautiful Annabel Lee;
And so, all the night-tide, I lie down by the side
Of my darling — my darling — my life and my bride,
    In the sepulchre there by the sea,
    In her tomb by the sounding sea.

---

[1]) Virginia, or "the Old Dominion," originally colonized under the auspices of Queen Elizabeth, is here poetically called "a kingdom by the sea."

Notwithstanding his infirmities, Poe had many warm and staunch friends, among whom were Mr. N. P. Willis (author of *Pencillings by the Way)*, and the poetess, Mrs. Frances Osgood. This lady said of him. in a letter to a friend, "I can sincerely say, that although I have frequently heard of aberrations on his part from 'the straight and narrow path,' I have never seen him otherwise than gentle, generous, well-bred. and fastidiously refined. To a sensitive and delicately nurtured woman, there was a peculiar and irresistible charm in the chivalric, graceful, and almost tender reverence with which he invariably approached all women who won his respect. It was this which first commanded and afterwards retained my regard for him."

H. R. Dana.

Henry Richard Dana (1787—1879), born at Cambridge, Massachusetts, is the author of *the Buccaneer* and other poems. The hero of the *Buccaneer* is a certain Matthew Lee, whose evil conscience continually conjures up before his mental vision the phantoms of the victims of his avarice and cruelty. In all probability the poem was suggested by Coleridge's *Ancient Mariner,* to which it has many points of resemblance. At the end of the poem the pirate is carried away by a spectre horse, which he feels himself mysteriously impelled to bestride, and from whose nostrils "streams a deathly light," which

> — lights the sea around their track —
> The curling comb and dark steel wave;
> There yet sits Lee the spectre's back —
> Gone! gone! and none to save!
> They're seen no more; the night has shut them in;
> May Heaven have pity on thee, man of sin!

As a more pleasing specimen of Mr. Dana's poetical style, we shall quote his verses on

THE POWER OF THE SOUL.

Life in itself, it life to all things gives;
For whatsoe'er it looks on, that thing lives,
Becomes an acting being, ill or good;
And, grateful to its giver, tenders food
For the Soul's health, or suffering change unblest,
Pours poison down to rankle in the breast.
As is the man, e'en so it bears its part
And answers, thought to thought, and heart to heart.

Yes, man reduplicates himself. You see
In yonder lake, reflected rock and tree.
Each leaf at rest, or quivering in the air,
Now rests, now stirs, as if a breeze were there,
Sweeping the crystal depths. How perfect all!
And see those slender top-boughs rise and fall;
The double strips of silvery sand unite
Above, below, each grain distinct and bright.
— Thou bird, that seek'st thy food upon that bough,
Peck not alone; that bird below, as thou,
Is busy after food, and happy too;
— They're gone! Both, pleased, away together flew.

And see we thus sent up, rock, sand, and wood,
Life, joy, and motion, from the sleepy flood?
The world, O man, is like that flood to thee:
Turn where thou wilt, thyself in all things see
Reflected back. As drives the blinding sand
Round Egypt's piles, where'er thou tak'st thy stand,
If that thy heart be barren, there will sweep
The drifting waste, like waves along the deep,
Fill up the vale, and choke the laughing streams
That run by grass and brake, with dancing beams.
Sear the fresh woods, and from thy heavy eye
Veil the wide-shifting glories of the sky,
And one still, sightless level make the earth,
Like thy dull lonely, joyless Soul, — a dearth.

The rill is tuneless to his ear, who feels
No harmony within; the south wind steals,
As silent as unseen, amongst the leaves.
Who has no inward beauty, none perceives.
Though all around is beautiful. Nay, more, —
In nature's calmest hour he hears the roar
Of winds and flinging waves, — puts out the light,
When high and angry passions meet in flight,
And, his own spirit into tumult hurled,
He makes a turmoil of a quiet world:

The fiends of his own bosom people air
With kindred fiends, that hunt him to despair.
Hates he his fellow-men? Why, then he deems
'Tis hate for hate. — As he, so each one seems.

Soul! fearful is thy power, which thus transforms
All things into its likeness: heaves in storms
The strong, proud sea, or lays it down to rest,
Like the hushed infant on its mother's breast, —
Which gives each outward circumstance its hue,
And shapes all others' acts and thoughts anew,
That so, they joy, or love, or hate impart,
As joy, love, hate, holds rule within the heart.

O. W. Holmes.

Oliver Wendell Holmes was born at Cambridge, Massachusetts, in 1809. After studying first law and then medicine at Harvard University, he visited Europe in 1833. In 1840 he obtained the chair of anatomy and physiology in Cambridge. "His fancy teems," says the *North-American Review*, "with bright and appropriate images, and these are woven into his plan usually with exquisite finish and grace. His artistic merits are very great; his versification is never slovenly, nor his diction meagre or coarse; and many of his shorter pieces are inwrought with so much fire and imagination, as to rank among our best lyrics." Between 1843 and 1850 Mr. Holmes published three poems, respectively entitled *Terpsichore, Urania,* and *Astraea, the Balance of Allusions;* and in 1858 he produced a series of agreeable and humorous essays, with the title, *the Autocrat of the Breakfast Table.* Of his more serious style of poetry we give two samples, the first of which was written at a time when it was proposed to break up and sell the materials of the old frigate *Constitution.*

OLD IRONSIDES.

Ay, tear her tatter'd ensign down!
 Long has it waved on high;
And many an eye has danced to see
 That banner in the sky;

Beneath it rung the battle shout,
  And burst the cannon's roar; —
The meteor of the ocean air
  Shall sweep the clouds no more!

Her deck, — once red with heroes' blood,
  Where knelt the vanquished foe,
When winds were hurrying o'er the flood,
  And waves were white below, —
No more shall feel the victor's tread
  Or know the conquer'd knee;
The harpies of the shore shall pluck
  The eagle of the sea!

Oh! better that her shatter'd hulk
  Should sink beneath the wave;
Her thunders shook the mighty deep,
  And there should be her grave:
Nail to the mast her holy flag,
  Set every threadbare sail;
And give her to the god of storms,
  The lightning and the gale!

THE STEAMBOAT.

See how yon flaming herald treads
  The ridged and rolling waves,
As crashing o'er their crested heads,
  She bows her surly slaves!
With foam before and fire behind,
  She rends the clinging sea,
That flies before the roaring wind,
  Beneath her hissing lee.

The morning spray, like sea-born flowers,
  With heap'd and glistening bells,
Falls round her fast in ringing showers,
  With every wave that swells;
And, flaming o'er the midnight deep,
  In lurid fringes thrown,
The living gems of ocean sweep
  Along her flashing zone.

With clashing wheel, and lifted keel,
  And smoking torch on high,
When winds are loud, and billows reel
  She thunders foaming by!
When seas are silent and serene,
  With even beam she glides,
The sunshine glimmering through the green
  That skirts her gleaming sides.

Now, like a wild nymph, far apart
  She veils her shadowy form,
The beating of her restless heart
  Still sounding through the storm;
Now answers, like a worthy dame,
  The reddening surges o'er,
With flying scarf of spargled flame,
  The Pharos of the shore.

To-night yon pilot shall not sleep,
  Who trims his narrow'd sail;
To-night yon frigate scarce shall keep
  Her broad breast to the gale;
And many a foresail scoop'd and strain'd,
  Shall break from yard and stay
Before this smoky wreath has stain'd
  The rising mist of day.

Hark! hark! I hear yon whistling shroud,
  I see yon quivering mast;
The black throat of the hunted cloud
  Is panting forth the blast!
An hour, and whirl'd like winnowing chaff,
  The giant surge shall fling
His tresses o'er yon pennon-staff,
  White as the sea-bird's wing.

Yet rest, ye wanderers of the deep;
  Nor wind nor wave shall tire
Those fleshless arms, whose pulses leap
  With floods of living fire;
Sleep on — and when the morning light
  Streams o'er the shining bay,
Oh, think of those for whom the night
  Shall never wake in day!

To his lighter style belong the verses:

OUR YANKEE GIRLS.

Let greener lands and bluer skies,
  If such the wide world shows,
With fairer cheeks and brighter eyes
  Match us the star and rose:
The winds that lift the Georgian's veil
  Or wave Circassia's curls
Waft to their shores the sultan's sail, —
  Who buys our Yankee girls?

The gay grisette, whose fingers touch
  Love's thousands chords so well;
The dark Italian, loving much,
  But more than one can tell;
And England's fair-haired, blue-eyed dame,
  Who binds her brow with pearls; —
Ye, who have seen them, can they shame
  Our own sweet Yankee girls?

And what if court or castle vaunt
  Its children loftier born?
Who heeds the silken tassel's flaunt
  Beside the golden corn?
They ask not for the dainty toil
  Of ribboned knights and earls,
The daughters of the virgin soil,
  Our free-born Yankee girls!

By every hill whose stately pines
  Wave their dark arms above
The home where some fair being shines,
  To warm the wilds with love;
From barest rock to bleakest shore
  Where farthest sail unfurls.
That stars and stripes are streaming o'er —
  God bless our Yankee girls!

Of Holmes's *humorous* poetry, the following is a good specimen:

CONTENTMENT.

Little I ask; my wants are few;
  I only wish a hut of stone,
(A very plain brown stone will do),
  That I may call my own; —
And close at hand is such a one,
In yonder street that fronts the sun.

Plain food is quite enough for me;
  Three courses are as good as ten;
If Nature can subsist on three,
  Thank Heaven for three Amen!
I always thought cold victual nice, —
My choice would be vanilla-ice.

I care not much for gold or land; —
  Give me a mortgage here and there,
Some good bank-stock, some note of hand,[1])
  Or trifling railroad-share, —

—————

[1]) In German, Schuldschein.

I only ask that Fortune send
A little more than I shall spend.

Honours are silly toys, I know,
  And titles are but empty names;
I would, p e r h a p s, be Plenipo —
  But only near St. James;[1]
I'm very sure I should not care
To fill our Gubernator's chair. [2]

Jewels are baubles; 'tis a sin
  To care for such unfruitful things;
One good-sized diamond in a pin,
  Some, not so large, in rings,
A ruby, and a pearl, or so,
Will do for me; I laugh at show.

My dame should dress in cheap attire
  (Good, heavy silks are never dear);
I own perhaps I *might* desire
  Some shawls of true Cashmere, —
Some marrowy crapes of China silk,
Like wrinkled skins on scalded milk.

Wealth's wasteful tricks I will not learn,
  Nor ape the glittering upstart fool;
Shall not carved tables serve my turn,
  But a l l must be of buhl?[3]
Give grasping pomp its double care, —
I ask but o n e recumbent chair.

Thus humble let me live and die,
  Nor long for Midas' golden touch;
If Heaven more generous gifts deny,
  I shall not miss them m u c h, —
Too grateful for the blessing lent
Of simple tastes and mind content!

---

[1] Plenipotentiary to the Court of St. James (the English Court); one of the highest and best paid of American diplomatic posts.
[2] The president of the United States has only the moderate yearly salary of 25,000 dollars, though his expenditure is necessarily large.
[3] Buhl-work, introduced by the Frenchman, Charles Boule, who died in 1732, is ebony or tortoise-shell, ingeniously inlaid with figures mostly of gold or brass.

Bayard Taylor.

Mr. *Bayard Taylor* (1825 — 1878), for some years before his death American ambassador in Berlin, wrote *Poems and Ballads*, *Poems of the Orient*, and several other works in both prose and poetry, but his principal glory will always be his unequalled translation of Goethe's *Faust*, of which the first part appeared in the autumn of 1870, and the second part in the spring of 1871.

Poetical translation is never easy, and previous translators of *Faust*, while indulging in a certain periphrastic diffuseness, and allowing themselves considerable latitude both in diction and metre, found they had undertaken a very serious task. But Mr. Taylor aspired to render the exact meaning, while he preserved the form and rhythm of the original. "It is useless to say," he remarks, "that the naked meaning is independent of the form; on the contrary, the form contributes essentially to the fulness of the meaning." Describing the method he had followed in his translation, he says: "The feminine and dactylic rhymes, which have been for the most part omitted by all metrical translators, except Mr. Brooks, are indispensable. The characteristic tone of many passages would be nearly lost without them. They give spirit and grace to the dialogue, point to the aphoristic portions (especially in the second part), and an even-changing music to the lyrical passages. The English language, though not so rich as the German in such rhymes, is less deficient than is generally supposed. The difficulty to be overcome is one of construction rather than of the vocabulary." We regret that our limited space forbids us to quote largely from this admirable translation, but we give a few passages as specimens, merely reminding the reader how difficult it is to judge of such a work by fragments. The two last stanzes of the *Dedication* (Sie hören nicht die folgenden Gesänge, etc.) are rendered by Mr. Taylor as follows:

> They hear no longer these succeeding measures,
> The souls to whom my earlier songs I sang:
> Dispersed the friendly troop with all its pleasures,
> And still, alas, the echoes first that rang!
> I bring the unknown multitude my treasures;
> Their very plaudits give my heart a pang,
> And those beside, whose joy my song so flattered,
> If still they live, wide through the world are scattered.
>
> And grasps me now a long-unwonted yearning
> For that serene and solemn Spirit-land:
> My song, to faint Aeolian murmurs turning,
> Sways like a harp-string by the breezes fanned.
> I thrill and tremble; tear on tear is burning,
> And the stern heart is tenderly unmanned.
> What I possess, I see far distant lying,
> And what I lost grows real and undying.

We pass on to the passage beginning with: Nun komm' herab, krystallne reine Schale, when Faustus resolves to put an end to his existence:

> And now come down, thou cup of crystal clearest!
> Fresh from thine ancient cover thou appearest,
> So many years forgotten to my thought!
> Thou shon'st at old ancestral banquets cheery, —
> The solemn guests thou madest merry,
> When one thy wassail to the other brought.
> The rich and skilful figures o'er thee wrought,
> The drinker's duty, rhyme-wise to explain them,
> Or in one breath below the mark to drain them,
> From many a night of youth my memory caught.
> Now to a neighbour shall I pass thee never,
> Nor on thy curious art to test my wit endeavour;
> Here is a juice whence sleep is swiftly born.
> It fills with browner flood thy crystal hollow;
> I chose, prepared it; thus I follow, —
> With all my soul the final drink I swallow,
> A solemn festal cup, a greeting to the morn!

The unversified scene, near the end of the first part, in which Faustus bitterly reproaches Mephistopheles with concealing from him the imprisonment and misery of Margaret, is finely translated in a rhythmical prose which approaches equally near the original. To the cynical reply of Mephistopheles: Sie ist die erste nicht, Faustus makes the indignant rejoinder (Hund, abscheuliches Unthier!):

Dog! abominable monster! Transform him, thou Infinite Spirit! transform the reptile again into his dog-shape, in which it pleased him often at night to scamper on before me, to roll himself at the feet of the unsuspecting wanderer, and hang upon his shoulders when he fell! Transform him again into his favourite likeness, that he may crawl upon his belly in the dust before me, — that I may trample him, the outlawed, under foot! Not the first! O woe! woe, which no human soul can grasp, that more than one being should sink into the depths of this misery, — that the first, in its writhing death-agony under the eyes of the Eternal Forgiver, did not expiate the guilt of all others! The misery of this single one pierces to the very marrow of my life; and thou art calmly grinning at the fate of thousands!

We give Mr. Taylor's translation of the König in Thule:

There was a King in Thule,
  Was faithful till the grave,
To whom his mistress, dying,
  A golden goblet gave.

He sat at the royal banquet
  With his knights of high degree;
In the lofty hall of his fathers
  In the castle by the sea.

Nought was to him more precious;
  He drained it at every bout:
His eyes with tears ran over
  As oft as he drank thereout.

There stood the old carouser,
  And drank the last life-glow;
And hurled the hallowed goblet
  Into the tide below.

When came his time of dying,
  The towns in his lands he told;
Nought else to his heir denying
  Except the goblet of gold.

He saw it plunging and filling,
  And sinking deep in the sea;
Then fell his eyelids for ever,
  And never more drank he!

In the still more arduous task of translating the second part of *Faust*, Mr. Taylor has acquitted himself with equal honour and success.

Three poems in drama-form have been written by Mr. Bayard Taylor: *the Prophet, the Masque of the Gods,* and *Prince Deukalion;* but they were never designed for representation on the stage.

W. C. Bryant.

William Cullen Bryant (1794 — 1879), one of the finest of the American poets, was the son of a physician in Cummington, a small place in Massachusetts. In his sixteenth year he entered Williams-College, and in 1815 settled in Great-Barrington, as a solicitor. But he soon gave up the uncongenial practice of the law, went to New-York, and made literature his profession. His most successful poems are: *Thanatopsis* (the View of Death), written in his eighteenth year; the *Ages*, a poem in which he traces the gradual intellectual development of the human race; the *Forest Hymn, Song of the Stars*, the *Fountain*, and the *Lapse of Time*. Bryant particularly excels in painting American scenery; and his poetry is elegant, forcible, and remarkably lucid. Passing over such of his verses as have been often re-printed, and are well known, we select as a specimen his exquisite lines on

THE ANTIQUITY OF FREEDOM.

Here are old trees, tall oaks and gnarled pines,
That stream with gray-green mosses; here the ground
Was never trenched by spade; and flowers spring up
Unsown, and die ungathered. It is sweet
To linger here, among the flitting birds,
And leaping squirrels, wandering brooks, and winds
That shake the leaves, and scatter, as they pass,
A fragrance from the cedars, thickly set
With pale blue berries. In these peaceful shades, —
Peaceful, unpruned, immeasurably old, —
My thoughts go up the long dim path of years,
Back to the earliest days of Liberty.

O Freedom! thou art not, as poets dream,
A fair young girl, with light and delicate limbs,
And wavy tresses gushing from the cap
With which the Roman master crowned his slave
When he took off the gyves. A bearded man,
Armed to the teeth, art thou; one mailed hand
Grasps the broad shield, and one the sword; thy brow,
Glorious in beauty though it be, is scarred
With tokens of old wars; thy massive limbs
Are long with struggling. Power at thee has launched
His bolts, and with his lightnings smitten thee;
They could not quench the life thou hast from heaven.
Merciless power has dug thy dungeon deep,
And his swart armorers, by a thousand fires,
Have forged thy chain; yet, while he deems thee bound,
The links are shivered, and the prison walls
Fall outward; terribly thou springest forth,
As springs the flame above a burning pile,
And shoutest to the nations, who return
Thy shoutings, while the pale oppressor flies.

Thy birthright was not given by human hands:
Thou wert twin-born with man. In pleasant fields,
While yet our race was few, thou sat'st with him,
To tend the quiet flock and watch the stars,
And teach the reed to utter simple airs.
Thou by his side, amid the tangled wood,
Didst war upon the panther and the wolf,
His only foes; and thou with him didst draw
The earliest furrows on the mountain side,
Soft with the deluge. Tyranny himself,
Thy enemy, although of reverend look,
Hoary with many years, and far obeyed,
Is later born than thou; and as he meets
The grave defiance of thine elder eye,
The usurper trembles in his fastnesses.

                      Oh! not yet
May'st thou unbrace thy corselet, nor lay by
Thy sword; nor yet, O Freedom! close thy lids
In slumber; for thine enemy never sleeps,
And thou must watch and combat till the day
Of the new earth and heaven. But wouldst thou rest
A while from tumult and the frauds of men,
These old and friendly solitudes invite
Thy visit. They, while yet the forest-trees
Were young upon the unviolated earth,
And yet the moss-stains on the rock were new,
Beheld thy glorious childhood, and rejoiced.

H. W. Longfellow.

Henry Wadsworth Longfellow (1807—1882), the best
known in Europe of all the American poets, was born
at Portland, in the State of Maine. He studied at
Bowdoin College, in which, a few years later, he
obtained the chair of modern languages; but on the
resignation of Mr. Ticknor, in 1835, he accepted the
same professorship in Harvard College, Cambridge. His
principal poetical works are: *Voices of the Night* (1839),
Ballads and other Poems (1841), *Poems on Slavery* (1842),
the Spanish Student, a play (1843), *Evangeline* (1847),
the Golden Legend (1851), *the Song of Hiawatha* (1855),
Miles Standish (1858), and *Tales of a Wayside Inn* (1863).
His numerous translations from the Spanish, Italian,

German, Danish, and other European languages, are generally excellent, though his Dante is not looked on as a success.

Three of Longfellow's poems have been dignified with the name of epics: *Evangeline, Hiawatha,* and *Miles Standish. Evangeline* is the story of the destruction by British and colonial troops, in war-time, of a village in Acadia, or Nova Scotia, inhabited by French emigrants. The incidents and characters are of course fictitious, and the original facts greatly exaggerated, to serve the purposes of poetry. Much finer and more thriving villages have been destroyed in many a European war than the group of rude log-huts known in their time as Grand-Pré. On the publication of the poem, it was regretted, in England, that Longfellow should have chosen the cumbrous hexameter measure, which Southey had already attempted, with very ill success, to adapt to English poetry. For a page or two, the hexameter sounds not amiss, and in the following lines it is pleasing enough:

This is the forest primeval.
The murmuring pines and the hemlocks
Bearded with moss, and in garments green, indistinct in the twilight,
Stand like Druids of old, with voices sad and prophetic
Stand like harpers hoar, with beards that rest on their bosoms.
Loud from its rocky caverns, the deep-voiced neighbouring ocean
Speaks, and in accents disconsolate answers the wail of the forest;

in so long a poem as *Evangeline,* however, this measure makes reading a real labour. The poem abounds in beauties; and we shall rarely find a sentiment and a simile so aptly joined, and so happily expressed, as in the passage we next quote:

Talk not of wasted affection, affection never was wasted;
If it enrich not the heart of another, its waters, returning
Back to their springs, like the rain, shall fill them full of refreshment;
That which the fountain sends forth returns again to the fountain.
Patience, accomplish thy labour; accomplish thy work of affection!
Sorrow and silence are strong, and patient endurance is godlike.

The poem concludes with a picture of the final resting-place of the two lovers in a small churchyard in the city of "Penn the apostle":

Daily the tides of life go ebbing and flowing beside them,
Thousands of throbbing hearts, where theirs are at rest for ever,
Thousands of aching brains, where theirs no longer are busy,
Thousands of toiling hands, where theirs have ceased from their labours,
Thousands of weary feet, where theirs have ceased from their journey.

"The *Song of Hiawatha*" — says the author, "this Indian Edda, if I may so call it — is founded on a tradition prevalent among the North-American Indians of a personage of miraculous birth, who was sent among them to clear their rivers, forests, and fishing-grounds, and to teach them the arts of peace. The scene of the poem is among the Ojibways, on the northern shore of Lake Superior." Such is the statement of the poet in his introduction, but in the poem itself he particularizes more fully the sources of the legend:

Should you ask me, whence these stories?
Whence these legends and traditions
With the odours of the forest
With the dew and damp of meadows,
With the curling smoke of wigwams,
With the rushing of great rivers,
With their frequent repetitions,
And their wild reverberations,
As of thunder in the mountain?
I should answer. I should tell you,
"From the forests and the prairies,
From the great lakes of the Northland,
From the land of the Ojibways,
From the land of the Dacotahs,
From the mountains, moors, and fenlands,
Where the heron, the Shuh-shuh-gah,
Feeds among the reeds and rushes.
I repeat them as I heard them
From the lips of Nawadaha,
The musician, the sweet singer.
All the wild-fowl sung them to him
In the moorlands and the fenlands,
In the melancholy marshes;
Chetowaik, the plover, sang them,
Mahng, the loon, the wild-goose, Wawa,
The blue heron, the Shuh-shuh-gah,
And the grouse, the Mushkodasa.

A little farther on, we learn that Hiawatha was the son of Wenonah, the daughter of Nokomis, who was daughter of the moon, and that his father was Mudjekeewis, the West-Wind, a very fickle husband, as it appears:

> Thus was born my Hiawatha,
> Thus was born the child of wonder;
> But the daughter of Nokomis,
> Hiawatha's gentle mother,
> In her anguish died deserted
> By the West-Wind, false and faithless,
> By the heartless Mudjekeewis.

Hiawatha was consequently reared by his grandmother, Nokomis, whose abode is thus described to us:

> By the shores of Gitche Gumee,
> By the shining Big Sea-Water,
> Stood the wigwam of Nokomis,
> Daughter of the Moon, Nokomis.
> Dark behind it rose the forest,
> Rose the black and gloomy pine-trees,
> Rose the firs with cones upon them;
> Bright before it beat the water,
> Beat the clear and sunny water,
> Beat the shining Big Sea-Water.

Hiawatha becomes a hunter, a warrior, and a traveller; and in one of his adventures he meets with Minnehaha, or Laughing Water, who awakens new feelings in his bosom, and leads him into new ponderings:

> "As unto the bow the cord is,
> So unto the man is woman;
> Though she bends him, she obeys him,
> Though she draws him, yet she follows."

> Thus the youthful Hiawatha
> Said within himself and pondered,
> Much perplexed with various feelings,
> Listless, longing, hoping, fearing,
> Dreaming still of Minnehaha,
> Of the lovely Laughing Water
> In the land of the Dacotahs.

Hiawatha marries Minnehaha, is converted to Christianity by the "Black Robe" or missionary, and at last sails away in a boat, like King Arthur, and is heard of no more:

> Westward, westward Hiawatha
> Sailed into the fiery sunset,
> Sailed into the purple vapours,
> Sailed into the dusk of evening.

On Hiawatha's childhood, his visit to Mudjekeewis, his fasting, his friends, his sailing, his fishing, his wooing, his combat with the great magician, Pearl-Feather, and his wedding-feast, we have no space to dwell. About the merits of the poem opinions are greatly divided. While it is cried up by some as the "great epic of America," it has been ridiculed and drolly parodied by others. It is said, that in the first year of its publication no less than thirty editions were sold; but it is impossible to decide whether curiosity or admiration had the greater share in its commercial success, for every one admitted that it was a most remarkable poem.

The Courtship of Miles Standish, the epic of New England, as it has been called, is again a poem in hexameters: a measure which in such a simple every-day story seems still more unsuitable than in *Evangeline.* We are at once introduced to the hero:

In the Old Colony days, in Plymouth, the land of the Pilgrims,
To and fro in a room of his simple and primitive dwelling
Clad in doublet and hose, and boots of Cordovan leather,
Strode, with a martial air, Miles Standish, the Puritan captain.

The soldier loves a maiden, called Priscilla, but not possessing himself the gift of eloquence, he seeks, and readily obtains the advocacy of his trusted friend, John Alden. Still Miles Standish's suit does not prosper, and one day, when Alden is unusually earnest and pressing, Priscilla, who has been compared to Anne Page, pettishly asks him, why he does not speak for himself. This question, or rather hint, is an unexpected revelation for Alden, and the end of the matter is, that he marries Priscilla himself. Miles Standish is, of course, at first highly incensed, but in time, some accidental circumstances aiding, he consents to forgive and forget. It is interesting to know that Miles Standish really existed, and that the poem is founded on fact.

Longfellow's *Tales of a Wayside Inn* are written in imitation of Chaucer's Canterbury Tales. They consist of seven stories in all; namely: 1. the Landlord's Tale; 2. the Student's Tale (Boccaccio's *Falcon*); 3. the Spanish Jew's Tale; 4. the Sicilian's Tale; 5. the

Musician's Tale (the Saga of King Olaf); 6. the Theologian's Tale (Torquemada); 7. the Poet's Tale (the Birds of Killingworth). As in Chaucer, the story-tellers meet accidentally

One Autumn evening in Sudbury town (in Massachusetts.)

The tales are interesting, and the individuality of the different personages is well maintained.

Of Longfellow's dramas, *the Spanish Student*, in three acts, seems to us the only one at all fitted for the stage. The hero is the student Victorian, and the heroine the gypsy girl, Preciosa. The dialogue is lively, the situations ingenious, and the interest well sustained till the last moment. In *the Golden Legend* we at once recognise an imitation of Goethe's *Faust*. Prince Henry corresponds pretty closely to *Faust* himself; Elise, in many if not in all respects, resembles Margaret, and Lucifer is Mephistopheles. The piece is in six parts, and the scene is successively Strasburgh, Genoa, Devil's Bridge, and some other places. Between the third and the fourth part a miracle play, *the Nativity,* is introduced: and there is an epilogue, with the two recording angels, the respective registrars of good and evil deeds, ascending to heaven. It is the most ambitious, but the most obscure of all that Longfellow has written, and we think he acted injudiciously in provoking a comparison with Goethe. In *the New England Tragedies,* which concern the persecutions of the Quakers and the cruel prosecution of supposed witches by the Puritan settlers in the seventeenth century, he is more at home. Still, as an English critical writer observes, in none of these pieces "has he been able to fulfil the main condition of dramatic interest;" in other words, to create "such entire individual personalities, each with an independent capability of existence and with a spring of action in himself, as the drama essentially requires."

After all, it must be admitted, that Longfellow's genius shines with the greatest brilliancy in his shorter poems and lyrical pieces. The subjoined selections may, we believe, be classed among the very finest of his compositions:

FOOTSTEPS OF ANGELS.

When the hours of Day are numbered,
  And the Voices of the Night
Wake the better soul that slumbered,
  To a holy, calm delight;

Ere the evening lamps are lighted,
  And, like phantoms grim and tall,
Shadows from the fitful fire-light
  Dance upon the parlour wall;

Then the forms of the departed
  Enter at the open door;
The beloved, the true-hearted,
  Come to visit me once more.

He the young and strong, who cherished
  Noble longings for the strife
By the road-side fell and perished,
  Weary with the march of life!

They, the holy ones and weakly,
  Who the cross of suffering bore,
Folded their pale hands so meekly,
  Spake with us on earth no more!

And with them the Being beauteous,
  Who unto my youth was given
More than all things else to love us,
  And is now a saint in heaven.

With a slow and noiseless footstep
  Comes that messenger divine,
Takes the vacant chair beside me,
  Lays her gentle hand on mine.

And she sits and gazes on me
  With those deep and tender eyes,
Like the stars, so still and saintlike,
  Looking downward from the skies.

Uttered not, yet comprehended,
  Is the spirit's voiceless prayer,
Soft rebukes, in blessings ended,
  Breathing from her lips of air.

Oh, though oft depressed and lonely,
  All my fears are laid aside;
If I but remember only
  Such as these have lived and died!

WRITTEN IN ITALY.

Bright star! whose soft familiar ray,
  In colder climes and gloomier skies,
I've watched so oft when closing day
  Had tinged the west with crimson dyes;

Perhaps to-night some friend I love,
  Beyond the deep, the distant sea,
Will gaze upon thy path above,
  And give one lingering thought to me.

THE LADDER OF ST. AUGUSTINE.

Saint Augustine! well hast thou said,
  That of our vices we can frame
A ladder, if we will but tread
  Beneath our feet each deed of shame!

All common things — each day's events,
  That with the hour begin and end;
Our pleasures and our discontents
  Are rounds by which we may ascend.

The low desire, the base design,
  That makes another's virtues less;
The revel of the giddy wine,
  And all occasions of excess

The longing for ignoble things,
  The strife for triumph more than truth,
The hardening of the heart, that brings
  Irreverence for the dreams of youth!

All thoughts of ill — all evil deeds,
  That have their root in thoughts of ill,
Whatever hinders or impedes
  The action of the nobler will!

All these must first be trampled down
  Beneath our feet, if we would gain
In the bright field of fair renown
  The right of eminent domain!

We have not wings, we cannot soar
  But we have feet to scale and climb
By slow degrees — by more and more —
  The cloudy summits of our time.

The mighty pyramids of stone
  That wedge-like cleave the desert airs,
When nearer seen and better known,
  Are but gigantic flights of stairs.

The distant mountains that uprear
  Their frowning foreheads to the skies
Are crossed by pathways that appear
  As we to higher levels rise.

The heights by great men reached and kept,
  Were not attained by sudden flight;
But they, while their companions slept,
  Were toiling upward in the night.

Standing on what too long we bore
  With shoulders bent and downcast eyes,
We may discern, unseen before,
  A path to higher destinies.

Nor deem the irrevocable past
  As wholly wasted, wholly vain,
If rising on its wrecks at last,
  To something nobler we attain.

TRUTH.

O holy and eternal truth! Thou art
  An emanation of the Eternal Mind!
A glorious attribute, — a noble part
  Of uncreated being! Who can find,
By diligent searching who can find thee.
The Incomprehensible, — the Deity!

The human mind is a reflection caught
  From thee, a trembling shadow of thy ray.
Thy glory beams around us, but the thought
  That heavenward wings its daring flight away,
Returns to where its flight was first begun
Blinded and beneath the noonday sun.

The soul of man, though sighing after thee,
  Hath never known thee, saving as it knows
. The stars of heaven, whose glorious light we see —
  The sun, whose radiance dazzles as it glows;
Something, that is beyond us, and above
The reach of human power, though not of human love.

Vainly Philosophy may strive to teach
      The secret of thy being. Its faint ray
Misguides our steps. Beyond the utmost reach
      Of its untiring wing, the eternal day
Of truth is shining on the longing eye
Distant, — unchanged, — changeless, pure and high!

And yet thou hast not left thyself without
      A revelation. All we feel and see
Within us and around, forbids the doubt,
      Yet speaks so darkly and mysteriously
Of what we are, and shall be evermore,
We doubt, and yet believe, and tremble and adore.

THE LIGHT OF STARS.

The night is come, but not too soon,
    And sinking silently,
All silently, the little moon
    Drops down behind the sky.

There is no light in earth or heaven
    But the cold light of stars;
And the first watch of night is given
    To the red planet Mars.

Is it the tender star of love?
    The star of love and dreams?
Oh, no! from that blue tent above
    A hero's armour gleams.

And earnest thoughts within me rise
    When I behold afar
Suspended in the evening skies
    The shield of that red star.

O star of strength! I see thee stand
    And smile upon my pain;
Thou beckonest with thy mailed hand,
    And I am strong again.

Within my breast there is no light
    But the cold light of stars;
I give the first watch of the night
    To the red planet Mars.

The star of the unconquered will,
    He rises in my breast,
Serene, and resolute, and still,
    And calm, and self-possessed.

And thou, too, whosoe'er thou art,
That readest this brief psalm,
As one by one thy hopes depart,
Be resolute and calm.

Oh, fear not in a world like this,
And thou shalt know ere long
Know how sublime a thing it is
To suffer and be strong.

"About Longfellow," says an American writer, "there is never any mawkish sentimentality, no versified cant, no drivelling, no diabolic gloom. His bold, broad brow catches the sunlight from the four points of heaven, and disperses it, glittering and fructifying through the homesteads of his readers. Longfellow is the healthiest, the heartiest, and the most harmonious of all the American poets."

Mrs. Osgood.

Mrs. *Frances Osgood* (Miss Locke) was born in Boston in the year 1816. In 1834 she married the painter, Mr. Osgood, and after travelling with him for some years in Europe, she returned to America in 1843, where she continued to reside till her death in 1850. She has been called "the American Hemans;" and it is true that her poems display much of the elegance and feminine delicacy of the English poetess, though, we think, with less warmth of feeling. We give two specimens of her poetry: the first entitled, *the Child playing with a Watch;* the other, an ode on a favourite horse, called *Lady Jane.*

THE CHILD PLAYING WITH A WATCH.

Art thou playing with Time in thy sweet baby-glee?
Will he pause on his pinions to frolic with thee?
Oh, show him those shadowless, innocent eyes,
That smile of bewildered and beaming surprise;
Let him look on that cheek where thy rich hair reposes,
Where dimples are playing "bopeep" with the roses:

His wrinkled brow press with light kisses and warm,
And clasp his rough neck with thy soft wreathing arm.
Perhaps thy bewitching and infantine sweetness
May win him, for once, to delay in his fleetness —
To pause, ere he rifle, relentless in flight,
A blossom so glowing of bloom and of light:
Then, then, would I keep thee, my beautiful child,
With thy blue eyes unshadowed, thy blush undefiled —
With thy innocence only to guard thee from ill;
In life's sunny dawning, a lily-bud still!
Laugh on, my own Ellen! that voice, which to me
Gives a warning so solemn, makes music for thee;
And while I at those sounds feel the idler's annoy,
Thou hear'st but the tick of the pretty gold toy;
Thou seest but a smile on the brow of the churl —
May his frown never awe thee, my own baby-girl.
And oh, may his step, as he wanders with thee,
Light and soft as thine own little fairy tread be!
While still in all seasons, in storms and fair weather,
May Time and my Ellen be playmates together.

LADY JANE.

Oh, saw ye e'er creature so queenly, so fine,
As this dainty, aërial darling of mine;
With a toss of her mane that is glossy as jet,
With a dance and a prance, and a sportive curvet
She is off — she is stepping superbly away,
Her dark, speaking eyes full of pride and of play.
Oh! she spurns the dull earth with a graceful disdain,
My fearless, my peerless, my loved Lady Jane.

Her silken ears lifted when danger is nigh,
How kindles the night in her resolute eye;
How stately she paces, as if to the sound
Of a proud, martial melody pealing around —
Now pauses at once, mid a light caracole,
To turn on her master a look full of soul —
Now, fleet, as a fairy, she speeds o'er the plain,
My dashing, my darling, my own Lady Jane.

Give her rein — let her go! like a shaft from the bow,
Like a bird on the wing she is glancing, I trow,
Light of heart, lithe of limb, with a spirit all fire
Yet swayed and subdued to my idlest desire;
Though daring, yet docile — and sportive, but true,
Her nature's the noblest that ever I knew:
Oh! she scorns the dull earth in her joyous disdain,
My beauty, my glory, my gay Lady Jane!

Charles Fenno Hoffman.

Mr. *Hoffman* was born in 1806 in the City of New York, and was admitted to practise at the bar when only twenty-one; but his natural tastes were altogether literary, and he soon began to furnish contributions to the magazines and newspapers, using a star as his signature. As a song-writer, he shares the popularity of Morris. Among his most admired poems and songs, we may instance *Moonlight on the Hudson, Love and Politics, the Myrtle and the Steel,* and the fine verses —

WHAT IS SOLITUDE?

Not in the shadowy wood,
  Not in the crag-hung glen,
Nor where the echoes brood
  In caves untrod by men;
Not by the bleak sea-shore,
  Where loitering surges break,
Not on the mountain hoar,
  Not by the breezeless lake,
Not on the desert plain,
  Where man hath never stood,
Whether on isle or main —
  Not there is solitude!

Birds are in woodland bowers,
  Voices in lonely dells,
Streams to the listening hours
  Talk in earth's secret cells;
Over the gray-ribb'd sand
  Breathe the ocean's foaming lips,
Over the still lake's strand
  The flower toward it dips;
Pluming the mountain's crest
  Life tosses in its pines;
Coursing the desert's breast,
  Life in the steed's mane shines.

Leave — if thou wouldst be lonely —
  Leave Nature for the crowd;
Seek there for one — one only —
  With kindred mind endow'd!
There — as with Nature erst
  Closely thou wouldst commune —
The deep soul-music, nursed
  In either heart, attune!

Heart-wearied, thou wilt own
Vainly that phantom woo'd,
That thou at last hast known
What is true solitude!

Elizabeth F. Ellet.

This lady, whose maiden name was Lummis, married at the age of seventeen Dr. W. H. Ellet, Professor of Chemistry in Columbia College. In 1833 she published a translation of Silvio Pellico's *Eufemia di Messina*, which was followed in 1835 by a tragedy of her own, *Teresa Contarini*, founded on Nicolini's *Antonio Foscarini*. Among her shorter poems few or none are sweeter or more touching than —

THE BURIAL.

We laid her in the hallowed place
  Beside the solemn deep,
Where the old woods by Greenwood's shore
  Keep watch o'er those who sleep:

We laid her there — the young and fair,
  The guileless, cherished one —
As if a part of life itself
  With her we loved were gone.

Like to the flowers she lived and bloomed,
  As bright, as pure as they;
And like a flower the blight had touched,
  She early passed away.

Oh, none might know her but to love,
  Nor name her but to praise,
Who only love for others knew
  Through life's brief vernal days.

Mrs. Ellet's principal prose works are: *the Characters of Schiller* (1841), and *Women of the American Revolution* (1848).

Anne Charlotte Lynch.

Miss Lynch belongs to an Irish family, her father having been a United Irishman, who emigrated to America after the failure of the Irish Rebellion in 1798. In 1841 she published in her native place, Providence, *the Rhode-Island Book*, a selection from Rhode-Island writers, including several poems by herself. Since that time she has given to the world sonnets and short poems, distinguished by their graceful style and easy flow. One of the most striking of these bears the title:

THOUGHTS IN A LIBRARY.

Speak low — tread softly through these halls;
  Here Genius lives enshrined;
Here reign, in silent majesty,
  The monarchs of the mind.

A mighty spirit-host they come,
  From every age and clime;
Above the buried wrecks of years,
  They breast the tide of Time.

And in their presence-chamber here
  They hold their regal state.
And round them throng a noble train,
  The gifted and the great.

Oh, child of Earth! when round thy path
  The storms of life arise,
And when thy brothers pass thee by
  With stern, unloving eyes —

Here shall the poets chant for thee
  Their sweetest, loftiest lays;
And prophets wait to guide thy steps
  In wisdom's pleasant ways.

Come, with these God-anointed kings
  Be thou companion here;
And in the mighty realm of mind
  Thou shalt go forth a peer.

J. G. Percival.

James Gates Percival was born in 1795 at a small place, called Berlin, in Connecticut. He has written *Prometheus*, the *Prevalence of Poetry, Consumption, Morning among the Hills*, and other poems, besides a tragedy called *Zamor*. Of poetry be elegantly says:

> The world is full of poetry — the air
> Is living with its spirit; and the waves
> Dance to the music of its melodies,
> And sparkle in its brightness. Earth is veiled
> And mantled with its beauty; and the walls
> That close the universe with crystal in
> Are eloquent with voices that proclaim
> The unseen glories of immensity
> In harmonies too perfect and too high
> For aught but beings of celestial mould,
> And speak to man in one eternal hymn
> Unfading beauty and unyielding power.

Mr. Percival died in 1857.

George Morris.

General Morris (born, according to Griswold, in New York, in the year 1800) is hardly less popular, as a song-writer, in England than in America. In 1823 he founded the *New York Mirror*, in conjunction with Mr. Samuel Woodworth. Among his numerous poetical effusions we select one, which is as yet but little known in Europe:

WOMAN.

> Ah, woman! — in this world of ours,
>   What boon can be compared to thee?
> How slow would drag life's weary hours
> Though man's proud brow were bound with flowers,
>   And his the wealth of land and sea,
> If destined to exist alone
> And ne'er call woman's heart is own!

My mother! at that holy name
  Within my bosom there's a gush
Of feeling which no time can tame,
A feeling which for years of fame
  I would not, could not crush!
And sisters! ye are dear as life
But when I look upon my wife
  My heart-blood gives a sudden rush, —
And all my fond affections blend
In mother, sisters, wife and friend!

Yes, woman's love is free from guile,
  And pure as bright Aurora's ray.
The heart will melt before her smile,
  And base-born passions fade away!
Were I the monarch of the earth,
  Or master of the swelling sea,
I would not estimate their worth,
  Dear woman, half the price of thee.

Emily Judson.

Mrs. *Judson* is still better known under her *nom de plume* of Fanny Forester. In 1846 she married the missionary, Mr. Judson, and accompanied him to Burmah. Two years before her marriage she published a poem in four cantos, called *Astaroga, or the Maid of the Rock.* As a specimen of her poetical style we subjoin her verses, *My Bird,* on the birth of a child in Jan. 1848, at Maulmain, in India:

Ere last year's moon had left the sky,
  A birdling sought my Indian nest,
And folded, oh! so lovingly,
  Its tiny wings upon my breast.

From morn till evening's purple tinge,
  In winsome helplessness she lies;
Two rose-leaves, with a silken fringe,
  Shut softly on her starry eyes.

There's not in Ind a lovelier bird;
  Broad earth owns not a happier nest;
O God, thou hast a fountain stirred,
  Whose waters never more shall rest!

This beautiful, mysterious thing,
  This seeming visitant from Heaven,
This bird with the immortal wing
  To me — to me, thy hand has given.

The pulse first caught its tiny stroke,
  The blood its crimson hue, from mine:
This life, which I have dared invoke,
  Henceforth is parallel with thine!

A silent awe is in my room —
  I tremble with delicious fear;
The future, with its light and gloom,
  Time and eternity are here.

Doubts, hopes, in eager tumults rise;
  Hear, O my God! one earnest prayer:
Room for my bird in paradise,
  And give her angel-plumage there!

Charles Sprague.

Mr. *Sprague* has been called "the American Pope," and in fact, both in his odes and his satires we may find much to remind us of the poet of Twickenham. He was born at Boston in 1791, and was for several years cashier in the Globe Bank in that city. The pungent satirist is a man of warm affections, so strongly attached to his family and. his friends, that he has seldom been able to leave them for even a brief absence. Besides his fine *Ode on Shakespeare,* his minor poems, *the Brothers, I see thee still, the Family Meeting,* and other poems and odes, he has written a satire, entitled *Curiosity*, in which he more especially lashes that pedantic school of critics, who, blind to the beauties of an author, are constantly hunting for obscure and insignificant allusions to annotate and explain. On this subject he writes:

How swells my theme! how vain my power I find,
To track the windings of the curious mind;
Let aught be hid, though useless, nothing boots,
Straightway it must be plucked up by the roots.
How oft we lay the volume down to ask
Of him, the victim in the Iron Mask;

The crusted metal rub with painful care
To spell the legend out — that is not there;
With dubious gaze o'er mossgrown tombstones bend
To find a name — the heralds never penned;
Dig through the lava-deluged city's breast,
Learn all we can, and wisely guess the rest;
Ancient or modern, sacred or profane, ·
All must be known, and all obscure made plain;
If 'twas a pippin tempted Eve to sin;
If glorious Byron drugged his Muse with gin;
If Troy e'er stood; if Shakespeare stole a deer;
If Israel's missing tribes found refuge here. [1])

We add one of his domestic pieces, and one of his odes:

THE BROTHERS.

We are but two — the others sleep
  Through death's untroubled night;
We are but two — oh, let us keep
  The link that binds us bright.

Heart leaps to heart — the sacred flood
  That warms us is the same;
That good old man — his honest blood
  Alike we fondly claim.

We in one mother's arms were lock'd —
  Long be her love repaid;
In that same cradle we were rock'd,
  Round the same hearth we play'd.

Our boyish sports were all the same,
  Each little joy and woe;
Let manhood keep alive the flame,
  Lit up so long ago.

We are but two — be that the band
  To hold us till we die;
Shoulder to shoulder let us stand,
  Till side by side we lie.

ODE ON ART.

When, from the sacred garden driven
  Man fled before his Maker's wrath,
An angel left her place in heaven,
  And crossed the wanderer's sunless path.

---

[1]) Alluding to a theory, that the American Indians are the descendants of the ten lost tribes of Israel.

'Twas Art! sweet Art! new radiance broke
  Where her light foot flew o'er the ground:
And thus with seraph voice she spoke, —
  "The Curse a Blessing shall be found."

She led him through the trackless wild,
  Where noontide sunbeam never blazed;
The thistle shrunk, the harvest smiled,
  And Nature gladdened, as she gazed.
Earth's thousand tribes of living things
  At Art's command, to him are given;
The village grows, the city springs,
  And point their spires of faith to heaven.

He rends the oak, — and bids it ride,
  To guard the shores its beauty graced;
He smites the rock, — upheaved in pride,
  See towers of strength and domes of taste.
Earth's teeming caves their wealth reveal,
  Fire bears his banner on the wave,
He bids the mortal poison heal,
  And leaps triumphant o'er the grave.

He plucks the pearls that stud the deep,
  Admiring Beauty's lap to fill;
He breaks the stubborn marble's sleep,
  And imitates creating skill.
With thoughts that swell his glowing soul,
  He bids the ore illume the page,
And proudly scorning Time's control,
  Converses with an unborn age.

In fields of air he writes his name,
  And treads the chambers of the sky;
He reads the stars, and grasps the flame,
  That quivers round the Throne on high.
In war renowned, in peace sublime,
  He moves in greatness and in grace;
His power, subduing space and time,
  Links realm to realm, and race to race.

J. G. Whittier.

John Greenleaf Whittier, the New-England quaker-
poet and moralist, born in 1807, has written *Mogg
Megone*, a story in verse of the struggles of the early
settlers with hostile Indian tribes; *Maud Müller*, a sad
but very popular poem, and a vast number of short

poems and verses on the Secession War and other public events. His lines on the great fire in Chicago (Oct. 8, 1871) are, we think, among his best:

Men said at vespers: "All is well!"
In one wild night the city fell;
Fell shrines of prayer and marts of grain
Before the fiery hurricane.

On three score spires had sunset shone,
Where ghastly sunrise looked on none,
Men clasped each other's hands, and said:
"The City of the West is dead!"

Brave hearts who fought, in slow retreat,
The fiends of fire from street to street,
Turned, powerless, to the blinding glare,
The dumb defiance of despair.

A sudden impulse thrilled each wire
That signalled round that sea of fire;
Swift words of cheer, warm heart-throbs came;
In tears of pity died the flame!

From East, from West, from South and North,
The messages of hope shot forth,
And, underneath the severing wave,
The world, full-handed, reached to save.

Rise, stricken city! — from thee throw
The ashen sackcloth of thy woe;
And build, as to Amphion's strain,
To songs of cheer thy walls again!

How shrivelled in thy hot distress
The primal sin of selfishness;
How instant rose, to take thy part,
The angel in the human heart!

Ah! not in vain the flames that tossed
Above thy dreadful holocaust.
The Christ again has preached through thee
The Gospel of Humanity!

Then lift once more thy towers on high,
And fret with spires the western sky,
To tell that God is yet with us,
And love is still miraculous!

J. R. Lowell.

James Russel Lowell, author of the *Indian Summer Reverie, Rosaline*, and the *Biglow Papers*, is often classed among the American humorists and satirists, but it would be doing him scanty justice to treat him as nothing more. Besides the above-mentioned productions he published, in 1868, *Under the Willows and other Poems*; in 1870 *Essays on Dryden, Shakespeare, Lessing, Rousseau*, etc.; besides an interesting work on witchcraft in New-England, two centuries ago. Of his vigorous and pregnant style the following verses will give some idea :

THE RICH MAN'S SON AND THE POOR MAN'S SON.

The rich man's son inherits lands,
And piles of brick, and stone, and gold ;
And he inherits soft, white hands,
And tender flesh that fears the cold ;
Nor dares to wear a garment old.
A heritage, it seems to me,
One would not care to hold in fee.

The rich man's son inherits cares ;
The bank may break, the factory burn ;
Some breath may burst his bubble shares,
And soft, white hands would hardly earn
A living that would suit his turn :
A heritage, it seems to me,
One would not care to hold in fee.

What does the poor man's son inherit ?
Stout muscles and a sinewy heart ;
A hardy frame, a hardier spirit ;
King of two hands ; he does his part.
In our useful toil and art :
A heritage, it seems to me,
A king might wish to hold in fee.

What does the poor man's son inherit ? —
Wishes o'erjoyed with humble things ;
A rank adjudged by toil-worn merit ;
Content that from employment springs ;
A heart that in his labour sings ;
A heritage, it seems to me,
A king might wish to hold in fee.

What does the poor man's son inherit? —
A patience learned by being poor,
  Courage, if sorrow come, to bear it,
  A fellow feeling that is sure
  To make the outcast bless his door:
  A heritage, it seems to me,
  A king might wish to hold in fee.

Oh, rich man's son, there is a toil
That with all others level stands:
  Large charity doth never soil,
  But only whitens soft, white hands:
  This is the best crop from the lands:
  A heritage, it seems to me,
  Worth being rich to hold in fee.

Oh! poor man's son, scorn not thy state; —
There is worse weariness than thine,
  In merely being rich and great;
  Work only makes the soul to shine,
  And makes rest fragrant and benign:
  A heritage, it seems to me,
  Worth being poor to hold in fee.

Both heirs to some six feet of sod,
Are equal in the earth at last;
  Both children of the same dear God;
  Prove title to your heirship vast,
  By record of a well-filled past:
  A heritage, it seems to me,
  Well worth a life to hold in fee.

The *Biglow Papers* consist of a series of humorous pieces in the American dialect and in rhyme, directed against the Mexican policy of the then existing Administration. Mr. Lowell is a native of Cambridge, Massachusetts, and was born in 1819. In 1879 he was appointed American Envoy Extraordinary and Minister Plenipotentiary in London. Mrs. *Maria Lowell* (Miss White) born at Watertown, Massachusetts, married Mr. Lowell in 1844. She has published several translations, besides some original poems, among which *the Morning Glory* and *the Maiden's Harvest* have found many admirers. Mrs. Lowell died Feb. 19, 1885.

Mrs. Sigourney.

Miss *Lydia Huntley*, born in 1791 at Norwich, Connecticut, gave early proofs of genius, for she began to write verses, when only eight years of age. In 1819 she married Mr. Sigourney, a merchant in Hartford, Connecticut, and for that time forward devoted all her leisure hours to literary pursuits, in which she was encouraged by her husband. After producing several small works, in the summer of 1840 she visited England and Scotland, and passed the winter in Paris. While in London she published a volume of poems, and soon after her return to America in 1841, the most elaborate of her longer poems, *Pocahontas*, appeared in New York. In 1842 she gave, under the title: *Pleasant Memories in Pleasant Lands*, an account in prose and verse of her wanderings abroad. This was succeeded by *Myrtis* in 1846; and in 1848 appeared a volume of her poems, with beautiful illustrations. She died in 1865.

Of Mrs. Sigourney's simpler style, the following may serve as a specimen:

THE THRIVING FAMILY.

Our father lives in Washington,
  And has a world of cares,
But gives his children each a farm,
  Enough for them and theirs.
Full thirty well-grown sons has he,
  A numerous race indeed,
Married and settled all, you see,
  With boys and girls to feed.
So, if we wisely till our lands,
  We're sure to earn a living,
And have a penny too to spare
  For spending or for giving.
A thriving family are we,
  No lordling need deride us;
For we know how to use our hands,
  And in our wits we pride us.
      Hail, brothers, hail!
Let nought on earth divide us.

Some of us dare the sharp north-east,
  Some clover-fields are mowing;
And others tend the cotton-plants
  That keep the looms a-going;
Some build and steer the whitewing'd ships,
  And few in speed can mate them,
While others rear the corn and wheat,
  Or grind the corn to freight them.
And if our neighbours o'er the sea
  Have e'er an empty larder,
To send a loaf their babes to cheer
  Will work a little harder.
        Hail, brothers, hail!
  Let nought on earth divide us.

Some faults we have, we can't deny,
  A foible here and there;
But other households have the same,
  And so we won't despair
'Twill do no good to fume and frown,
  And call hard names, you see,
And what a shame 'twould be to part
  So fine a family!
'Tis but a waste of time to fret,
  Since Nature made us one,
For every quarrel cuts a thread
  That healthful Love has spun.
Then draw the cords of union fast,
  Whatever may betide us,
And closer cling through every blast,
  For many a storm has tried us.
        Hail, brothers, hail!
  Let nought on earth divide us.

Of course, the "Family" here means the American people; and the "full thirty well-grown sons" are the 38 states of the American Union.

The subjoined verses contain much beauty and sublimity:

NIAGARA.

Flow on for ever, in thy glorious robe
Of terror and of beauty! Yea, flow on
Unfathomed and resistless! God hath set
His rainbow on thy forehead: and the cloud
Mantled around thy feet. And he doth give
Thy voice of thunder, power to speak of Him
Eternally, — bidding the lip of man
Keep silence, and upon thy rocky altar pour
Incense of awe-struck praise.

Ah! who can dare

To lift the insect trump of earthly hope,
Or love or sorrow, 'mid the peal sublime
Of thy tremendous hymn? Even Ocean shrinks
Back from thy brotherhood; and all his waves
Retire abashed. For he doth sometimes seem
To sleep like a spent labourer, and recall
His wearied billows from their vexing play
And lull them to a cradle calm, but thou
With everlasting, undecaying tide,
Dost rest not night or day. The morning stars,
When first they sang o'er young creation's birth,
Heard thy deep anthem; and those wrecking fires
That wait the archangel's signal to dissolve
This solid earth, shall find Jehovah's name
Graven as with a thousand diamond spears,
On thine unending volume.

Every leaf,

That lifts itself within thy wide domain,
Doth gather greenness from thy living spray
Yet tremble at the baptism. Lo! — yon birds
Do boldly venture near, and bathe their wing
Amid thy mist and foam. 'Tis meet for them
To touch thy garment's hem, and lightly stir
The snowy leaflets of thy vapour wreath,
For they may sport unharmed amid the cloud,
Or listen at the echoing gate of heaven
Without reproof. But, as for us, it seems
Scarce lawful, with our broken tones, to speak
Familiarly of thee. Methinks to tint
Thy glorious features with our pencil's point,
Or woo thee to the tablet of a song,
Were profanation.

Thou dost make the soul

A wondering witness of thy majesty;
But as it presses with delirious joy
To pierce thy vestibule, dost chain its step,
And tame its rapture with the humbling view
Of its own nothingness; bidding it stand
In the dread presence of the Invisible,
As if to answer to its God through thee.

In the verses, *Indian Names*, Mrs. Sigourney reveals her sympathy with a too often wronged and defamed race:

INDIAN NAMES.

Ye say that all have passed away,
    That noble race and brave;
That their light canoes have vanishèd
    From off the crested wave;

18*

That, 'mid the forests where they roamed,
  There rings no hunter's shout;
But their name is on your waters —
  Ye may not wash it out.

'Tis where Ontario's billow
  Like Ocean's surge is curled; .
Where strong Niagara's thunders wake
  The echo of the world;
Where red Missouri bringeth
  Rich tribute from the west;
And Rappahannock sweetly sleeps
  On green Virginia's breast.

Ye say their conelike cabins,
  That clustered o'er the vale,
Have disappeared, as withered leaves
  Before the autumn's gale:
But their memory liveth on your hills,
  Their baptism on your shore,
Your everlasting rivers speak
  Their dialect of yore.

Old Massachusetts wears it
  Within her lordly crown,
And broad Ohio bears it
  Amid his young renown;
Connecticut has wreathed it
  Where her quiet foliage waves,
And bold Kentucky breathes it hoarse
  Through all her ancient caves.

Wachusett hides its lingering voice
  Within its rocky heart,
And Alleghany graves its tone
  Throughout his lofty chart.
Monadnock, on his forehead hoar,
  Doth seal the sacred trust:
Your mountains build their monument,
  Though ye destroy their dust.

Joaquin Miller.

Joaquin Miller, the poet of the Far West (born in
Indiana in 1841), has published *Songs of the Sierras*,
a collection of songs or short poems, written in simple
and unpretending, yet often touching language. One
of these bears a title which tells its own story:

DEAD IN THE SIERRAS.

His footsteps have failed us,
  Where berries are red,
And madroños[1]) are rankest.
  The hunter is dead!

The grizzly may pass
  By his half-open door;
May pass and repass
  On his path, as of yore:

The panther may crouch
  In the leaves on his limb;
May scream and may scream, —
  It is nothing to him.

Prone, bearded and breasted,
  Like columns of stone;
And tall as a pine —
  As a pine overthrown!

His camp-fires gone,
  What else can be done
Than let him sleep on
  Till the light of the sun?

Ay, tombless! what of it?
  Marble is dust,
Cold and repellent;
  And iron is rust.

James Kirke Paulding.

Mr. Paulding was born in 1778, at a place called Pleasant Valley, in the State of New York; and he died in 1860. He has written a good deal of both prose and poetry; the scenes in Kentucky, in his *Westward Ho!* in particular, are very ably sketched. We give an extract from his *Backwoodsman:*

DOWN THE OHIO.

As down Ohio's ever-ebbing tide,
Oarless and sailless silently they glide,
How still the scene, how lifeless, yet how fair,
Was the lone land that met the stranger there!

---

[1]) The arbutus or strawberry-tree.

No smiling villages or curling smoke
The busy haunts of busy men bespoke;
No solitary hut, the banks along,
Sent forth blithe labour's homely, rustic song;
No urchin gamboll'd on the smooth, white sand,
Or hurl'd the skipping stone with playful hand,
While playmate dog plung'd in the clear blue wave,
And swam, in vain, the sinking prize to save.
Where now are seen, along the river side
Young, busy towns in buxom, painted pride,
And fleets of gliding boats, with riches crown'd,
To distant Orleans or St. Louis bound,
Nothing appeared but nature unsubdued,
One endless, voiceless, woodland solitude,
Or boundless prairie, that aye seem'd to be
As level and as lifeless as the sea;
They seem'd to breathe in this wide world alone,
Heirs of the earth — the land was all their own!

Mr. Paulding was one of the contributors to Washington Irving's humorous periodical *Salmagundi*.

H. T. Tuckerman.

The accomplished scholar and critic, *Henry Theodore Tuckerman*, has written some poetry of a pleasing and graceful, if not of a very vigorous character. He was born in the city of Boston in 1813, and after completing his collegiate studies, travelled for some years in Europe, whence he returned to America in 1838. From this time he was constantly occupied with literary labours till his death in 1871. Among his poetical effusions the most popular are *Mary, the Ringlet*, and the verses:

GIVE ME THE BOON OF LOVE.

Give me the boon of Love!
  I ask no more for fame;
For better one unpurchased heart
  Than Glory's proudest name.
Why wake a fever in the blood,
  Or damp the spirit now,
To gain a wreath whose leaves shall wave
  Above a withered brow?

Give me the boon of Love!
  Ambition's meed is vain;
Dearer Affection's earnest smile
  Than Honour's richest train.
I'd rather lean upon a breast
  Responsive to my own,
Than sit, pavilioned gorgeously,
  Upon a kingly throne.

Like the Chaldean sage,
  Fame's worshippers adore
The brilliant orbs that scatter light
  O'er heaven's azure floor;
But in their very hearts enshrined,
  The votaries of Love
Keep e'er the holy flame which once
  Illumed the courts above.

Give me the boon of Love!
  Renown is but a breath
Whose loudest echo ever floats
  From out the halls of death.
A loving eye beguiles me more
  Than Fame's emblazoned seal,
And one sweet tone of tenderness
  Than Triumph's wildest peal.

Give me the boon of Love!
  The path of Fame is drear,
And Glory's arch doth ever span
  A hill-side cold and sere.
One wild flower from the path of Love,
  All lowly though it lie,
Is dearer than the wreath that waves
  To stern Ambition's eye.

Give me the boon of Love!
  The lamp of Fame shines far,
But Love's soft light glows near and warm,
  A pure and household star.
One tender glance can fill the soul
  With a perennial fire;
But Glory's flame burns fitfully,
  A lone, funereal pyre.

Give me the boon of Love!
  Fame's trumpet-strains depart,
But Love's sweet lute breathes melody
  That lingers in the heart;

And the scroll of fame will burn,
  When sea and earth consume;
But the rose of Love, in a happier sphere,
  Will live in deathless bloom!

On the death of the young and promising poetess, Miss Lucy Hooper, in 1841, at the age of twenty-four, Tuckerman paid the following tribute to her memory:

And thou art gone! sweet daughter of the lyre,
  Whose strains we hoped to hear thee waken long;
Gone — as the stars in morning's light expire,
  Gone like the rapture of a passing song;
Gone from a circle who thy gifts have cherished
  With genial fondness and devoted care,
Whose dearest hopes with thee have sadly perished,
  And now can find no solace but in prayer;
Prayer to be like thee in so meekly bearing
  Both joy and sorrow from thy Maker's hand;
Prayer to put on the white robes thou art wearing,
  And join thy anthem in the better land.

Mrs. Welby.

Mrs. *Amelia B. Welby* (Miss Coppuck) was born in 1821 at St. Michael's, Maryland, and was married, in 1838, to Mr. B. Welby of Louisville, Kentucky. Her first poems appeared in 1844. Of all she has written we give a decided preference to her exquisite lines:

TO A SEA-SHELL.

  Shell of the bright sea-waves!
What is it that we hear in thy sad moan!
Is this unceasing music all thine own?
  Lute of the ocean-caves!

  Or does some spirit dwell
In the deep windings of thy chambers dim,
Breathing for ever in its mournful hymn,
  Of ocean's anthem-swell?

  Wert thou a murmurer long
In crystal palaces beneath the seas,
Ere from the blue sky thou hadst heard the breeze
  Pour its full tide of song?

      Another thing with thee:
Are there not gorgeous cities in the deep,
Buried with flashing gems that brightly sleep,
      Hid by the mighty sea?

      And say, O lone sea-shell!
Are there not costly things and sweet perfumes
Scattered in waste o'er that sea-gulf of tombs?
      Hush thy low moan and tell.

      But yet, and more than all —
Has not each foaming wave in fury tossed
O'er earth most beautiful, the brave, the lost,
      Like a dark funeral pall?

      'Tis vain — thou answerest not!
Thou hast no voice to whisper of the dead;
'Tis ours alone, with sighs like odours shed,
      To hold them unforgot!

      Thine is as sad a strain
As if the spirit in thy hidden cell
Pined to be with the many things that dwell
      In the wild, restless main.

      And yet there is no sound
Upon the waters, whispered by the waves,
But seemeth like a wail from many graves,
      Thrilling the air around.

      The earth, O moaning shell!
The earth hath melodies more sweet than these —
The music-gush of rills, the hum of bees
      Heard in each blossom's bell.

      Are not these tones of earth,
The rustling forest, with its shivering leaves,
Sweeter than sounds that e'en in moonlight eves
      Upon the seas have birth!

      Alas! thou still wilt moan —
Thou'rt like the heart that wastes itself in sighs,
E'en when amid bewildering melodies,
      If parted from its own.

Mrs. E. O. Smith.

Mrs. *Elizabeth Oakes-Smith* (Miss Prince), born near Portland, Maine, married at the ago of sixteen the poet and humorist, Mr. Seba Smith (Jack Downing). Her most popular poems are, *the Acorn*, *the Sinless Child*, *the April Rain*, *the Water*, and *the Brook*. Her finest lines are perhaps those on flowers in *the Sinless Child:*

> Each tiny leaf became a scroll
>   Inscribed with holy truth,
> A lesson that around the heart
>   Should keep the dew of youth;
> Bright missals from angelic throngs
>   In every by-way left —
> How were the earth of glory shorn,
>   Were it of flowers bereft!
>
> They tremble on the alpine height;
>   The fissured rock they press;
> The desert wild, with heat and sand,
>   Shares, too, their blessedness.
> And wheresoe'er the weary heart
>   Turns in its dim despair,
> The meek-eyed blossom upward looks,
>   Inviting it to prayer.

Mrs. E. O. Smith has produced two dramas: *the Roman Tribute,* the subject of which is the ransom of Constantinople, by a tribute paid to Attila by the Emperor Theodosius; the other, *Jacob Leisler,* a tragedy founded on an episode in American history about two centuries ago. The last-mentioned piece contains some powerful though painful scenes, particularly that in which the heroine, Elizabeth Howard, who had fled from a cruel and worthless husband in England, and then married Leisler, the New-York Masaniello, is obliged to confess her bigamy to her second husband; and again, when after the collapse of Leisler's revolution, she intreats her first husband, now a man of authority in America, to spare Leisler's life.

Mrs. Lewis.

Mrs. *Estella Anna Lewis* (Miss Robinson) is a native of Baltimore. In 1846 she published a volume of poems, with the title, *Records of the Heart*, some of which are of considerable length. In 1848 appeared *the Child of the Sea*, in which, among other fine passages, we find the following description of the Bay of Gibraltar:

> Fresh blows the breeze o'er Tarick's burnished bay,
> The silent sea-mews bend them through the spray;
> The beauty-freighted barges bound afar
> To the soft music of the gay guitar ......
> The sentry peal salutes the setting sun,
> The haven's hum and busy din are done,
> And weary sailors roam along the strand,
> Or stretch their brawny limbs upon the sand,
> Feast, revel, game, engage in sage dispute,
> Unthread the story, sound the tuneful lute;
> Or humming some rude air that stirs the heart,
> Clue up the sails, or spread them to depart.

Mrs. Lewis died in 1880.

The other principal American poets, verse-writers, and dramatists are: William Gilmore Simms *(Atlantis, a story of the sea,* etc.); Mrs. Mary H. C. Booth *(Wayside Blossoms among Flowers from German Gardens,* etc.); Miss L. H. Hooper (translations from *Geibel* and *Heine,* etc.); Miss E. Frothingham (translation of Goethe's *Hermann and Dorothea);* Washington Allston *(Sylphs of the Seasons,* etc.); J. Pierpoint *(Airs of Palestine,* etc.); J. A. Hillhouse (dramas: *Hadad, Percy's Mask, Demetria);* F. Bret Harte (songs and poems on the Civil War, *the Heathen Chinee;* drama: *Two Men of Sandy Bar);* Charles G. Leland (translations from the German; *Hans Breitmann's Ballad's,* etc.); E. C. Stedman *(the Diamond Wedding, Sumter,* etc.); Richard H. Stoddard *(Footprints,* etc.); Ch. G. Halpine, (various poems on the Civil War); Geo. H. Boker (dramas: *Calaynos; Anne Boleyn; Francesca da Rimini);* Henry Ware, jun. *(Ursa Major,* etc.); Ch. W. Everett *(Agriculture,* etc.); Ed. Everett *(Dirge of Alaric,* etc.); Epes Sargent (tragedy: *Velasco,* etc.); Mrs. Sawyer *(the Valley of Peace,* etc.); Mrs. A. C.

Mowatt (plays: *Gulzare, the Persian Slave; Fashion; Armand, the Child of the People)*; Sara J. Clarke *(Ariadne,* etc.); Miss Alice Carey *(the Handmaid,* etc.); Miss Phoebe Carey *(Light in Darkness,* etc.); the sisters, Mrs. Cather Warfield and Mrs. Eleanor Lee *(the Indian Chamber,* etc.); Mrs. J. W. Home *(Wordsworth,* etc.); Mrs. Maria Brooks *(Zophiel,* in six cantos). To these names we should perhaps add that of Walt Whitman *(Leaves of Grass),* though we confess we feel puzzled to decide whether his strange hybrid literary productions should be classed as prose or poetry. Before we conclude, we have a word to say about the *anonymous* poets. That much poetical talent exists among educated Americans is proved by the appearance, every now and again, in the newspapers or literary magazines, of verses possessing great merit, which are read, admired, and if not soon after re-published with the author's name. forgotten. To one of these anonymous poetical effusions, which appeared in a New York periodical, we should desire to give further publicity. The subject is that grand and comprehensive one, which Alexander Pope recommended as the proper study of mankind:"

MAN.

The human mind, — that lofty thing!
  The palace and the throne,
Where reason sits a sceptred king,
  And breathes his judgment tone.
Oh! who with silent step shall trace
The borders of that haunted place,
  Nor in his weakness own
That mystery and marvel bind
That lofty thing — the human mind!

The human heart, — that restless thing!
  The tempter and the tried;
The joyous, yet the suffering, —
  The source of pain and pride;
The gorgeous thronged, — the desolate,
The seat of love, the lair of late, —
  Self-stung, self-deified!
Yet do we bless thee as thou art,
  Thou restless thing, — the human heart!

The human soul, — that startling thing!
  Mysterious and sublime!
The angel sleeping on the wing
  Worn by the scoffs of time, —
The beautiful, the veiled, the bound,
The earth-enslaved, the glory-crowned,
  The stricken in its prime!
From heaven in tears to earth it stole,
That startling thing, — the human soul!

And this is man: — oh! ask of him
  The gifted and forgiven, —
While o'er his vision, drear and dim,
  The wrecks of time are driven,
If pride or passion in their power
Can chain the time, or charm the hour,
  Or stand in place of heaven?
He bends the brow, he bows the knee, —
"Creator, Father! none but thee!"

VOCABULARY.
(English and German.)

A.

Abdication, Abdankung.
aberrations, Verirrungen.
abigail, Kammerjungfer.
abreast, neben einander.
accessories, Nebensachen.
achieve (to), vollenden, zu Stande
    bringen.
acrimonious, beissend, bitter.
adamantine, demanten.
addled, faul, verdorben.
adulterous, ehebrecherisch.
aerial, ätherisch.
affect (to), [S. 174] lieb gewinnen.
affianced, verlobt.
agaric, Pilz.
aghast, erschrocken.
ain't, vulgär für isn't.
ajar, angelehnt.
akin, verwandt.
alderman, Stadtältester.
allegation, Behauptung.
almoner, Almosenspender.
amalgamation, Mischung.
a-maying (to go), Maiblumen
    sammeln.
amber, Bernstein.
ankle, Fussknöchel.
anon, in Kurzem.
antagonist, Widersacher.
anthem, Chorgesang.
appanage, Vorrecht.
approve (to), auf die Probe stellen,
    billigen.
aptitude, Fähigkeit, Begabung.

archery, das Bogenschiessen.
armorer, Waffenschmied.
articles of war, Kriegsgesetze.
aspen, Espe.
assafoetida, Teufelsdreck.
astute, schlau, hinterlistig.
athirst (poetisch), durstig.
athrob (poetisch), zitternd.
a-tiptoe, auf den Zehenspitzen.
atrabilious, schwermütig.
attune (to), in Einklang bringen.
auger-hole, Bohrloch.
aught, etwas.
avalanche, Lawine.
aver (to), beteuern.
average, Durchschnitt.
aversion, Abneigung.
ax (to), vulgär für ask.
aye, immer.

B.

Babble (to), schwatzen.
bait, Imbiss, Lockspeise.
ballot, die geheime Abstimmung.
balls (golden), Schild des Pfand-
    verleihers.
bamboozle (to), hintergehen.
ban, Fluch.
bandbox, Putzschachtel.
bantling, Kindlein.
bar, Hinderniss, Sandbank an der
    Mündung eines Flusses.
    (To be called to the bar,
    Advokat werden.)
barge, Barke.

bask (to), sich sonnen.
baton, Kommandostab.
battle-axe, Streitaxt.
beach, Strand, Ufer. (Beached, vom Strande eingeschlossen.)
bead-roll, Rosenkranz, Liste.
beads, (Glas-) Perlen.
beaker, Becher.
beam, Lichtstrahl; (von einem Schiff, with even beam, ganz gleichmässig).
bearer, Ueberbringer.
Beatrice and Benedick: vergl. Shakespeare's "Much Ado about Nothing."
beckon (to), zuwinken.
befit (to), anstehen.
beguile (to), betrügen.
bellow (to), brüllen.
bellows, Blasebalg.
bequeath (to), vermachen.
beset, bedrängt.
betrothed, verlobt.
bewail (to), beweinen.
bewilder (to), verwirren.
bicker (to), rauschen, zanken.
billow, Welle, Woge.
bit, Gebiss, Bischen.
blacksmith, Hufschmied.
blade, Klinge.
blaspheme (to), verfluchen.
blast, Wind, Sturm.
blast (to), austrocknen, beschimpfen.
bleak, kalt, unfreundlich.
bleat (to), blöken.
blemish, Mangel, Fleck.
blight (to), verderben, zu Grunde richten.
blink (to), verheimlichen.
blues, Blaustrümpfe.
blunder (to), einen Fehler machen.
blurred, verschwommen.
bohea, eine Sorte Thee.
Bohemian Girl (Oper), die Zigeunerin.
bolt (thunder-), Donnerkeil.
bonnie, schön, freundlich.
boon, Gunst, Gefallen.

boots (nothing), es hilft nichts.
bopeep, Versteckenspiel.
borough, Wahlflecken.
bother the gibberish! der Henker hole das Kauderwälsch.
bothie (schottisch), Wirthshaus.
boundary, Grenze.
bounden, verpflichtet.
bowery, laubreich.
brackish, salzig.
brae (schottisch), Anhöhe.
braid, Gewebe.
brake, Farrnkraut.
brand, Schwert, Fackel.
brandy, Cognac.
brawl, Zank, Aufruhr.
brawny, muskulös.
bribe (to), bestechen.
bridesmaid, Brautjungfer.
bristles, Borsten; (S. 167), Bart.
brittle, zerbrechlich.
broom, Ginster.
brow, Augenbraue, Stirnrunzeln, Rand.
browse (to), weiden.
bruise, Wunde, Schlag.
Brussels (carpet), Brüsseler Teppich.
buckle, Schnalle.
bud, Knospe.
buff-coat, Büffelwamms.
bugle, Jagdhorn.
bump along (to), auf holprigem Wege fahren.
bumper, Humpen.
buoy up (to), schwimmend erhalten.
burden, Bürde, Refrain.
burglar, Einbrecher.
burnished, glänzend.
bustling, Gewühl.
buxom, fröhlich.
by-the-by, beiläufig gesagt.

C.

Cabal (to), sich gegen etwas verschwören.
callous, abgehärtet.
cancel (to), vernichten, ausstreichen.

canker (to), verderben (bei Rosen, anfressen).
cant (S. 260), Heuchelei.
canto, Gesang.
canvass (to), erörtern.
cap, Mütze.
carcase, Leiche.
carnage, Blutbad.
carol, Gesang.
carrion, Aas.
casement (poetisch), Fenster.
castigate (to), züchtigen.
Cathay, China.
caw (to), krächzen.
cemetery, Gottesacker.
cerulean, himmelblau.
chaff, Spreu.
chair, Stuhl, Präsidentenstuhl.
chalet, Sennhütte.
challenge, herausfordern, auswählen.
chart, Seekarte.
chaste, rein, züchtig.
chats, Plaudereien.
check, Einhalt, karriertes Muster.
cheek-strap, Backenriemen.
cheesemonger, Käsehändler.
chime, Glockengeläut.
chimney-sweep question, Frage betreffend die Verwendung von Kindern beim Schornsteinfegen.
chipp'd, gesprungen.
chirp, Gezwitscher.
choir, Kirchenchor.
church-rates, Kirchensteuer.
churl, Bauer, Kerl.
cider, Apfelwein.
cite (to), anführen.
civet, Zibethkatze und ein aus einer Drüse derselben bereitetes Parfüm.
claim, Anspruch.
clamour, Geräusch.
clang (to), schallen.
clasp, Schloss am Buch.
clod, Erdscholle.
clomb (poetisch) = climbed.
clot, Klümpchen Blut.
clover, Klee.

clue up (to), zusammenziehen.
coat-of-arms, Wappen.
cobweb, Spinngewebe.
coil around (to), umschlingen.
coin, Münze.
collaboration, Mitwirkung, gemeinschaftliche Arbeit.
collation, Erfrischung.
colloquy, Gespräch.
colourings, Bemäntelung.
comb, Kamm, Wellenrücken.
comfits and cates, Konfekt und Leckerbissen.
commiseration, Mitleid.
commune (to), verkehren, sich beraten.
competition, Konkurrenz, Wetteifer.
concede (to), zugeben.
confederate, verbündet.
confound! verwünscht sei —
connoisseur, Kenner.
consort with (to), verkehren mit.
constituency, Wählerschaft.
consummate, vollkommen.
contrast (to), entgegenstellen.
contumacy, Hartnäckigkeit.
convalescent, genesend.
co-operation, Mitwirkung.
coot, Wasserhuhn.
cope, Chorrock.
copse, Gebüsch.
corduroy, ein sehr starkes geripptes Zeug zu Beinkleidern.
coronet, Herzog-, Grafenkrone.
corpse-candle, Irrlicht.
corse (poetisch für corpse), Leichnam.
corselet, Brustharnisch.
counter, Ladentisch.
counterfeit, falsch, nachgemacht.
court-martial, Kriegsgericht.
course, Gang.
covet (to), begehren (S. 238, nicht gönnen).
coward, Feigling.
cowl, Kaputze.
cowslip, Primel.

coyness, Zurückhaltung. Sprödig-
keit.
cozy, gemütlich.
cracked, gesprungen.
craft, Fahrzeug.
crag, Fels.
Cranmer, englischer Reformator,
der im Jahre 1556
als Ketzer verbrannt
wurde.
crash, Zusammensturz, Krach.
crave (to), erflehen.
crazy, baufällig, verrückt.
creed, Lehre, Glaubensbekennt-
niss.
crew, Mannschaft.
croak (to), krächzen.
crosier, Bischofsstab.
crossing, Fussweg, der über eine
Fahrstrasse führt.
croup, Kreuz des Pferdes, Kruppe.
crown-stamp, officieller Stempel.
crumpled, zusammengeschrumpft.
crypt, Gruft.
cuff (to), mit der Faust schlagen.
culinary, zur Küche gehörig.
culprit, der Schuldige.
cumbrous, schwerfällig, ungelenk.
curdle (to), gerinnen.
currency, Geld, Währung.
curricle, leichter zweispänniger
Wagen.
curriculum, Kursus, Unterrichts-
plan.
curry, eine scharfe indische Sauce.
curse, Fluch.
curtsey, Knix.
custard, Eiercrême.
cutlass, Enterschwert.
cycle, Cyclus.

D.

Daffodil, die gelbe Narzisse.
dainty, fein, zierlich.
Dan, Herr (lat. dominus.)
dangle (to), baumeln.
dapper, klein, niedlich.
dapple-grey, apfelgrau.

darling, Liebling.
dart, Pfeil.
dashing, fliessend, kühn.
dearth, Mangel, Unfruchtbarkeit.
debauchery, Ausschweifung.
defiantly, trotzend.
deformed, missgestaltet.
degenerate (to), ausarten.
deify (to), vergöttern.
deluge, Sündfluth.
demarcation (line of), Grenzlinie.
department, Fach.
destiny, Schicksal.
deter (to), abschrecken, abhalten.
dexterity, Gewandtheit.
dilate on (to), weitläuftig erörtern.
dimple, Grübchen.
dint, Spur eines Schlages. (By
dint of, kraft, vermöge.)
disappointment, Enttäuschung.
discreetness, Mass, Klugheit.
disembowel (to), den Leib auf-
schlitzen.
disfranchise (to), einer Stadt das
Wahlrecht (der Be-
stechlichkeit halber)
entziehen.
disgrace, Schande.
disguise, Verkleidung.
disjointed, unzusammenhängend,
inconsequent.
dismay, Bestürzung.
dispart (to), auseinandergehen.
dissever (to), trennen.
dissipated, liederlich.
dissolution, Auflösung.
dissolve (to), sich auflösen.
ditty, Lied.
dizzy, schwindelig.
doat on (to), zärtlich lieben.
dole (to), sparsam verteilen.
domain, Gebiet.
dotard, kindisch gewordener
Greis.
doublet, Wamms.
Downs (the), Ankerplatz unweit
der englischen Stadt
Deal.
doze, Schlummer.
dragon-fly, Wasserjungfer, Libelle.

drain (to), austrinken.
drench, Regen, Nässe.
drivelling, Faselei.
drowning (S. 160), in Thränen
  schwimmend.
drudge (to), sich abarbeiten.
drysaltery, Viktualienhandlung.
dull (to), dämpfen, abstumpfen.
dungeon, Kerker.
dyes, Farben.

E.

Ecstasy, Entzücken.
ee = eye, Auge.
effective, wirkungsvoll.
eke = also, auch.
elaborate, sorgsam ausgearbeitet.
elk, das Elentier.
elucidation, Erklärung.
emanation, Ausfluss.
emblazoned, berühmt machend.
embody (to), verkörpern.
empty, leer, zwecklos.
enamelled, emailliert, mit Adern
  durchzogen.
encampment, Lager.
endearment, Liebkosung.
engine,   Mittel,   Werkzeug,
  Maschine.
enthralled,   besiegt,   gefangen
  gehalten.
ephemeral, vorübergehend, von
  kurzer Dauer.
ermine, Hermelin.
erroneously, irrtümlich.
estranged, entfremdet.
eulogium, Lobrede.
euphony, Wohlklang.
evade (to), ausweichen.
exasperate (to), reizen, heraus-
  fordern.
exemplified, verkörpert.
exotic, ausländisches Gewächs.
expanse, ausgedehnte Fläche.
explicit, bestimmt, deutlich.
expostulation, Erörterung.
expunge (to), ausstreichen.
eye-socket, Augenhöhle.

F.

Failure, Misslingen.
fain, gern.
fairy, Fee.
fallow, Brachfeld.
falter, stammeln; (S. 75) schüch-
  tern hervordringen.
fanged, in Form einer Kralle.
fanned, angehaucht.
farce, Posse.
fare (to), gut oder schlecht an-
  kommen.
fascination, Zauber, Bezauberung.
fastidious, eigen, schwer zu be-
  friedigen.
fay = fairy.
feat, That, Heldenthat.
fee (to hold in), zu Lehen haben.
fester (to), schwären, eitern.
fickle, unbeständig.
fiend, Dämon, Teufel.
figure-head, Gallion.
fillip (to), leise oder scherzhaft
  schlagen.
fir, Tanne.
fire-bucket, Feuereimer.
fire up (to), Feuer fangen.
fissure, Riss.
fitful, unbeständig, launig.
flag (to), schwächer werden.
flat (Musik), Bmoll.
flaunt, Prunk.
flaw (S. 165), Regenschauer mit
  Wind.
flawn, Fladen.
fleshly (S. 147), unzüchtig.
flight of stairs, Treppe.
flirt (to), kokettieren.
flitting, Umzug.
flout (to), spotten, necken.
fold, Schafhürde.
forecastle, die Back.
forego (to), auf etwas verzichten.
foretaste, Vorgeschmack.
fore-yardarm, die Fockraa.
forfeit (to), verwirken.
fosterage, Pflege, Aufziehen bei
  einer Amme.
foster-brother, Milchbruder.

fraught, voll, vereint mit.
freak, frecher Streich.
freighted, befrachtet.
fret (to), verzehren, sich grämen.
frigid, kalt.
fringe, Franse.
fugitive (poetry), Gelegenheits-
      Gedichte.
fume (to), wütend werden.

G.

Gadfly, Stechfliege, leichtsinniger
      Mensch.
gait (schottisch), Weg.
galingale, der Galgen.
gall (to), schmerzen.
gambol (to), spielen, hüpfen.
gamut (Musik), Skala.
gang (schottisch) (to), gehen.
gangway (starboard), Gang auf
      der rechten Seite eines
      Schiffes.
gaol, Gefängniss.
gap, Lücke.
garb, Gewand.
garish, blendend.
garlic, Knoblauch.
gaud, Juwel, Zierrat.
gauntlet (to run the), Spiessruten
      laufen.
Gazette (the London), das offizielle
      Blatt, in welchem die
      Anstellung von Civil-
      und Militär-Beamten
      und Offizieren, die etwa
      stattfindende Aende-
      rung des Familien-
      Namens, ebenso wie
      die Liste der Falliten,
      veröffentlicht wird.
geniality, Sympathie, Menschen-
      freundlichkeit.
ghastly, entsetzlich.
Ghoul, Dämon, Vampyr.
glade, Lichtung.
glare, blendendes Licht.
glean (to), sammeln, auslesen.
glee, Freude.

glen, Schlucht, Thal.
glimpse, flüchtiger Blick.
gloat on (to), verliebt anschauen.
glossy, glänzend.
gnat, Mücke.
gnaw (to), nagen.
god one's self (to), sich vergöttern.
gorge, Bergschlund.
gorgeous, prachtvoll.
gorse, Stechginster, Pfriemen-
      kraut.
gossamer, Sommerwebe.
grant (to), gewähren.
grate, Feuerrost.
grayling, die Aesche.
greeting, Gruss, Empfang.
grim, grimmig.
grizzly (bear), der graue Bär.
groan (to), ächzen.
grocer, Gewürzkrämer.
grouse, Auerhahn.
grudge (to), missgönnen.
guilt, Schuld.
gull, Seemöve, Gimpel, Tropf.
gun-brig, Kanonenbrick.
gust, Windstoss.
gymnastics, Turnübungen.
gypsy, Zigeuner.
gyves, Fesseln.

H.

Haggardness, Hagerkeit.
halo, Hof um einen Stern.
harbinger, Vorläufer,
harebell, Glockenblume.
hasp, Haspe.
hawk, Habicht, Falke.
haze, leichter Nebel.
heartiness, Herzlichkeit.
hebdomadally, wöchentlich.
heed, Acht.
helpmate, Gehülfin.
hem, Saum.
hemlock (pine), Schierlingstanne.
hempseed, Hanfsamen; (S. 222,
      Anspielung auf den
      Strick des Henkers).
heron, Reiher.

hest = behest, Befehl, Verlangen.
hideous, schreckhaft.
hit (S. 221), Erfolg.
hive (to), (S. 65) einsammeln,
    heimbringen.
hoad (to). aufhäufen.
hobble (to), hinken.
hod, Mörteltrog.
holly, Stechpalme.
holt, Hölzchen.
homestead, Heimstätte.
homily, Predigt.
horn-book, das ABC-Buch.
hostage, Geissel.
hothouse, Treibhaus.
hour-glass, Sandglas.
hues, Farbenwechsel.
hulk, Rumpf eines Schiffes.
humanities. das Menschliche.
hunchback, der Buckelige.
hustle (to), mit den Elbogen
    stossen.
huxter, Krämer.
hybrid, zwitterartig.

I.

Idlesse, Unthätigkeit.
ignoble, unedel, verächtlich.
ill-omened, unglückverkündend.
immersed, vertieft, versunken.
immunity, Vorrecht.
impecunious, arm, von Geld ent-
    blösst.
imperative, gebieterisch.
implacable, unversöhnlich.
incense, Weihrauch.
incumbrance, Last.
indigence, Armut.
ineffable, unbeschreiblich.
infelicitous, schlecht angebracht.
infidelity, Untreue.
initiate (to), einführen.
injured, beleidigt.
innovation, Neuerung.
insinuation, boshafte Anspielung.
insolence, Uebermut.
installation, Einführung.
instigate (to), verleiten.
interchange, Austausch.

intervention, Dazwischenkunft.
intoxicated, berauscht.
investigation, Untersuchung.
irrelevant, der Sache fremd.
islet, kleine Insel.

J.

Jack-boots, Stulpenstiefel.
jackdaw, Dohle.
jangle (to), misstönen.
javelin, Wurfspiess.
jaws of Death, Todesrachen.
jerky, unebenmässig.
jet, Gagat.
jilt (to), mutwillig abweisen.
jump at (to), mit Eifer, gierig
    ergreifen.
juniper, Wachholder.
jury, Geschworengericht.
justling, Getümmel.
jut (to), hervorragen.

K.

Keg, Tönnchen.
kindred, verwandt.
knapsack, Tornister.
knight, Ritter; knight hospi-
    taler, Ritter des Mal-
    teserordens.
knitted (S. 65), gewunden.

L.

Lace, Spitzen.
lack, Mangel.
lackey, Diener.
lad, laddie, Bursch.
lair, Lager.
lap (to), schlappen (wie eine Katze.)
larder, Vorratskammer.
lattice, Gitter.
launch (to), schleudern.
laureate, Hofdichter.
lavish, verschwenderisch.
lawn (S. 91), Schleierleinwand;
    (S. 106) Rasenplatz.
league (to), sich verbünden.

league (a), drei englische Meilen.
ledger, Hauptbuch, Register.
leech, Arzt (auch Blutegel.)
legislation, Gesetzgebung.
liberal (S. 139), frei, offen.
license (special), Erlaubniss seitens der geistlichen Behörde zur sofortigen Trauung, ohne den Verlauf der gewöhnlichen Frist von drei Wochen abwarten zu müssen.
lie away (to), (S. 76), den guten Ruf durch Lügen untergraben.
limes, Lindenbäume.
limn'd, gezeichnet.
lineage, Herkunft.
link, Kettenglied.
loan, Darlehen.
loath, abgeneigt.
loathe (to), hassen, verabscheuen.
lock in an embrace (to), fest umarmen.
log (S.80), Holzklotz (zum Brennen.)
look-out (to be on the), auf der Lauer sein.
loom, Weberstuhl.
loon, Art Schwimmvogel.
lore, Wissenschaft, Lektüre.
lot (bei einer Auktion) Partie.
lucrative, gewinnbringend.
lunch, das zweite Frühstück.
lurid, düster.
luscious, saftig.

M.

Machination, listiger Streich, Komplott.
maggot, Made.
maid-of-all-work, Mädchen für Alles.
mail (S. 43), Panzerhemd.
main, hauptsächlich.
make up one's mind (to), sich zu etwas entschliessen.
make up a cap (to), eine Haube zurechtmachen, anfertigen.

man-of-war, Kriegsschiff.
margeut = margin, Rand.
marrowy, schwer, von guter Qualität.
mastiff, Dogge.
match one (to), Jemand gewachsen sein.
Match (S. 225), Heirat.
mate (to), sich zugesellen.
mated (S. 90), ehelich verbunden.
maternity, Mutterschaft.
mawkish, wenig schmackhaft, ekelhaft.
mellow, sanft, reif.
me'em, vulgär für ma'am, Madam.
mercenaries, Söldner.
meseems, es däucht mir.
midshipman, Seekadet.
mince-meat, klein geschnittenes Fleisch.
minister (to), dienen.
mire, Strassenkot.
mischievous, schädlich.
misguide (to), irreführen.
miss (to), verfehlen, versäumen.
miss (a), Fehlschuss.
missal, Gebetbuch, Messbuch.
mist, Nebel; (S. 66) Rätsel.
mistress (S. 137), Ehehälfte.
mite, Käsemade.
mitre, Bischofshut.
moan (to), stöhnen.
mock-disease, Scheinkrankheit.
mockery, Spott, Schein.
modish, nach der Mode gerichtet.
mole, Maulwurf.
molten, geschmolzen.
monitor, Ermahner.
monster, Ungeheuer, Unmensch.
mote, Stäubchen.
motley, bunt.
mottled, roth angelaufen.
mountebank, Quacksalber, Akrobat.
mouthpiece, Organ, Vertreter.
muffled, gedämpft.
mummy, Mumie.
murky, dunkel, düster.
musk, Moschus.

N.

Narrowing (S. 97), engherzig-
machend.
naughty, unartig, nichtswürdig.
nautch, indische Tänzerin.
newt, Sumpfeidechse.
nickname, Spitzname.
niddle-noddle, (to) hin und her
wackeln.
nidificate (to), ein Nest bauen.
niggardly, kärglich.
nightmare, der Alp.
night-rack, die dunkeln Sturm-
wolken.
noon, Mittag.
notelessness, Unberühmtheit.
nuncheon, Imbiss um 12 Uhr
Mittag.
nurse a thought (to), einen Ge-
danken hegen.
nurture (to), aufziehen.

O.

Odd, sonderbar.
onion stone, schlichter einfarbiger
Stein.
orange blossoms, Orangenblüten
(von englischen Damen
bei der Trauung ge-
tragen.)
out-babying, an Kindereien über-
treffend.
out-of-the-way, ungewöhnlich,
wenig verbreitet.

P.

Pace, Schritt.
padded, gepolstert.
Paddy, allgemeiner Name für die
Irländer.
paean, Triumpfgesang.
palfrey, Reitpferd.
pall, Talar, Mantel.
pall (to), schal werden.
palliatives, Milderungsgründe.
palmy, glücklich.
palpitate (to), zittern, pochen.

pamphlet, Broschüre.
pander, Kuppler.
panoply, Rüstung.
parchment, Pergament.
parricide, Vatermord.
pastime, Zeitvertreib.
patchwork pastoral, zusammenge-
flicktes Schäfergedicht.
pattering, klappernd.
pavilion, Thronhimmel, Zelt.
peep (to), gucken, nachsehen.
peer (to), durchblicken, erscheinen.
peerless, unvergleichlich.
pencilling, Skizze.
pennon, Wimpel.
perennial, immerwährend.
periodical, Zeitschrift.
periwinkle, das Immergrün.
personalities, Anzüglichkeiten.
pervade (to), durchdringen.
petrel, Sturmvogel.
pettishly, mutwillig.
Pharos, Leuchtturm.
pied, bunt angezogen.
pile, Gebäude, Haufen.
pilfer, stehlen, mausen.
pillaw, Reis in Fett gekocht.
pinafore, Kinderschürze, Lätzchen.
pine (to), schmachten.
pinion, Flügel, Fittich.
pincushion, Nadelkissen.
pippin, der Pippingapfel.
pitching, Stossen.
plague, Pest.
plaudits, Beifall.
pleading, Fürsprache.
Pleiades, Siebengestirn.
plinth, Sockel.
plodder, Grübler.
plot, Handlung, Intrigue.
plover, Kibitz.
plumage, Gefieder.
plump (to), füttern.
poach (to), Wilddieberei treiben.
point-blank, geradezu, ent-
schieden.
poker, Ofengabel.
ponder (to), erwägen.
poppy, Mohn.
portent, Vorbedeutung.

posies, Blumen.
pranks, tolle Streiche.
prate (to), schwatzen.
precarious, unsicher.
pregnant, inhaltsvoll.
presumptuous, anmassend.
prey, Beute.
prime, Blütezeit.
primeval (forest), Urwald.
primrose, Primel.
principality, Fürstentum.
prints, Zeitungen, auch Holz-
    schnitte u. s. w.
proceeding (the) das Verfahren.
proctor, Universitäts-Behörde.
profligate, lasterhaft.
progeny, Kinder, Nachkommen.
prone (to sink), zu Boden fallen.
provender, Proviant.
provocation, Reiz, Antrieb.
puling, weinerlich.
pun, Wortspiel.
puncheon, Oxhoft.
punctilious, formell, ceremoniös.
pupil, Zögling.
purloined conceits, gestohlene
    Einfälle.
puss, Katze (vergl. civet.)
puzzle, Rätsel, Schwierigkeit.
pyre, Holzstoss zur Leichen-
    verbrennung.

Q.

Quaff(to), in grossen Zügen trinken.
quarry, Steinbruch; (S. 164) Beute,
    Opfer.
quivering, zitternde Bewegung.

R.

Rail (to), wüten, schimpfen.
rank, üppig wachsend, ekelhaft.
rankle (to), eitern, um sich fressen.
ransom, Lösegeld.
rapacious, raubgierig.
realm, Reich.
recalcitrant, widerspenstig.
reck (to), sich bewusst sein.
recreant, verräterisch, abtrünnig.

recumbent chair, Lehnstuhl.
reduplicate, (to) verdoppeln,
    wiederholen.
rehearse (to), probieren, vortragen.
reinforce (to), verstärken.
reiterated, wiederholt.
rejoinder, Erwiderung.
reminiscence, Erinnerung.
renounce (to), entsagen.
renovate (to), erneuern.
repellent, widerlich.
replete, sprudelnd.
residuary legatee, Universalerbe.
retail, Kleinhandel.
reverberation, Wiederhall.
reverses, Glückswechsel.
reviewer, Recensent.
revoke (to), zurücknehmen.
riddle, Rätsel.
ridge, Furche.
rill, Flüsschen.
riven, geraubt.
rivet (to), befestigen, nieten.
roam (to), wandern.
roan (horse), Fuchs.
rochet, feines Chorhemd.
rock (to), eine Wiege in Bewegung
    halten.
rolls (hot), warme Semmel.
roseate, rosenfarben.
rouge, Schminke.
round, Sprosse einer Leiter.
Roundhead, Puritaner.
rout, Rotte, Niederlage.
routs, Festlichkeiten.
rub-dub (to), wie eine Trommel
    tönen.
ruff, Halskrause.
russet, braunrot.
rut, Geleise.
rutty, holperig.

S.

Sacrilege, Entweihung.
sample, Probe.
sampler, Stickmuster.
sap, Saft.
satchel, Bücher, Provianttasche.
scale (to), erklimmen.

scalp, Hirnschale.
scamp. Taugenichts.
scanty. knapp.
scar, Narbe.
scoff (to), spötteln.
scooped and strained, vom Winde
      straff gespannt.
scope, Platz, Raum.
scourge, Peitsche.
scrivener, Notar.
scullion, Küchenjunge.
scroll, Papierrolle.
scythe, Sense.
sear (to), ausbrennen.
sensuous, unzüchtig.
sentence, Urteilsspruch.
sepulchre, Ruhestätte.
sergeant, Rechtsgelehrter, Ser-
      geant.
shaft, Pfeil.
shallow, Untiefe.
sharp (Musik), Kreuz, Erhöhungs-
      zeichen.
shattered, zerrüttet, zerstreut.
shed (to) (S. 123), ablegen.
shell, Muschel, Sprengkugel.
shift (to), ziehen, sich ändern.
shingly, voll flacher Steine.
shirk (to), ausweichen.
shoot, Schössling, Zweig.
shrew, Spitzmaus.
shrine, Altar.
shrivel (to), zusammenschrumpfen.
shroud, Leichentuch, das Wanttau.
sire (poetisch), Vater, König.
skirt (to), begrenzen.
skittles oder ninepins, Kegelspiel.
sledge, Schlitten.
sleek, schlau, gewandt, fett.
sleeve (to laugh in one's), sich
      ins Fäustchen lachen.
smouldering, glimmend.
snub (to), grob abweisen.
snubby, plattgedrückt.
soar (to), aufsteigen.
sob (to), schluchzen.
spectre, Gespenst.
spell, Zauber.
spent, erschöpft, ermüdet.
spray, Zweig, Seeschaum.

sprightly. lebhaft, lustig.
sprite (poetisch für spirit), Geist.
spume-flakes, Schaumflocken.
squalid, schmutzig, unordentlich.
squall, Windstoss.
squander (to), vergeuden.
squat, kurz und dick.
squeeze (to), fest drücken.
squirrel, Eichhörnchen.
stab, Stichwunde.
stagger (to), wanken.
stagnant (Wasser, etc.), still-
      stehend.
stake, Scheiterhaufen, Einsatz.
stall, Verkaufsstand.
stamp (to), auszeichnen.
stanch (to), Blut stillen.
stars and stripes, die ameri-
      kanische Flagge.
startish game, furchtsames Wild.
staunch, fest, beständig.
stave (to), den Boden aus-
      schlagen.
stay, ein Stag (Schiffstau.)
stays, Corsett.
steadfast, standhaft.
steed, Ross.
stem the tide (to), wider den
      Strom schwimmen.
steward, Verwalter.
stingy, geizig.
stirrup, Steigbügel.
stock, Fonds, Aktien.
stole, Festgewand.
store, Vorrat.
stove, Heizofen.
strain (Musik), Arie.
strait, eng.
strait, Meerenge.
stratagem, List.
streamer (S. 85), Nordlicht.
strenuous, beherzt, mannhaft.
stripes, Schläge.
strown (S. 149), [mit Muscheln]
      bedeckt.
stubble, Strohhalm.
studded, besetzt.
studio, Atelier.
subordinate, Untergebener.
substantiate (to), beweisen.

succinctly, kurz; (S. 138) an-
geschmiegt.
succulent, nahrhaft.
suggestion, Wink, Einflüsterung.
suit (of clothes), Anzug.
suitor, Freier.
summary, Auszug, Compendium.
summon (to), herbeirufen.
surf, Brandung.
surfeit, Unverdaulichkeit.
surge, Woge.
surly, mürrisch.
sway (to), lenken, beherrschen;
in leiser Bewegung er-
zittern.
swing, Schaukel.
swoon (to), in Ohnmacht fallen.
swart, schwarz.
sweep (to), fegen.

T.

Tamarisk, Tamariskenbaum.
tamper (to),heimlich unterhandeln.
tangled, verwickelt.
tap (to), picken, anklopfen.
tarnish'd, ausgeblasst.
tattered, zerrissen.
tawny, braungelb.
tax, Steuer, Abgabe.
tease (to), quälen, necken.
teem (to), reich an etwas sein.
Temple - Bar, altes Stadtthor in
London.
tenant (S. 163), Gast.
terms of intimacy (on), auf
freundschaftlichem
Fusse.
tender (to), anbieten.
tether (to), anbinden.
thaw (to), aufthauen.
Theirs (S. 112), ihnen gebührte
es nicht.
thraldom, Knechtschaft; in thral-
dom (S 165), nach-
gebend.
threadbare, fadenscheinig.
thrill, Wonneschauer, Durch-
schauern.
thrive (to), gedeihen.

throb (to), schlagen, beben.
thrust (to) and parry, stossen
und parieren.
thrust, Stoss, Stich.
tie, Band.
tiger-moth, Tigermotte.
tilt, Turnier.
tinge, Anstrich.
tingling, zitternd, wallend.
tinkle (to), rauschen, läuten.
tinsel, Flittergold.
tint, Farbenton.
tintinnabulation, Klingen, Tönen.
tip-tilted, aufgestülpt.
tit für tomtit, Kohlmeise.
toad, Kröte.
toll (to), läuten.
tombstone, Grabstein.
topple over (to), zu Boden schlagen.
tortoise-shell, Schildpatt.
toss (to) [S. 69], sich hin und her
werfen.
totter (to), wanken.
tournament, Turnier.
toy, Spielzeug.
Trades' Unions, Handwerker-
Vereine.
train (an einem Damenkleide),
Schleppe.
trance, Ohnmacht, Scheintod.
trap-ball, Schlagballspiel.
trappings, Putz.
trash, Schofel.
treachery, Verrath.
treble, dreifach; (Musik), Diskant.
trefoil, Klee.
tremor, Zittern, Befürchtung.
trench (to), abstechen.
trifling, unbedeutend.
trim (to), putzen.
tripe, Kaldaunen.
trout, Forelle.
trowel, Maurerkelle.
trunk, Reisekoffer.
tuft, Büschel.
turbulency, Ungestüm.
turbulent, aufrührerisch, unruhig.
Turlough (gh stumm), irischer
Taufname.
turmoil, Aufruhr, Getümmel.

turnkey, Gefängnisswärter.
turtle-dove, Turteltaube.
tutelar, schützend.
tutor, Lehrer, Meister.
twain = two, zwei.
twang (to), dröhnen.
twin, Zwilling.
twinkle (to), funkeln.

U.

Udder, Euter.
umpire, Schiedsrichter.
unanimously, einstimmig.
uncongenial, unsympathisch.
uncouth, linkisch, bauernhaft.
undergraduate, Student der noch
   nicht promovirt hat.
underplot, Nebenhandlung.
unequivocal, unzweifelhaft, un-
   zweideutig.
unfathomed, unergründet.
unfurled (S. 40), noch nicht ent-
   hüllt.
unquestionably, zweifellos.
unstinted, unbeschränkt.
upbraid (to), beschuldigen, vor-
   werfen.
uphold (to), unterstützen.
upstart, Emporkömmling.
urchin, Knabe, Zaunigel.
usher, Hilfslehrer.
uttermost (to the), aufs Aeusserste.

V.

Vacant (S. 110), nichtssagend, leer.
vat (cheese-), Käsefass.
vault, Gruft.
veins, Adern.
vent (to find), sich Luft machen.
verdict, Ausspruch, Entscheidung.
viand, Speise.
vie (to), wetteifern.
vigil, Nachtwache.
vivid, lebhaft.
void, Leere.
volley (to), krachen.
voluptuary, Wollüstling.
voter, Stimmgeber.

W.

Wail, Wehklage.
waive (to), auf etwas verzichten.
wake, das Kielwasser eines Schiffes.
wand, Zauberstab.
wanton (S. 209), ein leichtsinniges
   Frauenzimmer.
warble (to), trillern, schmettern.
ward, Mündel.
warden, Vormund, Beschützer.
waterbreak, Wellenbruch.
wedge, Keil.
weed, Unkraut.
welling, hervorsprudelnd.
well-tempered (S. 136), passend
   gehärtet.
well-to-do, wohlhabend.
wench (veraltet), Mädchen od. Frau.
whistle, Pfeife.
wield (to), handhaben, gebrauchen.
wight, Bursch, Jüngling.
willow, Weidenbaum.
window-ledge, Fensterbrüstung.
winnow chaff (to), Spreu aus-
   sondern.
winsome, gewinnend, einnehmend.
wisp, Strohwisch.
wits' end (to be at one's), sich nicht
   mehr zu helfen wissen.
Witan oder Witangemote, angel-
   sächsischer Staatsrat.
wizard, Zauberer.
womb (S. 66), Schoss.
woof, Gewebe, Faden.
worry, Plage, Qual.
worst (to), besiegen.
would-be (man möchte sein) Nach-
   ahmer.
wrangle (to), hadern.
wreck, Wrack, Trümmer.
wrestle (to), ringen.
wrongs, gelittene Unbill.

Y.

Yard-arm, der Arm der Raa.
yell (to), gellen.
yeoman, Freisasse.
yew-tree, Taxus.
yore (of), aus anderen Zeiten.